IMAGES
of America

STEILACOOM

ON THE COVER: Lafayette Street became Steilacoom's second commercial district. Pictured around 1905 are, from left to right, John Downey, Fred Doyne, Fred Chelius, Harry Gaul, and Charlie Armstrong. The others in this photograph are unidentified. The man in the white apron is presumably the butcher. (Steilacoom Historical Museum Association.)

IMAGES
of America

STEILACOOM

Sunny Pepin and the
Steilacoom Historical Museum Association

ARCADIA
PUBLISHING

ISBN 978-0-7385-5820-2

Published by Arcadia Publishing
Charleston SC, Chicago IL, Portsmouth NH, San Francisco CA

Printed in the United States of America

Library of Congress Catalog Card Number: 2007941838

For all general information contact Arcadia Publishing at:
Telephone 843-853-2070
Fax 843-853-0044
E-mail sales@arcadiapublishing.com
For customer service and orders:
Toll-Free 1-888-313-2665

Visit us on the Internet at www.arcadiapublishing.com

This book is dedicated to early-day pioneers and their families, including E. A. Light, Sam McCaw, Dr. John Webber, William Downey, Rev. George Sloan, John Bradley, Miles West, Phillip Keach, Andrew Byrd, Warren Gove, Louisa Goodtime, Isaac Pincus, Adolph Packscher, James Hughes, Julius Dickens, William M. Clendenin, Levant Thompson, Charles Prosch, Albert Balch, George Gallagher, Hill Harmon, Lemuel Bills, Robert More, John Latham, and Ezra Meeker.

Contents

ACKNOWLEDGMENTS

The book *Town on the Sound*—stories of Steilacoom published in 1988 by the Steilacoom Historical Museum Association—was the inspiration for this book. Thank you to the Steilacoom Historical Museum for opening your archives and for the permission to print and share your rich history with all who are interested. Without the dedicated people of Steilacoom and their countless hours of volunteer service, it would not be possible to tell the story of the people and events that shaped where we live today. Joan Curtis, thank you for the many hours that you have so generously given me. Thank you for editing 36 years of the *Steilacoom Historical Museum Quarterly* and then sharing your copies to piece this project together. Without the Davidson family collection and their passion for preservation, valuable local history would have been lost. Thank you to those who have entrusted photographs and stories to the Steilacoom Museum archives to share with future generations. All of the photographs, except where noted, were provided by the Steilacoom Historical Museum Association.

Thank you to the brave and adventurous settlers who wanted to go first and pave the way so someday we could call Puget Sound home. Research resources included *Memory Trails of Steilacoom* (the Pioneer Memory Group), *Reminiscences of the Washington Territory* by Charles Prosch, *History of Pierce County* by W. P. Bonney, *South on the Sound* by Murray and Rosa Morgan, and the *Steilacoom Historical Museum Quarterly*. Thank you to my grandparents Bill and Joy Johnston for selling us our home on Anderson Island above the Puget Sound. Driving through the town of Steilacoom and waiting for the ferry perpetuated my interest in local history. Liz Galentine, thank you for your support and encouragement with this project. Thank you to my editor, Julie Albright, who has eagerly shared the gift of perspective and humor. My sweet baby Annabelle, thank you for asking so many questions and most importantly listening to the answers. Thank you to my husband, Joey, who unconditionally loves, supports, and encourages me no matter how outrageous the dream.

INTRODUCTION

Steilacoom, "The Town of Firsts," was named after a pink flower that bloomed on the prairies of what is now Lakewood-Steilacoom. Before European white settlers came west, there were approximately 600 Native American people in five bands occupying the Tacoma drainage basin: Steilacoom, Sastuck, Spanaway, Tlithlow, and Segwallitchu. In 1792, when George Vancouver and the British Royal Navy explored the region, Peter Puget saw Native Americans camped at what is now Chambers Creek. The Hudson Bay Company founded Fort Nisqually in 1833, southwest of what became Steilacoom. Joseph Heath was a tenant farmer of the Puget Sound Agricultural Company, a subsidiary of the Hudson Bay Company. In the 1840s, exploration of the region continued. Lt. Charles Wilkes and the U.S. Navy surveyed and explored the waterways on behalf of the U.S. government. In 1846, Great Britain and the United States agreed that the 49th parallel would be the boundary between Canada and the United States of America. The treaty between the two countries would open the land north of the Columbia River for settlement. In 1849, Joseph Heath died and the U.S. Army rented the land from the Hudson Bay Company to establish Fort Steilacoom.

In 1851, when Port Steilacoom and Steilacoom City were founded, planning and establishing a settlement was immediate, and Fort Steilacoom would give protection to settlers. After an act by the Washington Territorial legislature merged the two establishments, Steilacoom became the first incorporated town in the Washington Territory and also served as the Pierce County seat. Seattle was hardly visible by passing ships in the early 1850s, and it appeared that Steilacoom would surpass Olympia and Vancouver as the largest town in the territory. It was believed that Steilacoom was destined to be a great city: It is geographically located in the most protected and easily navigable waters in the Sound, and there was a seemingly endless supply of lumber shipping from Steilacoom Bay to San Francisco for trade. The town boomed quickly and served the needs of citizens and visitors alike with the conveniences of the day. Many of the Washington Territory's "firsts" happened in Steilacoom: The first post office was established in 1852; the first Protestant church was built in 1854; Steilacoom was incorporated as the first territorial town in 1854; the first public library in the Washington Territory was organized; and the first brewery and the first territorial jail were built in 1858.

Steilacoom's future was shaped by several notable events that would transform one of the fastest growing settlements into a scenic small town. Steilacoom's peak of prosperity was during the Fraser Gold Rush. At that time, there were 40 businesses in operation, homes and roads were built, and Steilacoom's port was the busiest on Puget Sound. At the end of the 1860s, the population was 631.

The next two decades would bring change to the frontier. In 1868, Fort Steilacoom was abandoned as a U.S. Army post. A territorial hospital for the mentally ill was established utilizing the former army buildings and property, now named Western State Hospital. The Northern Pacific Railroad announced Tacoma would be the terminus for the transcontinental railroad. In 1880, the county seat was moved to Tacoma. In 1888, the population of Steilacoom was 250 people.

The town had two churches, an organized school system, and employment. The 1890s brought the electric streetcar line that ran between Tacoma and Steilacoom, and W. L. Bair built the first commercial building on Lafayette Street. Steilacoom became a tourist destination for those seeking recreation and small-town atmosphere.

In 1910, the Northern Pacific Railroad began purchasing the beachfront property for the Tacoma line. Subsequently Steilacoom was no longer considered a vacation destination. It was realized that Steilacoom, with its population of 230, was not intended to become the metropolis that it had hoped for half a century earlier but a scenic waterfront suburb to its once rival cities.

Through the next century, Fort Lewis expanded into Steilacoom's borders, farms became housing developments, and the need for more schools was met. Steilacoom happily settled into a small-town pace. Currently nearly 7,000 people call Steilacoom home. There are still no stoplights, and the breathtaking view of the Puget Sound and Olympic Mountains looks the same as the day Lafayette Balch landed on the shore. The new and historic homes dot the hillside. The residents have embraced their history and proudly refer to Steilacoom as "The Town of Firsts."

One

ESTABLISHING A TOWN

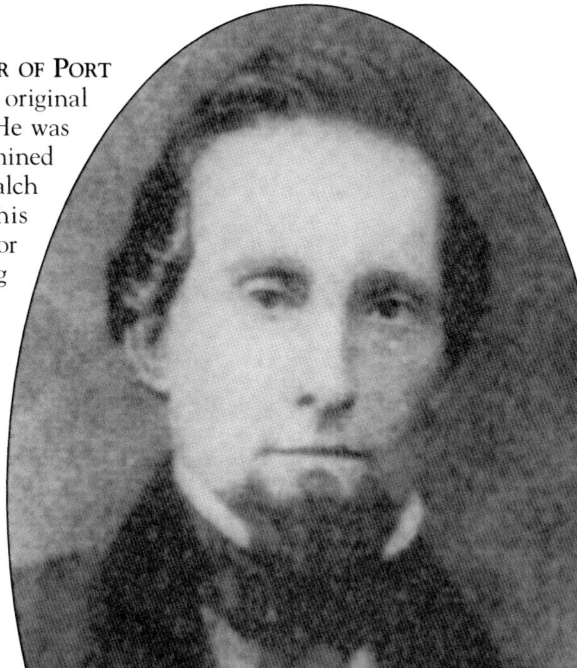

CAPT. LAFAYETTE BALCH, FOUNDER OF PORT STEILACOOM. Lafayette Balch is the original settler and founder of Steilacoom. He was an accomplished captain and a determined businessman. From San Francisco, Balch set out with the Puget Sound as his destination in search of land suitable for trade. His seaworthy vessels—the brig *George Emory* and the sloop *Demaris Cove*—were loaded with merchandise and lumber to build. After a failed attempt to settle in Olympia and then spending Christmas Eve 1850 at Fort Nisqually, Balch found what he was looking for on January 10, 1851. Subsequently Balch laid claim to 315.6 acres under the Oregon Land Law, naming the settlement Port Steilacoom. Without delay, he built a store and a home in his newly established settlement. During the first few years of the Steilacoom settlement, Balch had many enterprises, including a general store, Balch's Wharf, a sawmill at the mouth of Sequalitchew Creek (near Solo Point), a lumberyard at Pier 20 in San Francisco, and a thriving trade business. He would take the lumber to San Francisco, and on the return trips, he would bring back merchandise for his store. He was Steilacoom's chief promoter. Capt. Lafayette Balch died suddenly in San Francisco in 1862.

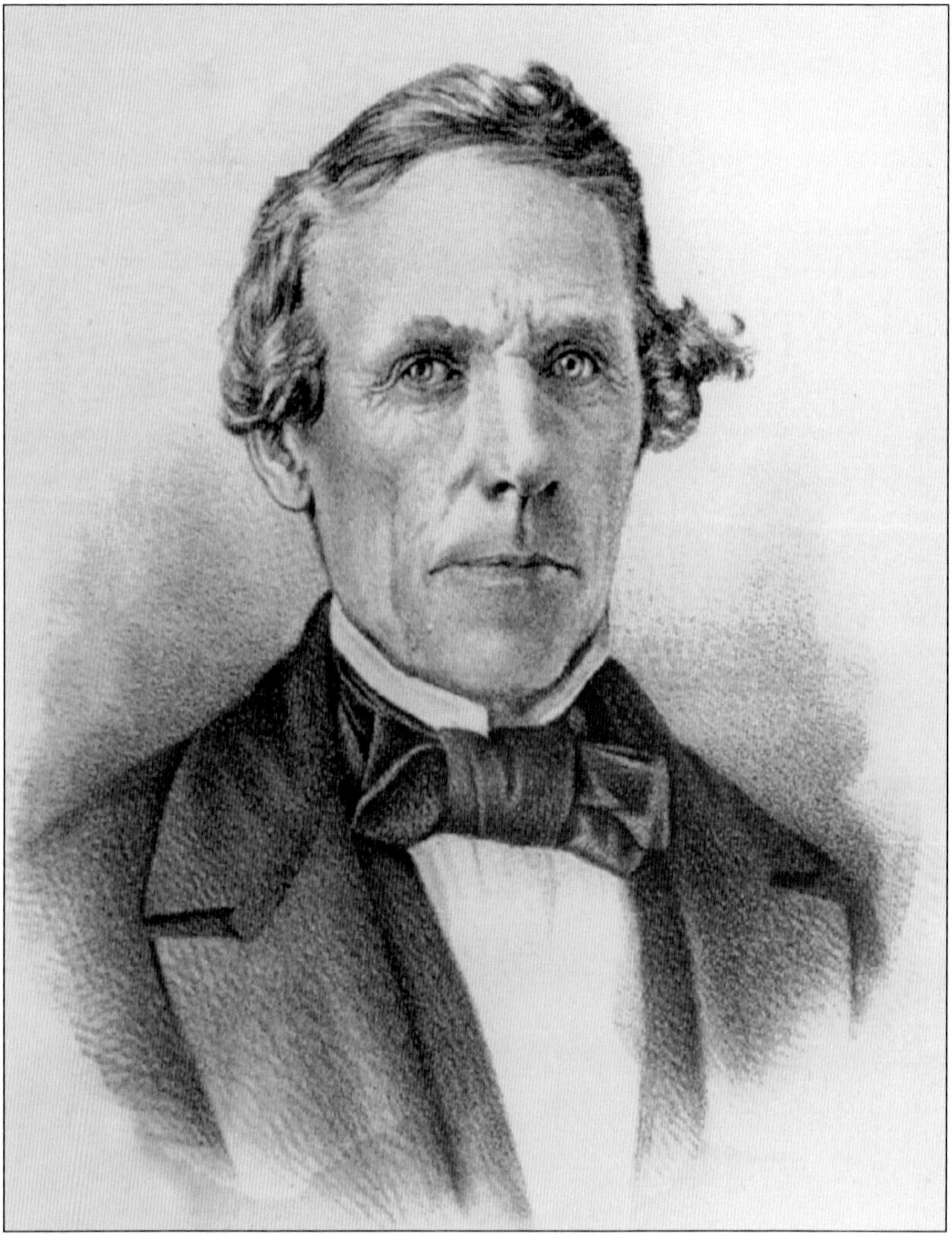

STEILACOOM CITY. John Butler Chapman was the founder of Steilacoom City. Chapman tried unsuccessfully several times to establish towns in the Oregon and Washington Territories. In June 1851, he happened upon the beautiful waters of south Puget Sound and laid claim adjacent to Balch's Port Steilacoom, naming his settlement Steilacoom City. In July 1851, Chapman was elected judge of Lewis County and county commissioner. Although he tried unsuccessfully to secure official appointments as a delegate in Washington Territory, he finally received a clerkship at the Treasury Department in Washington, D.C. John B. Chapman handed off his claim of 312 acres to his son John M. Chapman, who settled in Steilacoom for a time.

The Reverend John DeVore. In 1853, Steilacoom was a large frontier establishment with hundreds of new settlers, Fort Steilacoom soldiers, and the native people. Steilacoom had an authentic Wild West atmosphere. There was no church, but there were many saloons and retail shops. When Capt. Lafayette Balch heard that the Reverend John DeVore from Illinois would be stopping at Alki Point on his way to his new assignment in Olympia, Balch gathered a group of townspeople and went by canoe to persuade the reverend to start his church in Steilacoom instead of Olympia. Perhaps in an effort to persuade, Balch explained that Olympia already had a minister and a case of smallpox. The Reverend John DeVore preached his first sermon on August 28, 1853. The church was completed in March 1854.

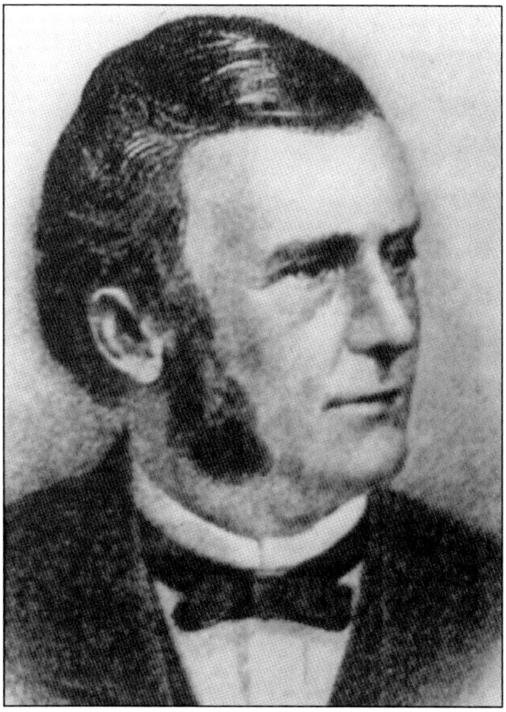

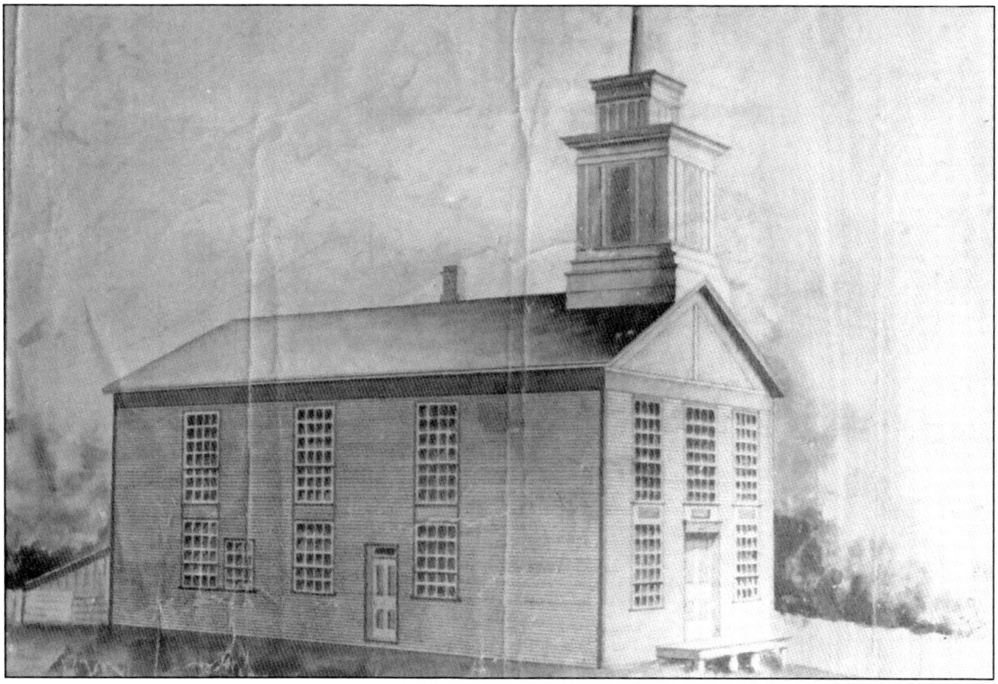

The First Church in the Washington Territory. The church was built on two lots donated by Lafayette Balch. The Methodist Episcopal church was the first Protestant church building north of the Columbia River. The initial cost of the church was $2,300, and it was financed by residents of Pierce County and Steilacoom. The lumber was shipped from McCallister Creek (formerly Medicine Creek) in the Nisqually Valley and delivered to Steilacoom Landing.

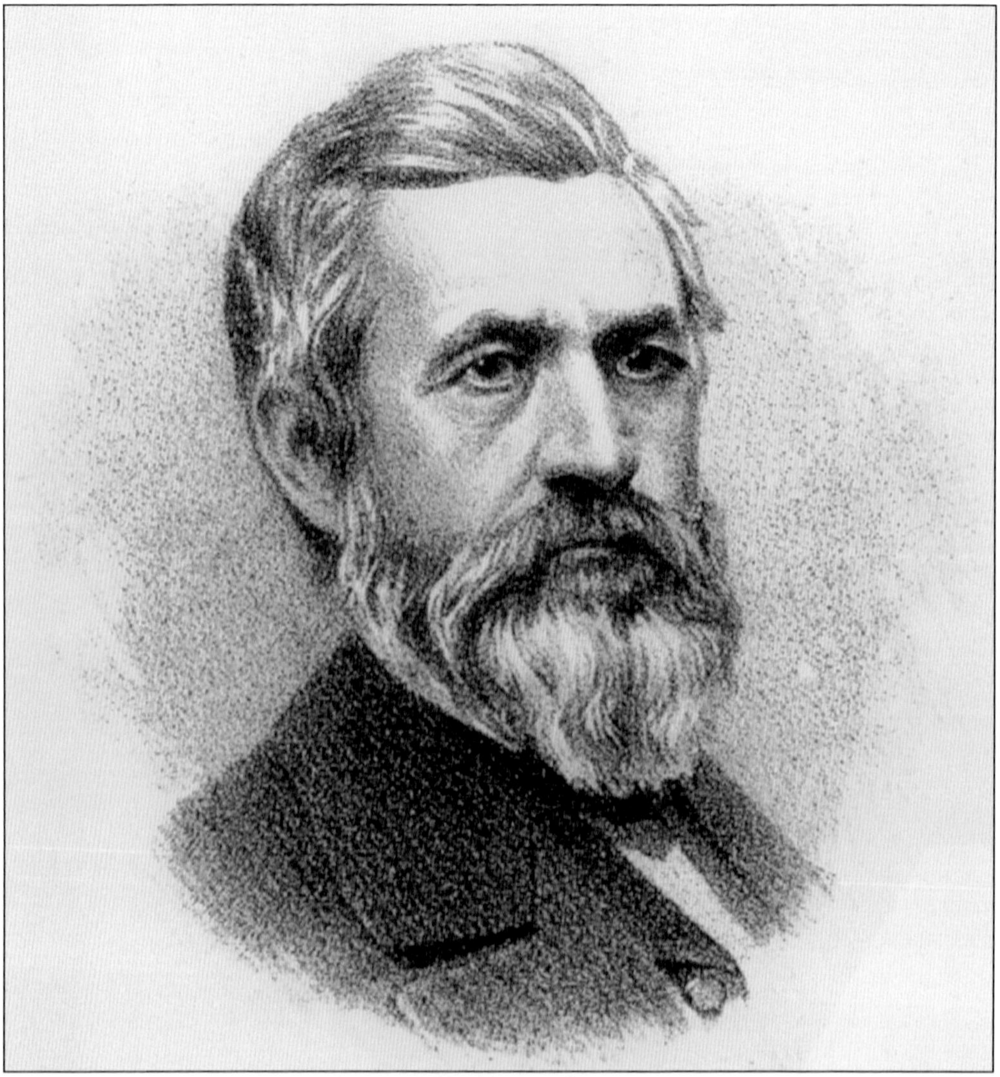

GOVERNOR WALLACE. Col. William Wallace from Indiana arrived in Steilacoom in 1853 with experience as a soldier, lawyer, and politician. He quickly began practicing law in Washington Territory. He won and lost elections for local offices and appointments. Colonel Wallace's affiliation with newly elected Pres. Abraham Lincoln resulted in an appointment as governor of the Washington Territory in 1861 after he took a trip to personally congratulate his old friend on winning the election. Upon Colonel Wallace's return to the Washington Territory, he learned that he had also been nominated to represent the territory in Congress and gladly accepted. When his term expired, he accepted a second appointment from President Lincoln to be the first governor of Idaho and also served as a delegate to Congress for Idaho. The morning of April 14, 1865, Wallace met with President Lincoln and was assured that he would be reappointed as the governor of Idaho. Colonel Wallace and his wife, Luzena, were invited to accompany the Lincolns to the theater that evening and declined the invitation because Luzena was ill. President Lincoln was assassinated that night. Colonel Wallace was a pallbearer at his friend's funeral. The Wallaces returned to Steilacoom, where he was elected as one of the first mayors of Steilacoom, and they happily lived out their days in Steilacoom. Colonel Wallace was buried in the cemetery at Fort Steilacoom in 1879.

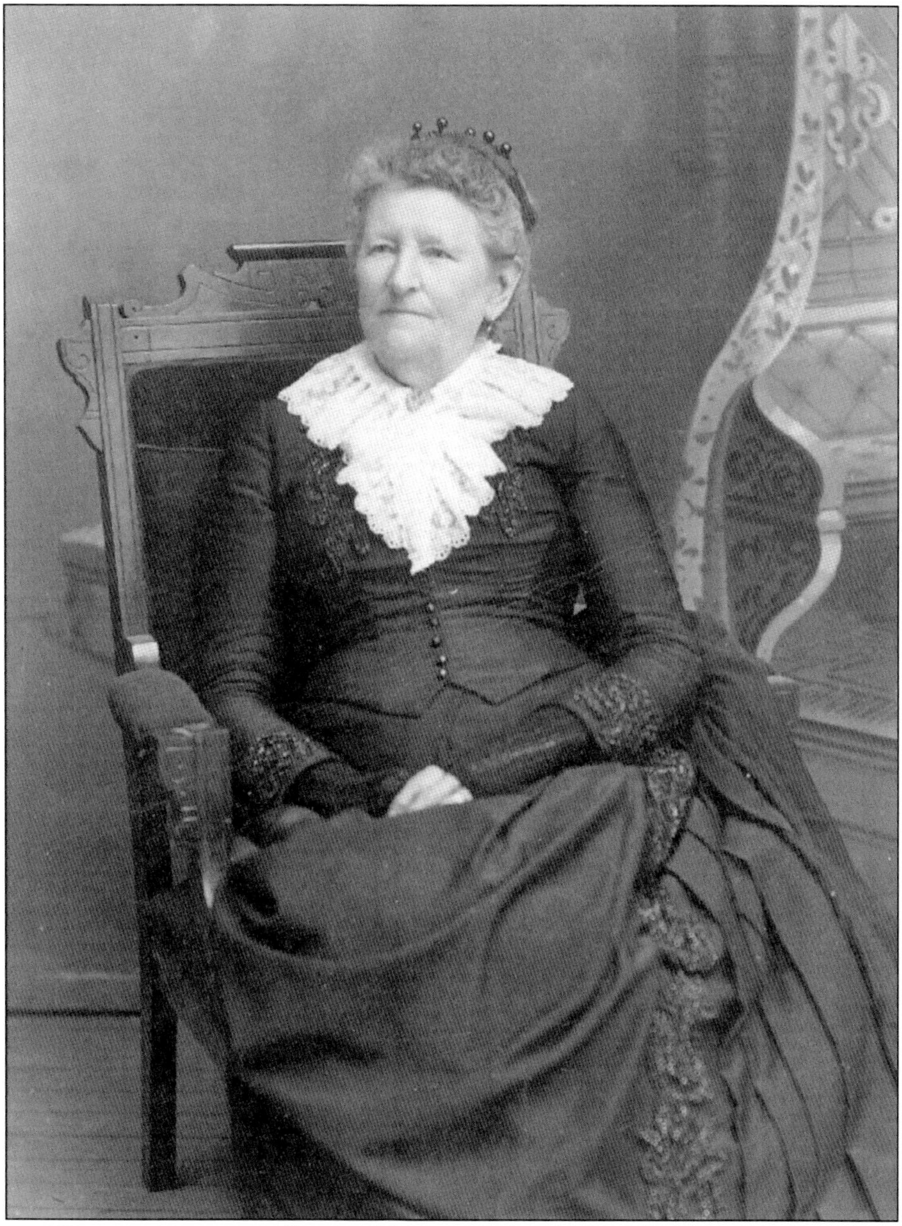

LUZENA WALLACE. Luzena Wallace and her son William made the trip to Steilacoom in 1854 to be reunited with Colonel Wallace. The two traveled from New York through Panama, ending in San Francisco, with the expectation her husband would be waiting. Since Colonel Wallace was not there, Luzena decided to make the trip to Puget Sound to search for him. She eventually found him in Seattle, where he was attending court. They were reunited, and after that, she commonly accompanied her husband for court dates and delegation responsibilities whenever possible. Luzena was apart from him again during the Native American uprising in the 1850s, when she and her son sought refuge at Fort Steilacoom with other settlers. Colonel Wallace wrote the bill to enact Idaho as a territory, and Luzena named the territory for her niece, who was in turn named after a beautiful Native American chief's daughter from Colorado Springs. Idaho means "gem of the mountain."

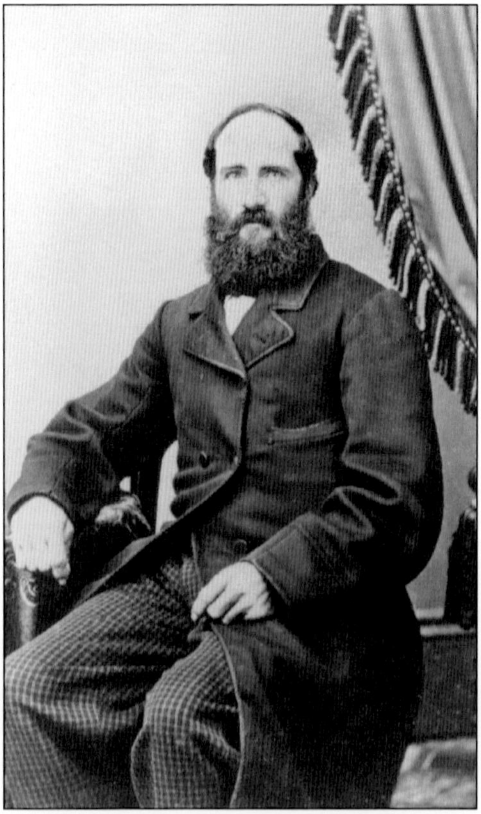

CAPTAIN BLACK. Born in Nova Scotia, Capt. George Black was a bachelor sea captain who came to Steilacoom in 1860. He regularly sailed out of Steilacoom to San Francisco. He was known to have captained the *Clara Light*, a vessel built in Steilacoom.

THE CAPTAIN'S HOUSE. This home was built by Captain Black on Lafayette Street in the 1860s. The home was built on Steilacoom City's side of Union Avenue. The home is still occupied and has been remodeled in recent years. It probably looks even more beautiful than it did the day it was built.

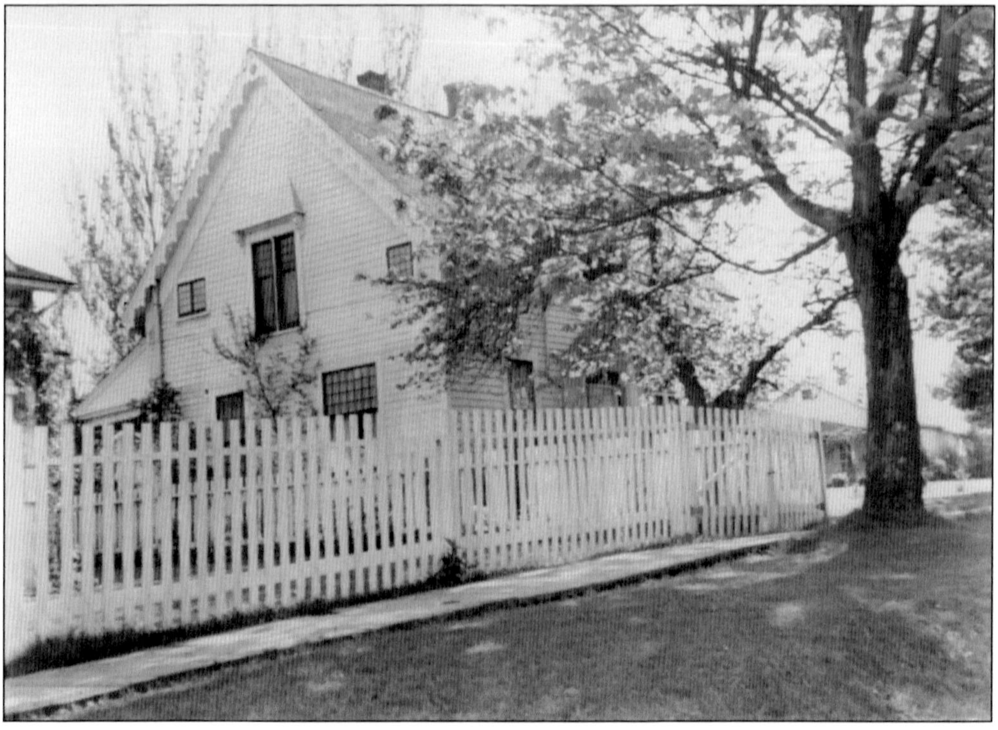

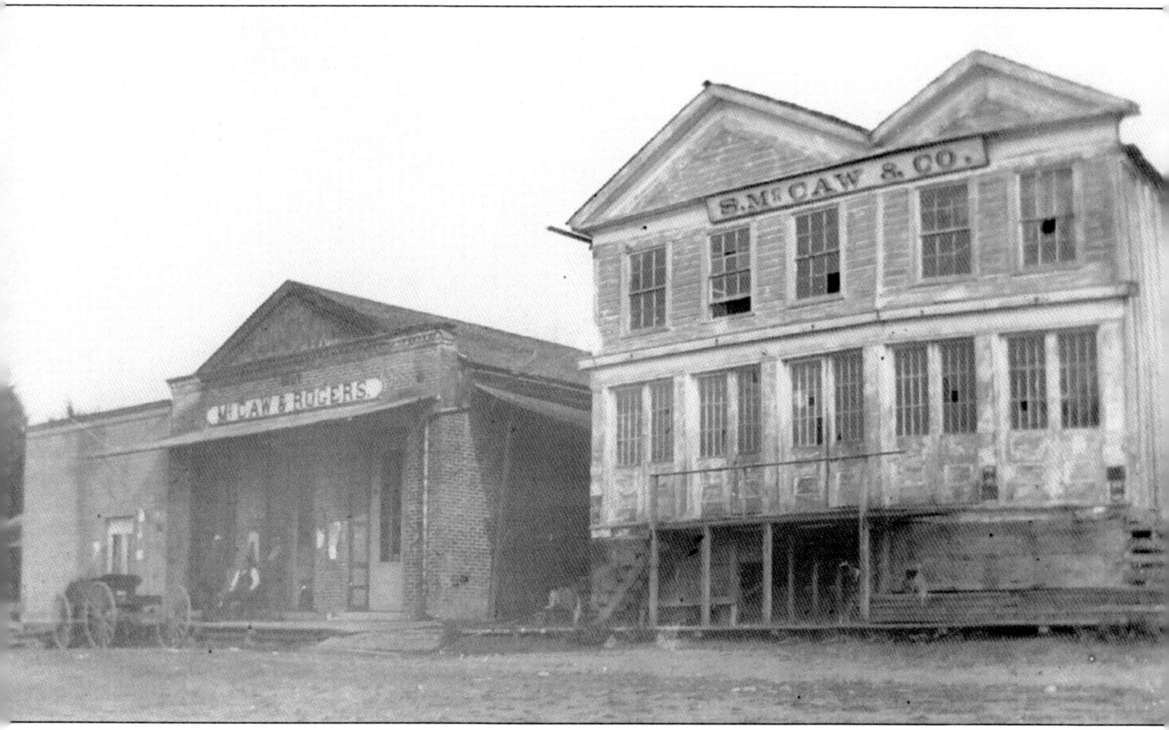

THE FIRST BRICK BUILDING. The McCaw and Rogers Building was the first brick building in the Washington Territory. The building was constructed in 1859. Samuel McCaw and E. R. Rogers were sellers of general merchandise and were both politically active. In the early days of Steilacoom, it was used not only to conduct business but also as a gathering place for the community. McCaw died in 1881, and Rogers relocated the store in 1898. Samuel McCaw built the wooden building on the right in 1854.

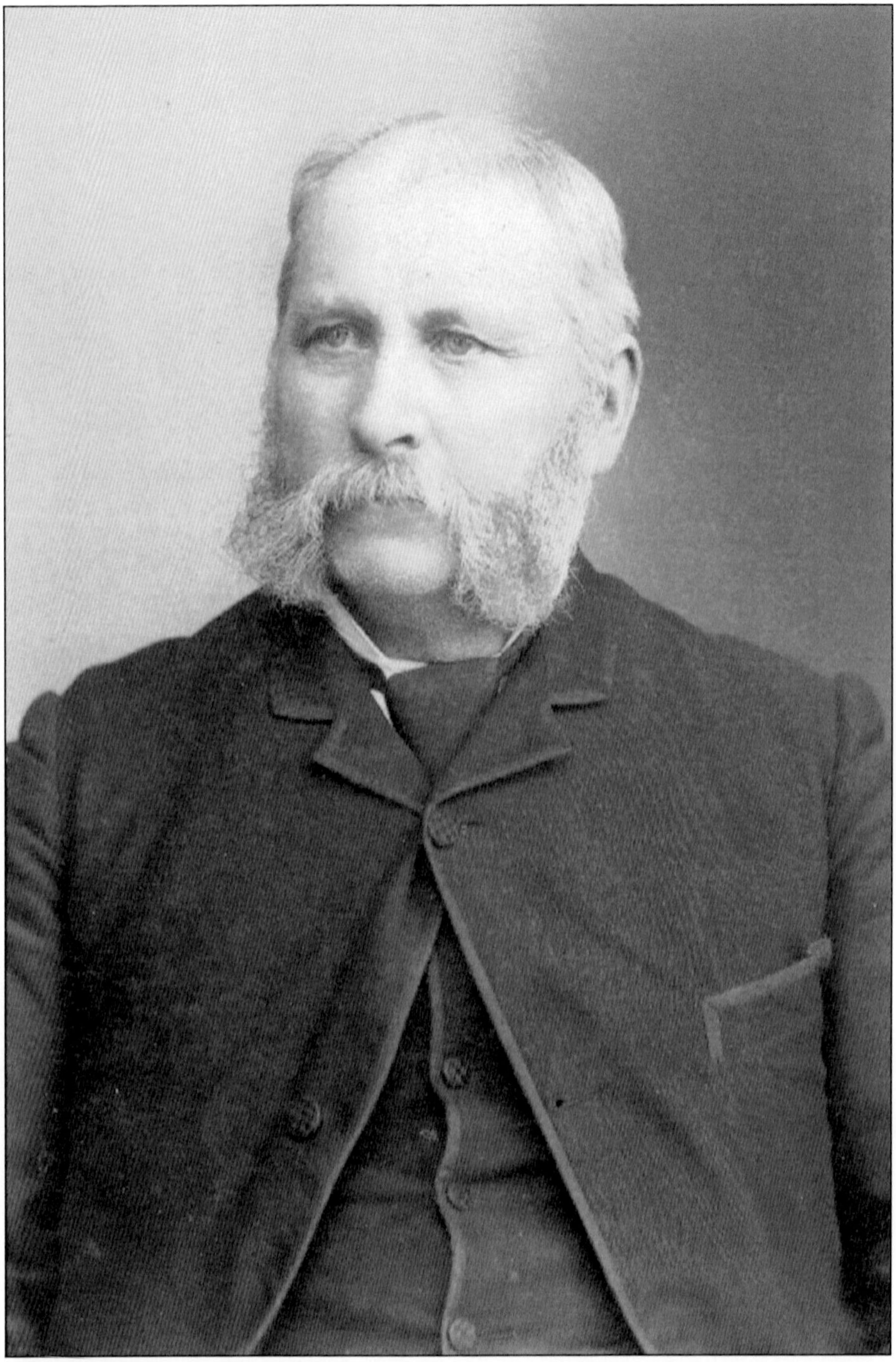

E. R. ROGERS. Edwin R. Rogers was a pioneer, sailor, merchant, and justice of the peace. E. R. was a partner in the McCaw and Rogers Store and was instrumental in building a successful town and establishing the library association. Today the E. R. Rogers name is synonymous with a stately 17-room mansion overlooking Puget Sound that he built for his wife, Catherine. The couple only lived in the house for a very short time before the Panic of 1893 forced them to move back to their original home right next door. Rogers died in his bed in August 1906 at the age of 76.

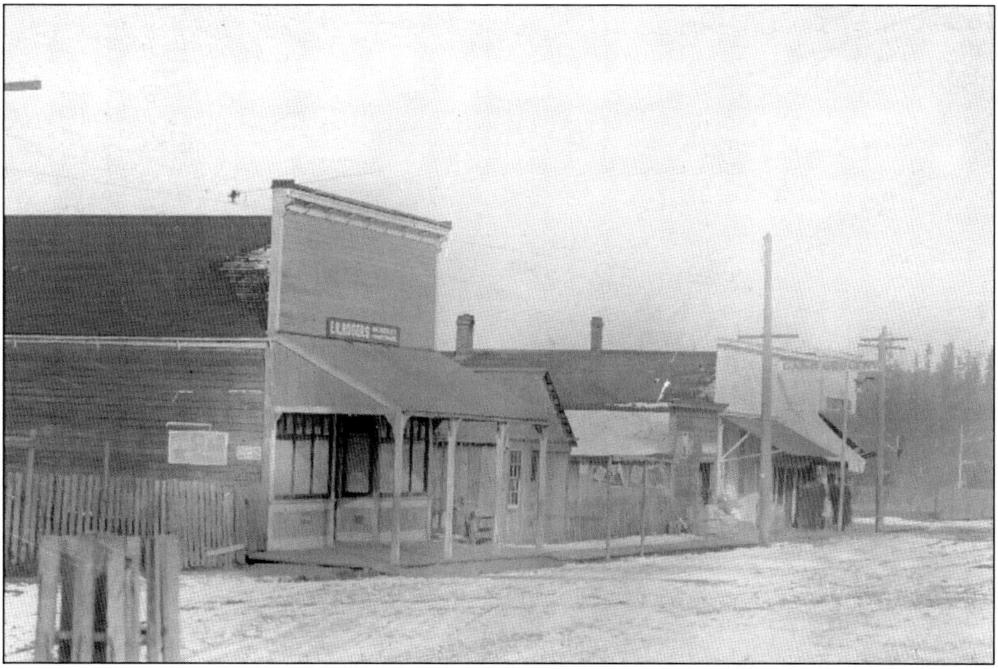

THE STORE ON LAFAYETTE. By the end of the 1890s, businesses were beginning to relocate to Lafayette Street from Commercial Street, where the center of business had been for nearly 50 years of commerce in Steilacoom. The new Rogers store occupied the Derville Building on Lafayette Street.

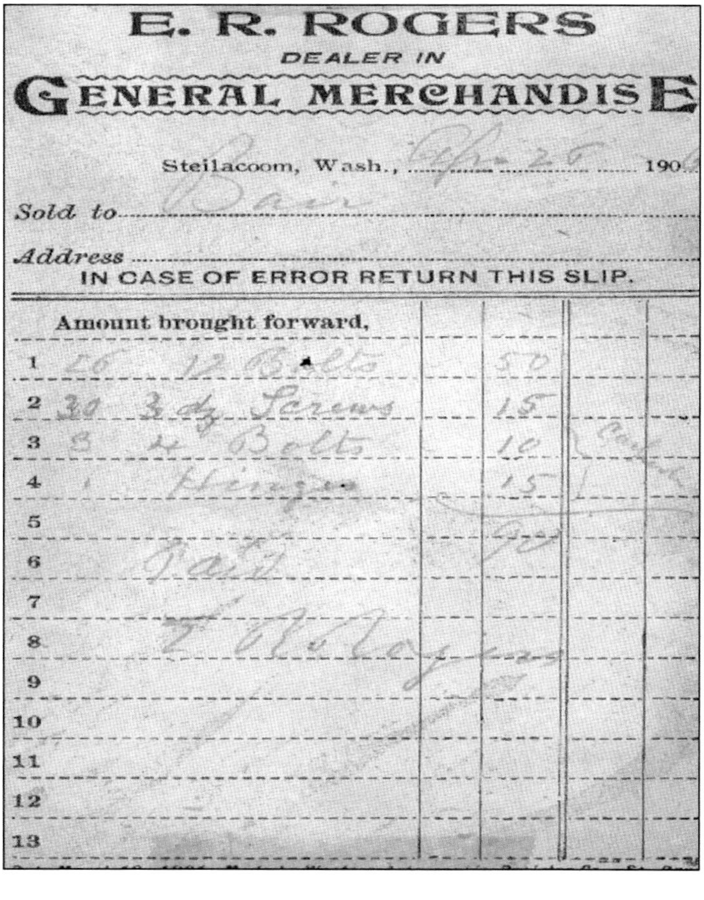

E. R. ROGERS
DEALER IN
GENERAL MERCHANDISE

Steilacoom, Wash., ... 190

Sold to ....

Address ....

IN CASE OF ERROR RETURN THIS SLIP.

Amount brought forward,

1
2
3
4
5
6
7
8
9
10
11
12
13

PROOF OF PURCHASE. This receipt was written exactly five months before E. R. Rogers died, which was on August 26, 1906. He was selling these items to the Bair Store, which was then located just a few doors down the street.

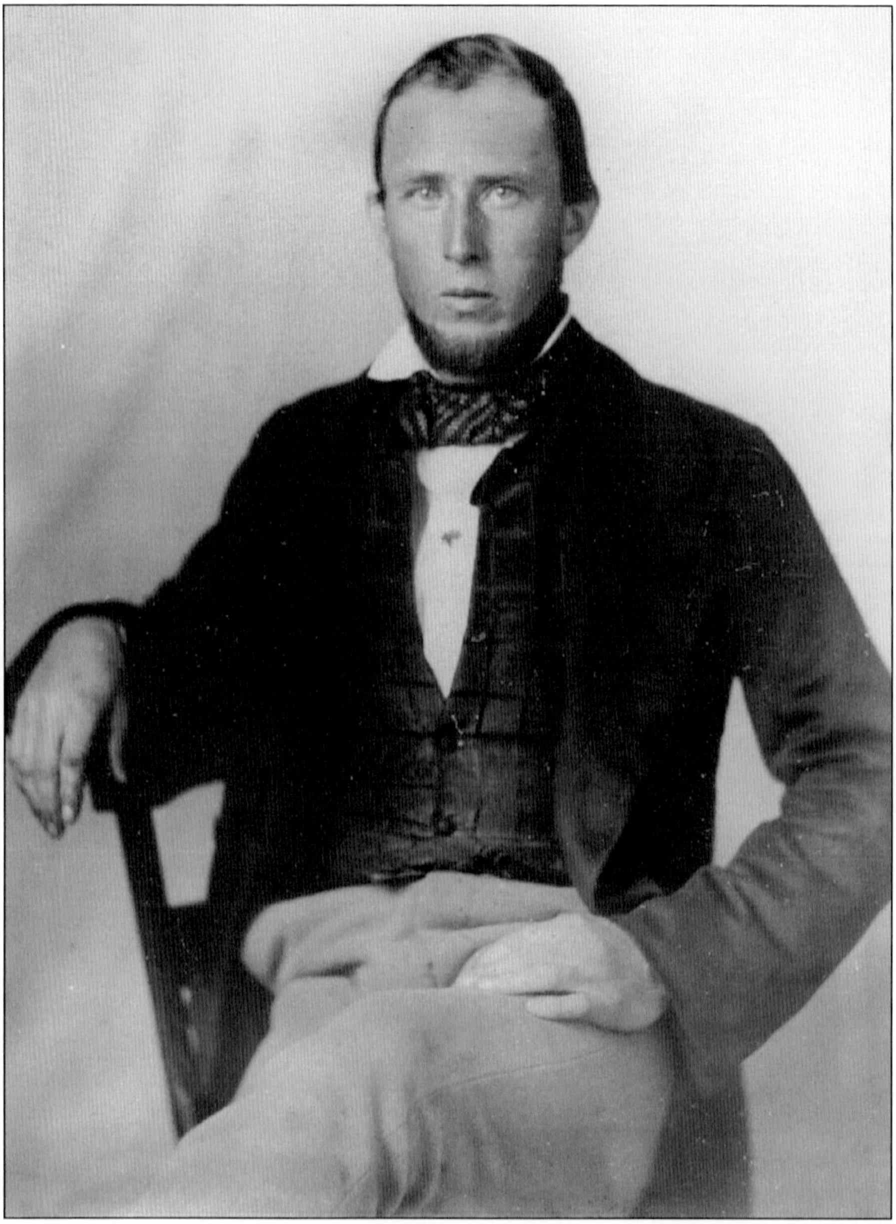

NATHANIEL ORR. As a young pioneer cabinetmaker, Nathaniel Orr came to Steilacoom in the fall of 1852. Upon landing on Balch's Wharf, he was so hungry that he traded the shirt off his back to a Native American walking by with a freshly caught salmon; the man offered to cook it as well. Orr was captivated by the beauty of Anderson Island (sometimes known as Wallace Island) across the bay from Steilacoom. He laid claim to 160 acres on what is now called Oro Bay. According to the obituary of Christine Anderson, whose family purchased nearby property, the bay was originally named Orr Bay. When the Indian War of 1855–1856 began, Orr purchased the island property outright and went back to Steilacoom to sign up with the volunteers. After that, he built his wagon shop on Rainier Street. Orr was an active citizen. He helped establish the library and served as the clerk on the school board and as a town councilman. With others, he worked on the road connecting the city of Steilacoom to the town of Seattle.

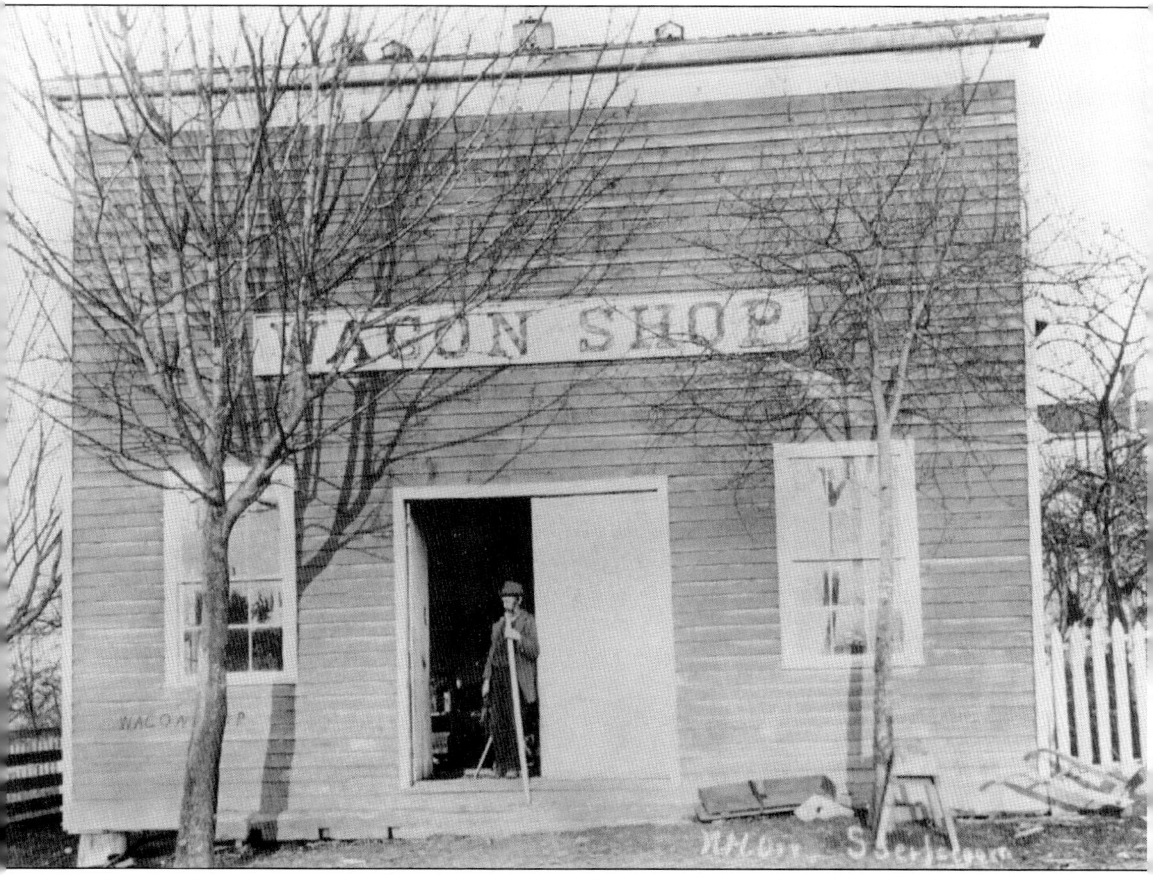

WAGON SHOP. Orr was an accomplished woodworker skilled in crafting furniture, coffins, cabinets, looms, spinning wheels, and, of course, wagons. Orr operated the first horse-powered lathe and would allow the teenage boys in town to make their own baseball bats and spinning tops. Bringing wool from farms on the prairie was indeed a lucrative day for Orr at his wagon shop. Farmers would bring their wool to the ships at the wharf to be traded elsewhere. Then they would take their wagons in for much-needed repairs. The wagon shop has been rehabilitated and contains Orr's original tools.

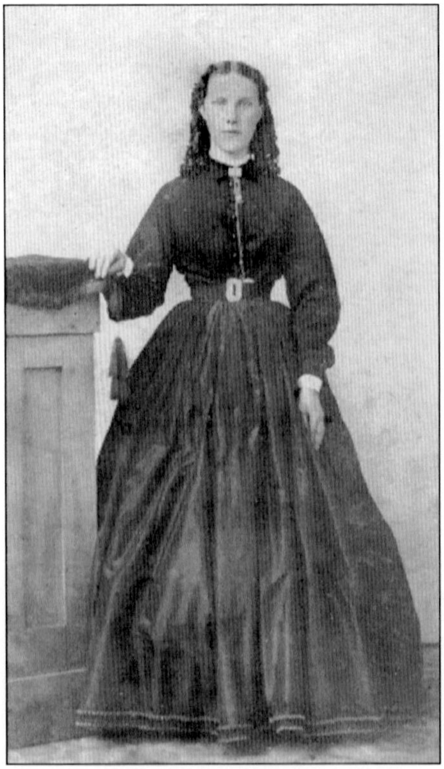

EMMA ORR. Nathaniel Orr met his fair bride, Emma Thompson, on the hill behind his wagon shop. The white pitcher that she carried that day always had a place of honor in their home. She was a beautiful girl with a talent for music. She and Nathanial became the parents of eight children within 20 years.

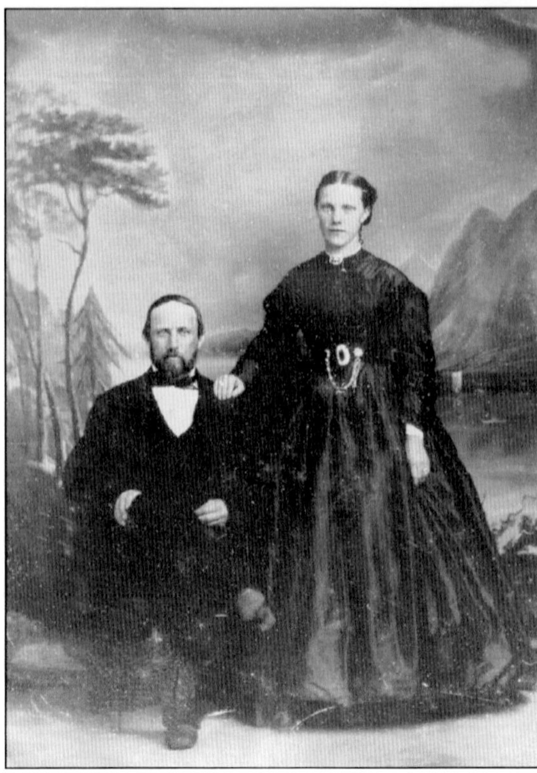

MAY 11, 1868. The young couple married in Victoria on May 11, 1868. The wagon shop had to be converted to a home for their large family. Although Nathaniel was a skilled furniture maker, he meticulously chose their furnishings from fine stores in Victoria and had the pieces shipped to their new home.

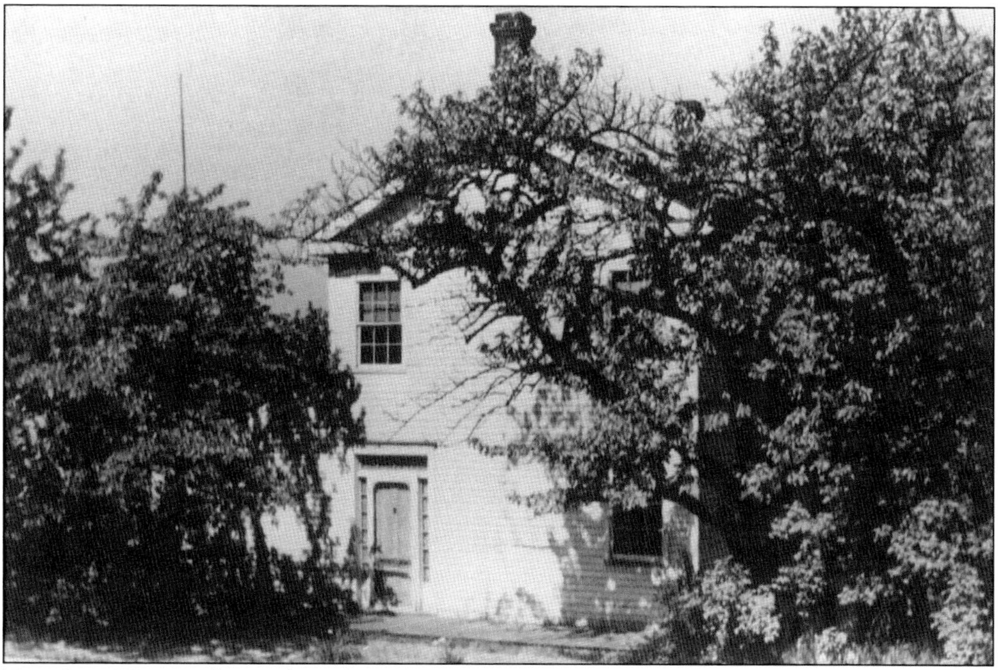

The Orr Home. The Nathaniel Orr home was built in 1857. The home sits on the corner of Main and Rainier Streets. The orchard that Orr planted produced plums, apples, cherries, and pears, and a few of the trees still exist today. Their home was filled with music from the grand piano that he had shipped from New York for Emma. The Orrs lived out their lives in Steilacoom and were buried in the Masonic Cemetery on land that they sold to Steilacoom Lodge No. 2 for the sum of $50 in 1883.

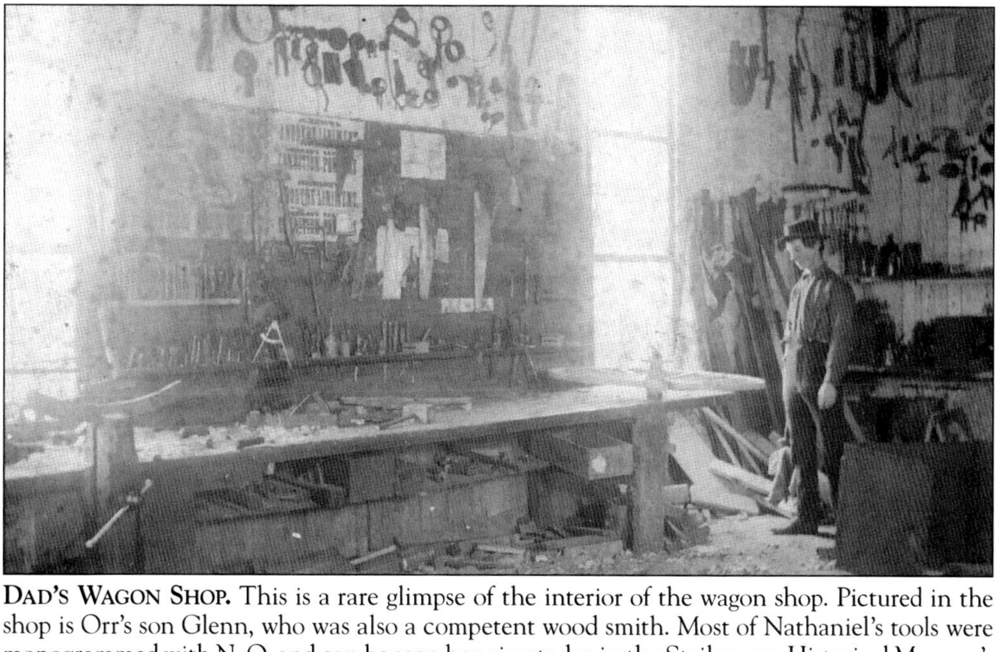

Dad's Wagon Shop. This is a rare glimpse of the interior of the wagon shop. Pictured in the shop is Orr's son Glenn, who was also a competent wood smith. Most of Nathaniel's tools were monogrammed with N. O. and can be seen hanging today in the Steilacoom Historical Museum's reconstructed wagon shop.

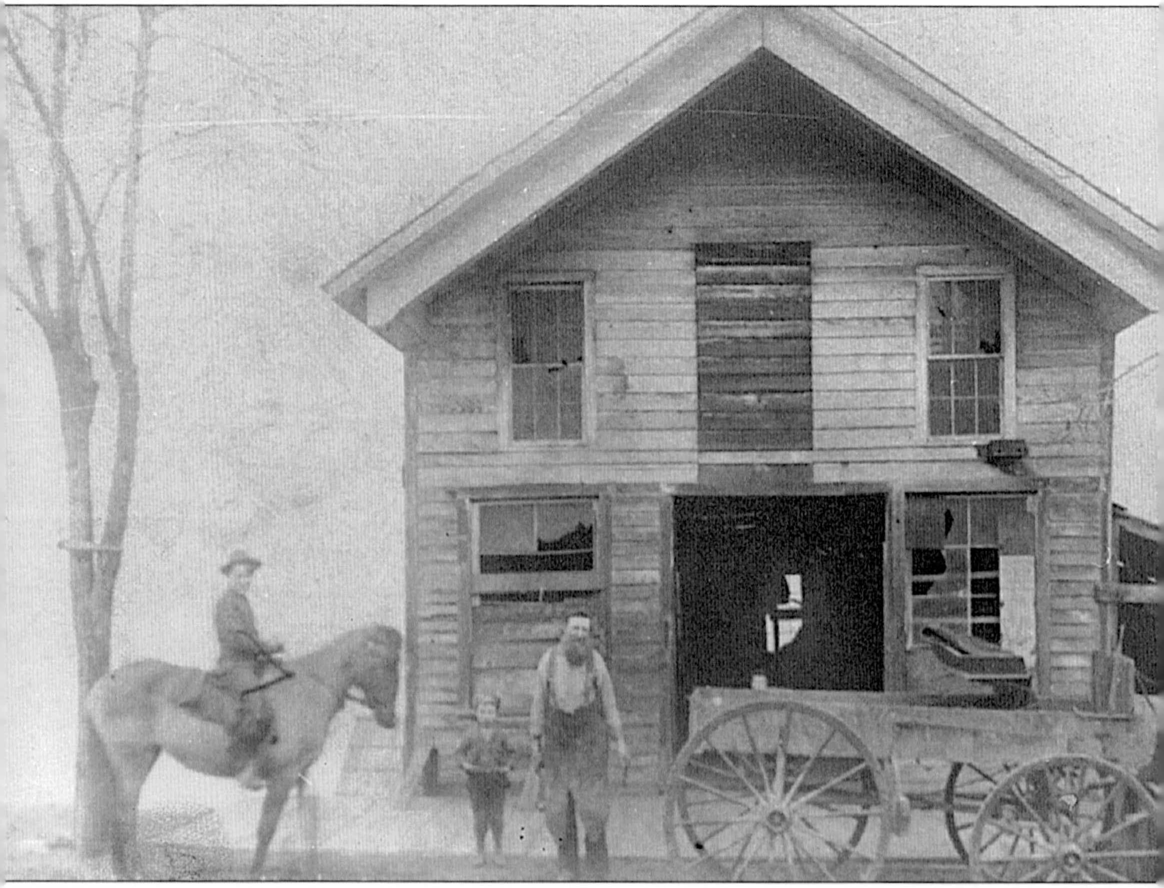

THE TOWN FARRIER. Peter Runquist was a Steilacoom pioneer and blacksmith. Runquist originally came to Steilacoom by way of the army in 1849. He operated four different blacksmith shops in Steilacoom; this one was located on Commercial Street. He ran an advertisement in the paper, the *Sunbeam*, printed in 1883: "P-Runquist BLACK-SMITH Steilacoom W. T., Parties that have their horses shod at my shop once never go elsewhere." Peter Runquist died in 1899; his descendants continue to live in Steilacoom.

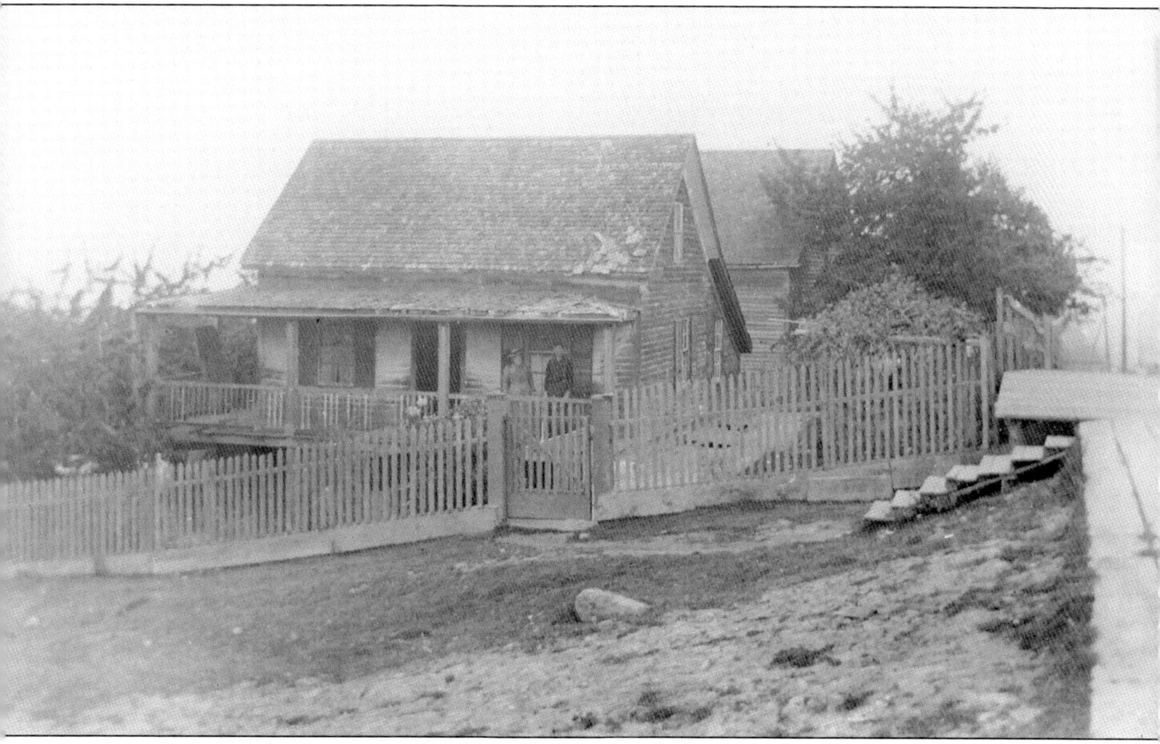

The Runquist Home. This home once belonged to the Peter Runquist family; the people in the picture are unidentified. By 1910, the Northern Pacific Railroad had purchased the property on the water side of Commercial Street. This is one of several structures that were moved up one block to Lafayette Street with the help of Nick Doering and his mighty team of horses.

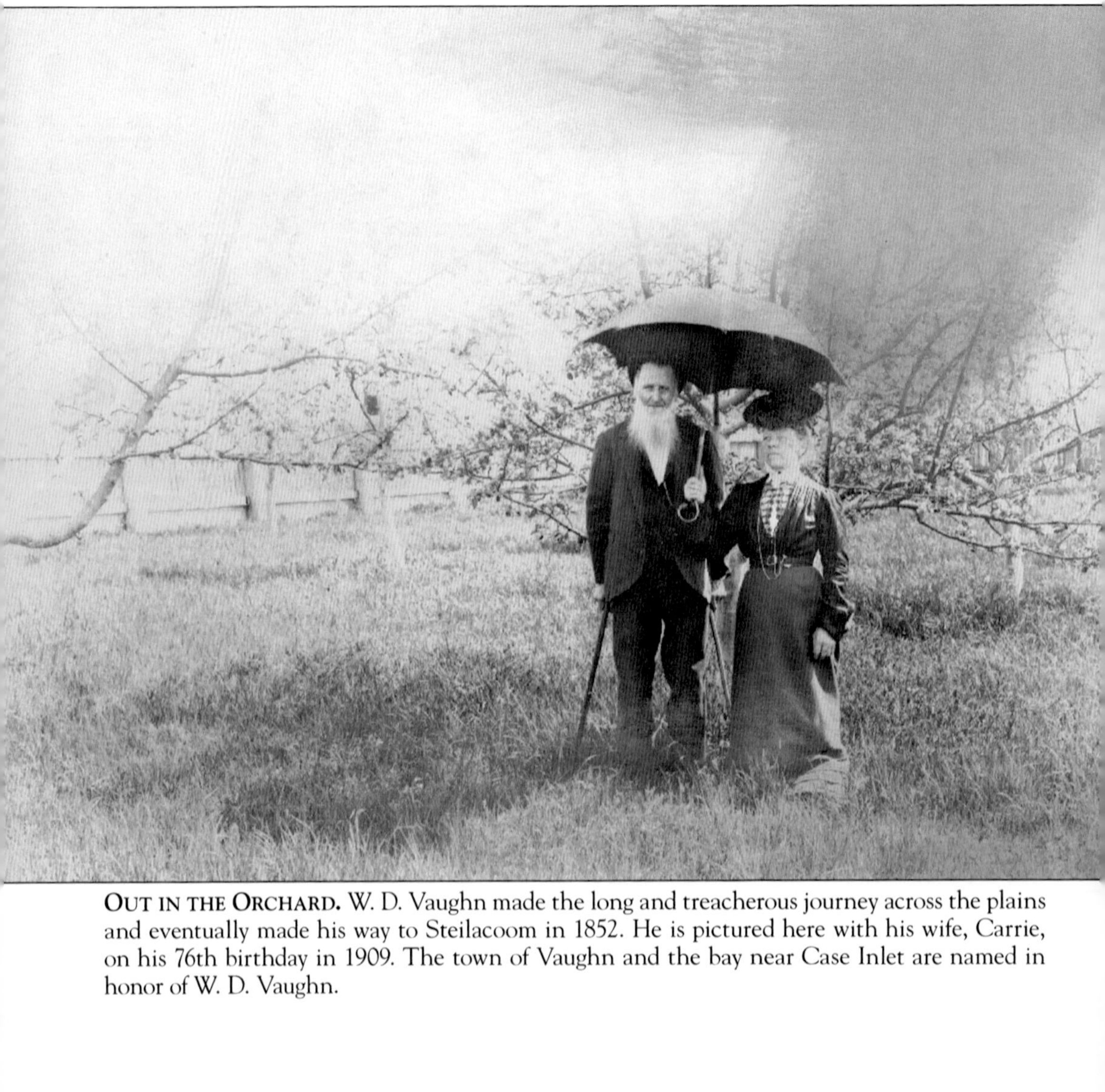

OUT IN THE ORCHARD. W. D. Vaughn made the long and treacherous journey across the plains and eventually made his way to Steilacoom in 1852. He is pictured here with his wife, Carrie, on his 76th birthday in 1909. The town of Vaughn and the bay near Case Inlet are named in honor of W. D. Vaughn.

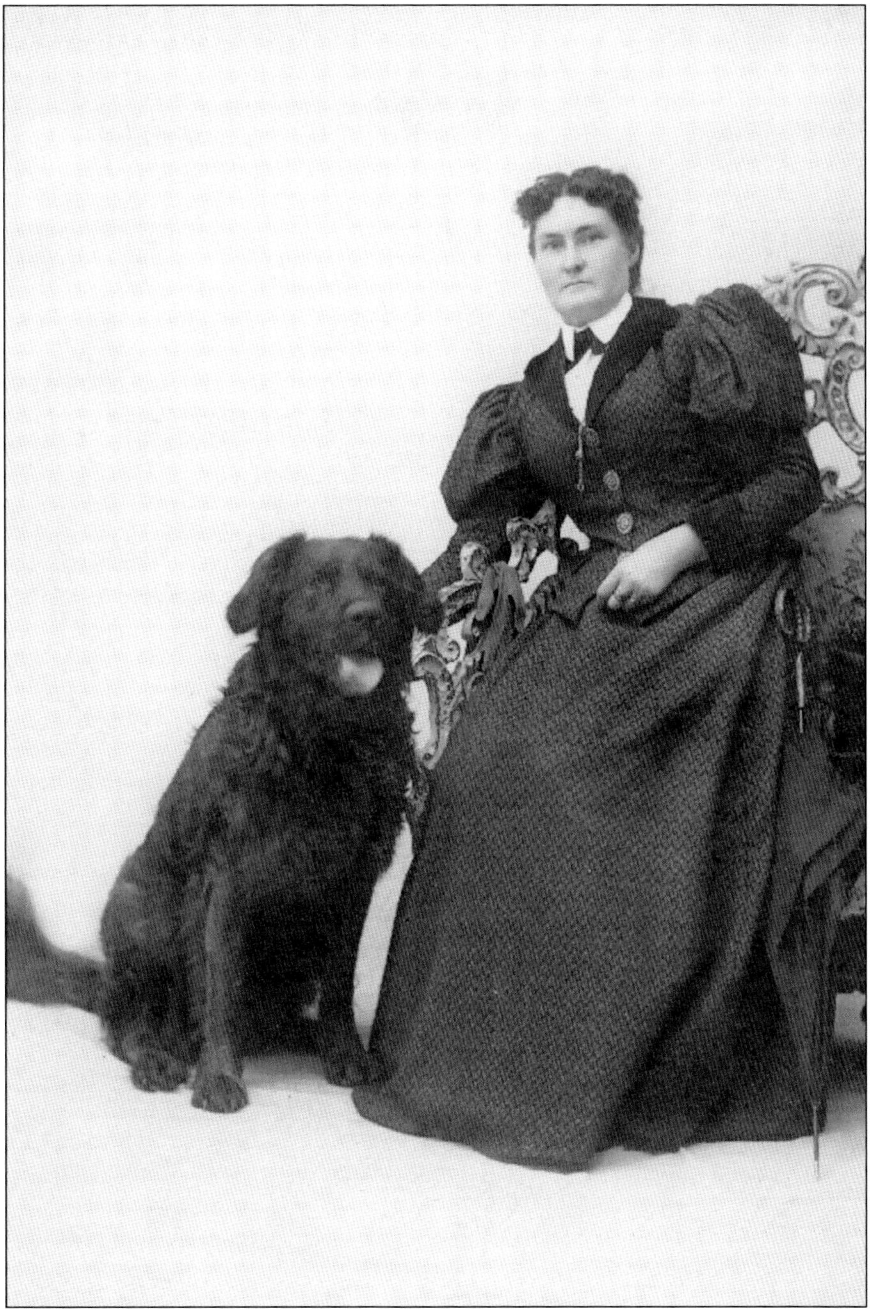

LAURA BELLE DOWNEY BARTLETT. This remarkable woman began her journey West at the age of two years via wagon train across Naches Pass with her parents and 10 siblings. Laura Belle Downey Bartlett was an accomplished woman. She was an author, a translator, a miner, a historian, and an avid supporter of musical arts. Laura Belle Bartlett was also known as a preservationist of Chinook Jargon and acted as an interpreter between political figures and the Quinault Indians. Chinook Jargon was the universal language of settlers, Native Americans, and traders alike. Laura Belle was widowed after only a few years of marriage. Her husband, Nehamiah, drowned in a boating accident off Fox Island.

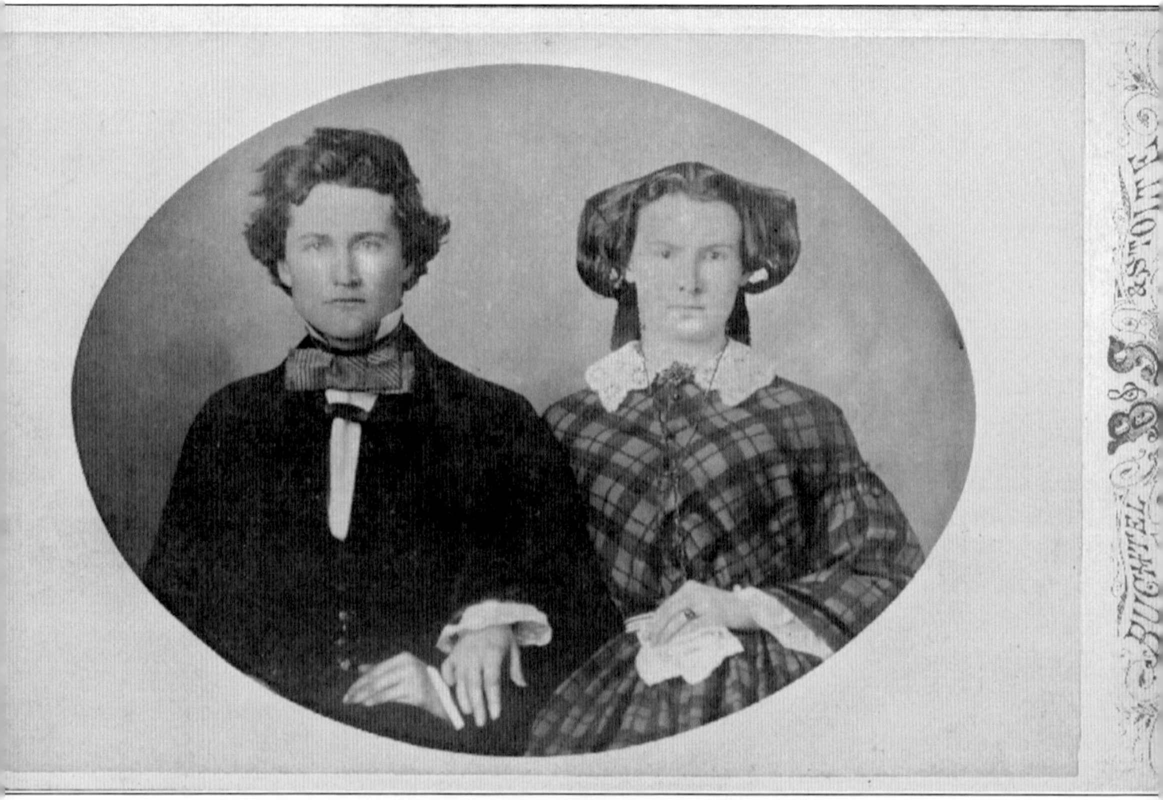

PIONEER WEDDING. Frank Clark came to Steilacoom in 1852 at the age of 18. He set out from San Francisco aboard the *George Emory* under the command of Lafayette Balch. When Clark arrived, he was fresh out of law school but with little funds. He worked at the Balch-Thompson mill at Sequalitchew Creek until he could save enough money to start his practice. In 1853, he purchased a lot on Main and Lafayette Streets and constructed a small building. He hung a sign that read, "Frank Clark—Attorney-at-Law." On New Year's Day 1856, he married Elizabeth Jane Downey, pictured above. Frank and Elizabeth had four daughters and one son. Elizabeth died in 1867, and he remarried Lena Scholfield. Frank and Lena had one son. Frank Clark rose to prominence as a lawyer and legislator. He was able to practice in all branches of law, although he is most known for his involvement in the high-profile case of Chief Leschi. Much to the disapproval of the citizens, Clark was able to temporarily delay Leschi's execution. In 1875, Clark was serving as the Northern Pacific attorney and decided to move to New Tacoma. He built a large home on the southwest corner of A and Tenth Streets. Frank Clark died at the age of 49 en route to court aboard a Northern Pacific train.

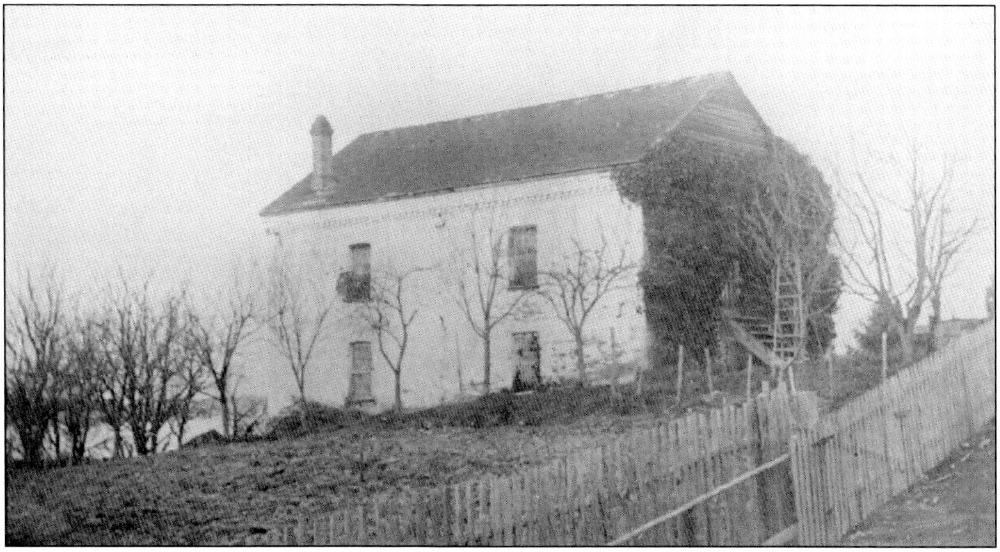

The First Jail in the Territory. Although this structure looks more like a residence, it was the first jail in the territory and began operation in 1858. The jail also housed federal prisoners until a federal prison site was established on McNeil Island in 1875. The jail was dismantled with the intention of relocating the building. It was never reassembled, and a few iron bars are all that remain. They can be seen at the Steilacoom Historical Museum.

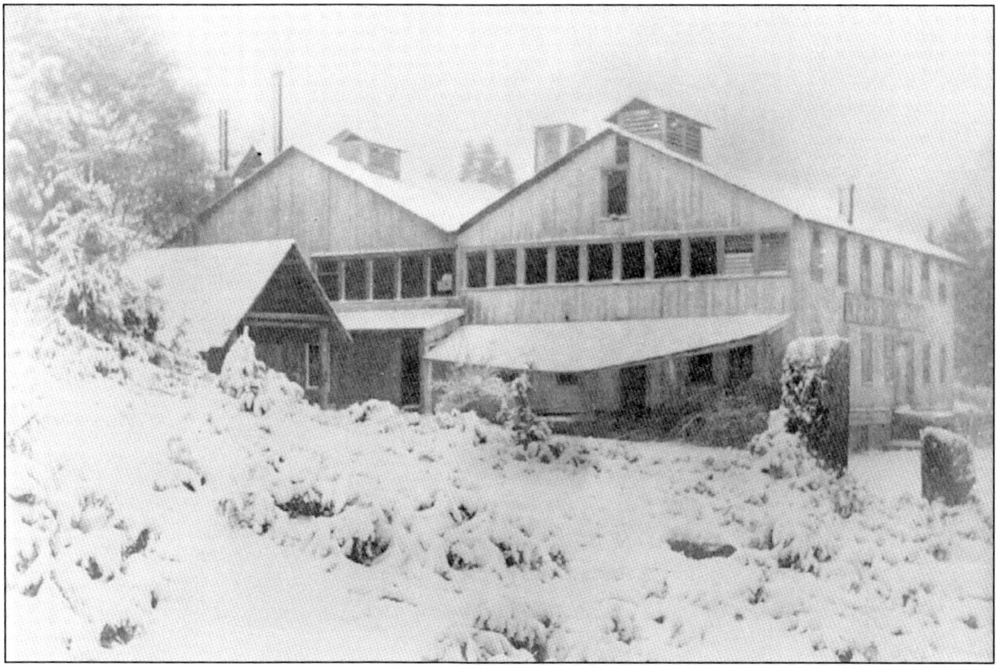

The First Brewery. The year 1858 brought the first brewery to the territory. The specialty was lager beer, which most people had never tasted. The brewery was a very profitable business for Martin Schmeig. The beer was shipped all over the region with the promise that the customer could be confident of "prompt attention paid to all orders." In the early 1870s, Wolf Schafer came to Steilacoom and established the Northern Pacific Railroad Brewery on Starling Street, seen here.

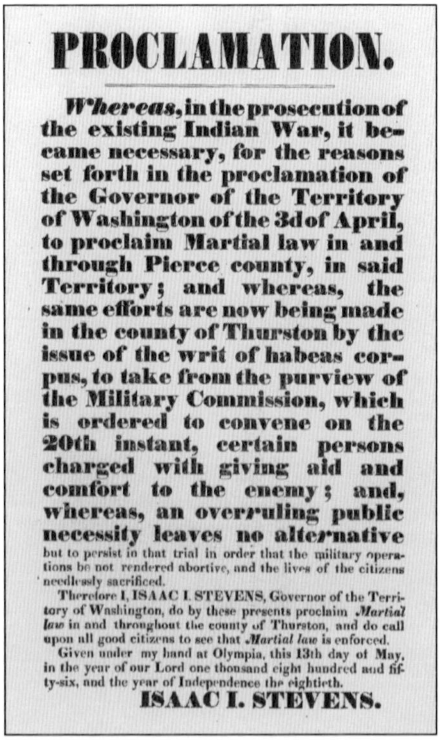

PROCLAMATION.

Whereas, in the prosecution of the existing Indian War, it became necessary, for the reasons set forth in the proclamation of the Governor of the Territory of Washington of the 3d of April, to proclaim Martial law in and through Pierce county, in said Territory; and whereas, the same efforts are now being made in the county of Thurston by the issue of the writ of habeas corpus, to take from the purview of the Military Commission, which is ordered to convene on the 20th instant, certain persons charged with giving aid and comfort to the enemy; and, whereas, an overruling public necessity leaves no alternative but to persist in that trial in order that the military operations be not rendered abortive, and the lives of the citizens needlessly sacrificed.

Therefore I, ISAAC I. STEVENS, Governor of the Territory of Washington, do by these presents proclaim *Martial law* in and throughout the county of Thurston, and do call upon all good citizens to see that *Martial law* is enforced.

Given under my hand at Olympia, this 13th day of May, in the year of our Lord one thousand eight hundred and fifty-six, and the year of Independence the eightieth.

ISAAC I. STEVENS.

MARSHALL LAW PROCLAIMED. Appointed by Pres. Franklin Pierce, Isaac Stevens became the first governor of Washington Territory and superintendent of Indian Affairs. Concerned with the growing conflict between the incoming settlers seeking land and the Native American people who had always claimed the land, Governor Stevens conducted treaty negotiations throughout the territory, beginning at Medicine Creek in December 1854. Conflict resulted in the Indian War of 1855–1856 as the tribes were moved to reservations, often far from their original hunting and fishing grounds.

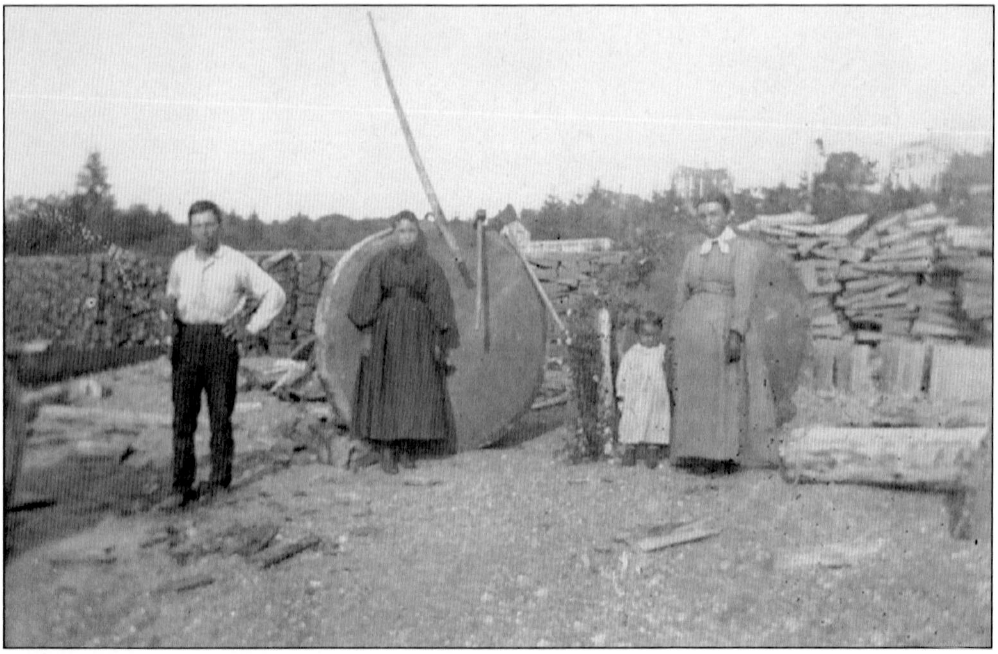

NATIVE FAMILY, C. 1909. Shown here are "Indian Jim" and his family. He was one of the many native people who stayed in Steilacoom. Half a century earlier, tribal leader Sam Young made every effort to establish a Steilacoom reservation. He is quoted as saying, "My home is Shilicum (Steilacoom) Creek, and there is where I want to live and die. . . . I wish to tell the Governor that every Indian loves his native land best. Every Indian loves his own people best."

VOLUNTEERS NEEDED. The call for action from the territorial government was directed at its settlers to volunteer to serve in the Indian War. Those who did not serve in the equivalent of the "reserves" sought refuge at Fort Steilacoom.

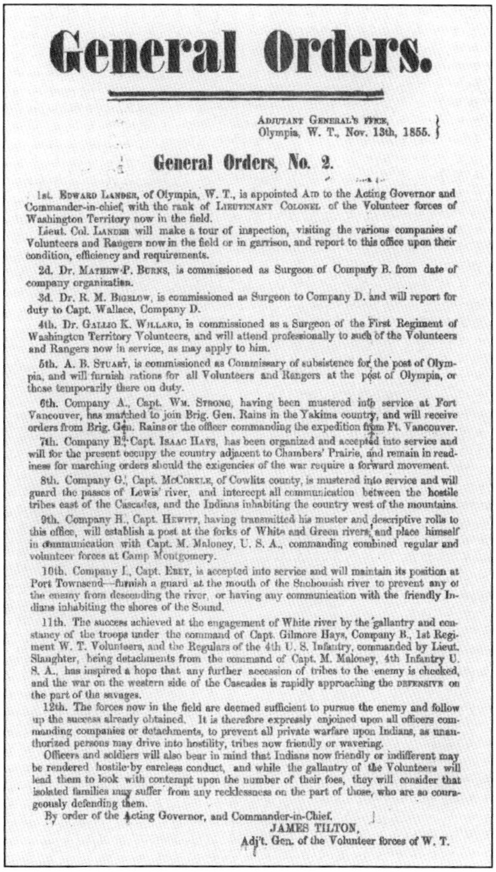

General Orders.

ADJUTANT GENERAL'S FFICE,
Olympia, W. T., Nov. 13th, 1855.

General Orders, No. 2.

1st. EDWARD LANDER, of Olympia, W. T., is appointed AID to the Acting Governor and Commander-in-chief, with the rank of LIEUTENANT COLONEL of the Volunteer forces of Washington Territory now in the field.

Lieut. Col. LANDER will make a tour of inspection, visiting the various companies of Volunteers and Rangers now in the field or in garrison, and report to this office upon their condition, efficiency and requirements.

2d. Dr. MATHEW P. BURNS, is commissioned as Surgeon of Company B. from date of company organization.

3d. Dr. R. M. BIGELOW, is commissioned as Surgeon to Company D. and will report for duty to Capt. Wallace, Company D.

4th. Dr. GALLIO K. WILLARD, is commissioned as a Surgeon of the First Regiment of Washington Territory Volunteers, and will attend professionally to such of the Volunteers and Rangers now in service, as may apply to him.

5th. A. B. STUART, is commissioned as Commissary of subsistence for the post of Olympia, and will furnish rations for all Volunteers and Rangers at the post of Olympia, or those temporarily there on duty.

6th. Company A., Capt. WM. STRONG, having been mustered into service at Fort Vancouver, has marched to join Brig. Gen. Rains in the Yakima country, and will receive orders from Brig. Gen. Rains or the officer commanding the expedition from Ft. Vancouver.

7th. Company E., Capt. ISAAC HAYS, has been organized and accepted into service and will for the present occupy the country adjacent to Chambers' Prairie, and remain in readiness for marching orders should the exigencies of the war require a forward movement.

8th. Company G., Capt. MCCORKLE, of Cowlitz county, is mustered into service and will guard the passes of Lewis' river, and intercept all communication between the hostile tribes east of the Cascades, and the Indians inhabiting the country west of the mountains.

9th. Company H., Capt. HEWITT, having transmitted his muster and descriptive rolls to this office, will establish a post at the forks of White and Green rivers, and place himself in communication with Capt. M. Maloney, U. S. A., commanding combined regular and volunteer forces at Camp Montgomery.

10th. Company I., Capt. EBEY, is accepted into service and will maintain its position at Port Townsend—furnish a guard at the mouth of the Snohomish river to prevent any of the enemy from descending the river, or having any communication with the friendly Indians inhabiting the shores of the Sound.

11th. The success achieved at the engagement of White river by the gallantry and constancy of the troops under the command of Capt. Gilmore Hays, Company B., 1st Regiment W. T. Volunteers, and the Regulars of the 4th U. S. Infantry, commanded by Lieut. Slaughter, being detachments from the command of Capt. M. Maloney, 4th Infantry U. S. A., has inspired a hope that any further accession of tribes to the enemy is checked, and the war on the western side of the Cascades is rapidly approaching the DEFENSIVE on the part of the savages.

12th. The forces now in the field are deemed sufficient to pursue the enemy and follow up the success already obtained. It is therefore expressly enjoined upon all officers commanding companies or detachments, to prevent all private warfare upon Indians, as unauthorized persons may drive into hostility, tribes now friendly or wavering.

Officers and soldiers will also bear in mind that Indians now friendly or indifferent may be rendered hostile by careless conduct, and while the gallantry of the Volunteers will lead them to look with contempt upon the number of their foes, they will consider that isolated families may suffer from any recklessness on the part of those, who are so courageously defending them.

By order of the Acting Governor, and Commander-in-Chief.

JAMES TILTON,
Adj't. Gen. of the Volunteer forces of W. T.

"STEILACOOM JOHN" AND "STEILACOOM ANNIE." These two native Steilacoom people stayed in Steilacoom until their deaths. They lived in a home along the beach until it was destroyed by a grading project that eventually made way for the streetcar. The townspeople helped John and Annie build their float home. John and Annie earned their living by fishing, harvesting shellfish, making baskets, and selling blackberries. Note the canoes tied to their float home.

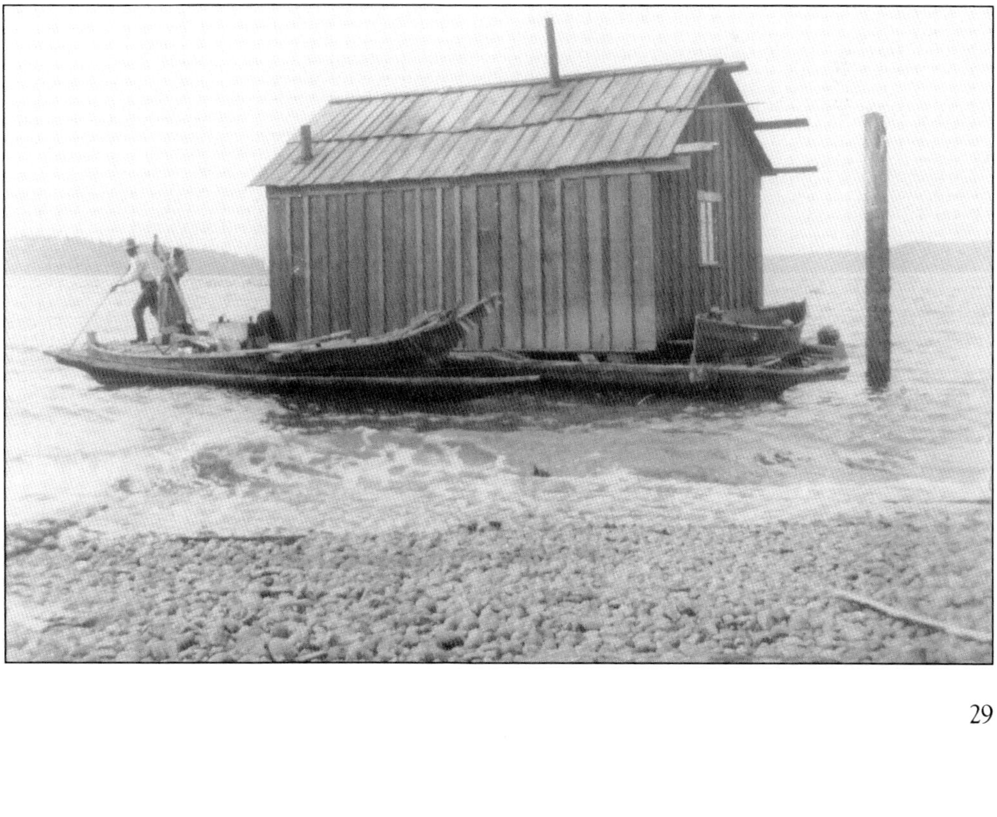

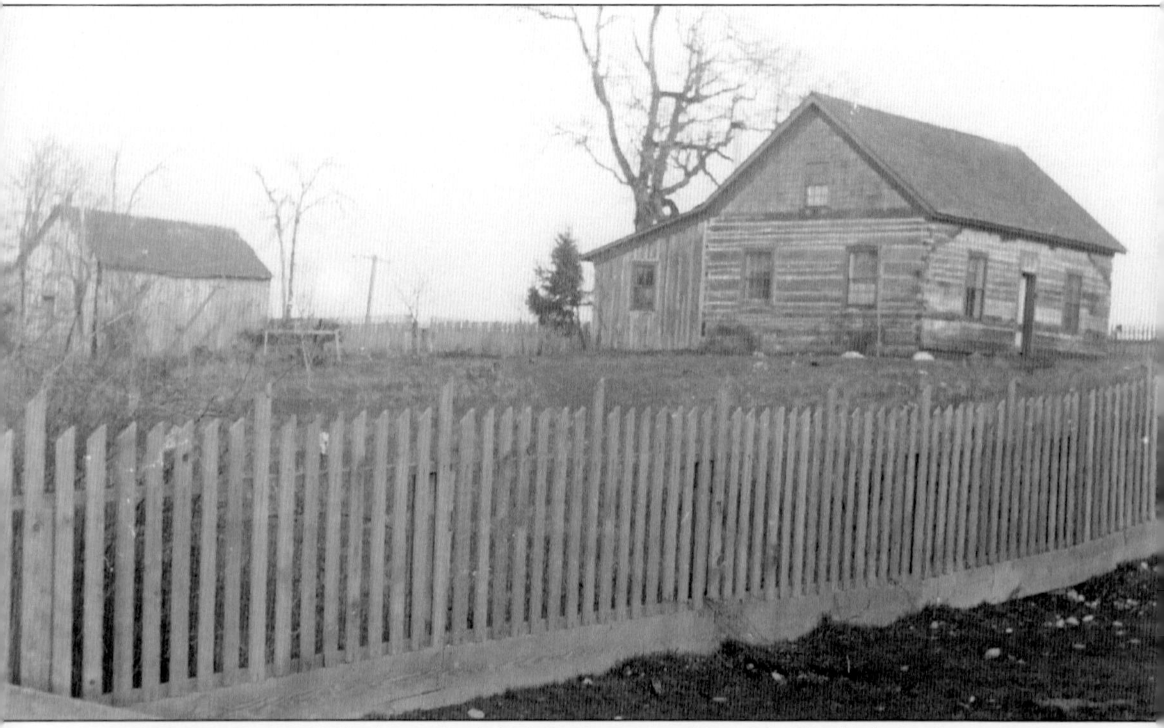

THE RIGNEY CABIN. This home, built by John Rigney and his wife, Elizabeth, is where they began raising their 10 children. John Rigney served in the army and was stationed at Fort Vancouver; from there, he was reassigned to Fort Steilacoom. Elizabeth was able to accompany her husband to the Puget Sound area because she was employed as a laundress in the army. After his discharge, he had earned a claim of 640 acres. Rigney Hill is now known as Manitou Park. The family's cabin was located on what is now Sixty-fourth and Orchard Streets in Tacoma. The Rigney family moved to Steilacoom in 1880.

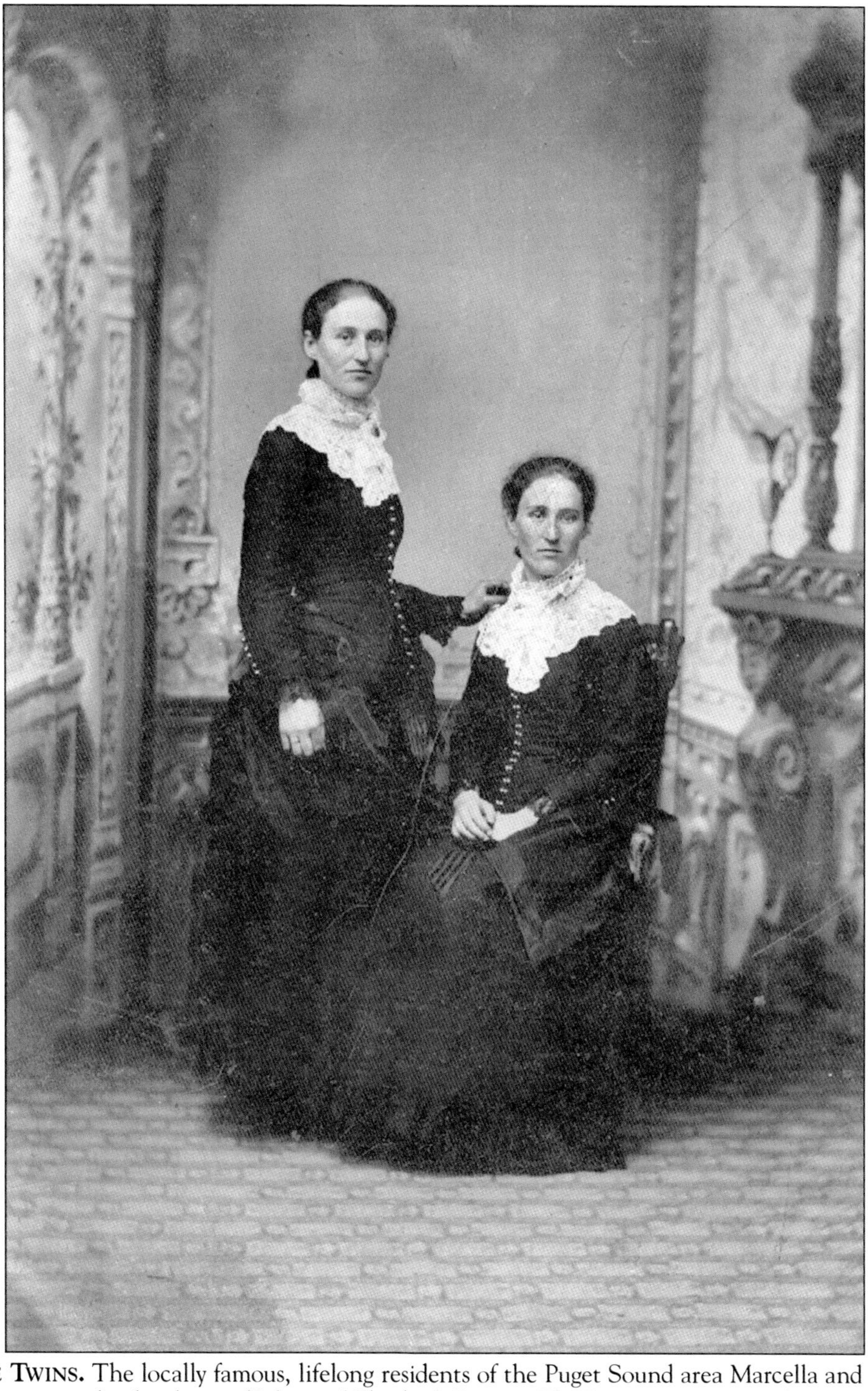

THE TWINS. The locally famous, lifelong residents of the Puget Sound area Marcella and Rose Rigney were the daughters of John and Elizabeth Rigney. The Rigney twins were the second set of twins in their family. The women married and stayed in Steilacoom. They eventually took over the family's Western Union business in 1886, continuing until Western Union merged with the phone company in 1911.

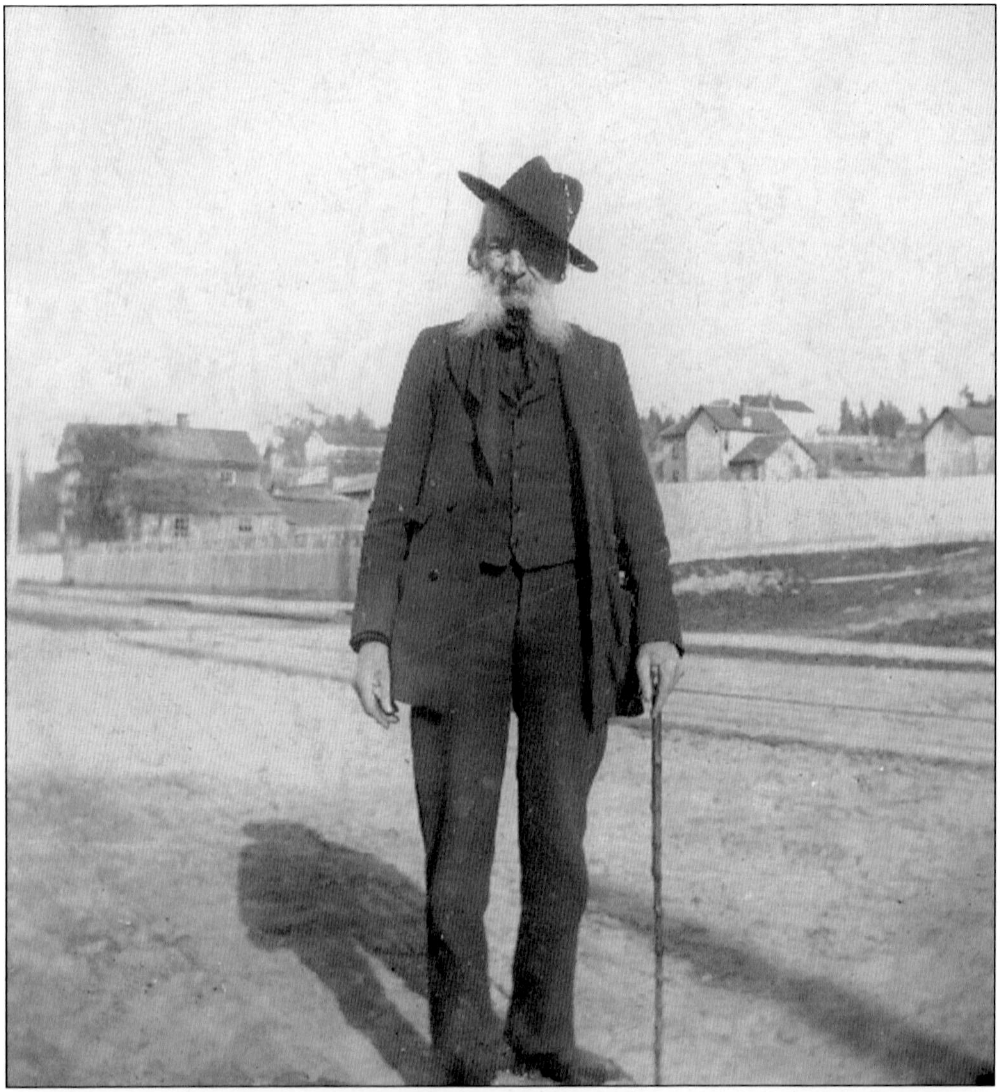

CAPT. JOHN SALTAR. Born in Philadelphia in 1814, the captain came to Steilacoom by way of San Francisco in the 1860s. John Saltar was the clerk of the U.S. District Court from 1863 until 1880, when the Pierce County seat was moved to Tacoma. He was the collector and assessor for the U.S. Bureau of Internal Revenue for Idaho and Washington Territories. With his long white sideburns, Van Dyke beard, wide felt hat, flowing tie, and courtly Southern manners, the captain cut a striking figure as he walked down the wooden sidewalks of early Steilacoom. He stood 6 feet, 4 inches tall and always carried a bone-handled cane on the long walks for which he was noted. It is said that he walked from Tacoma to Steilacoom while in his early 80s. Captain Saltar died in 1889 in his 85th year and was buried in the Masonic Cemetery.

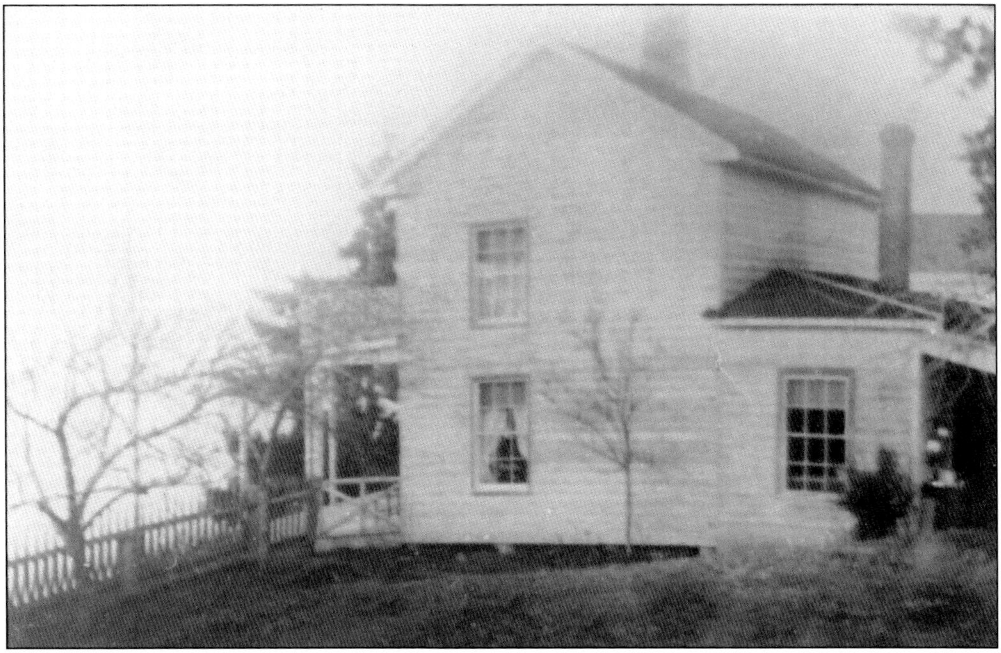

The Saltar Home. Pictured above is the house John Saltar built, according to navigation charts on Gordon's Point, known locally as Saltar's Point. The home was torn down to make way for pending construction of the railroad. The home had a veranda with French-style doors opening toward Puget Sound.

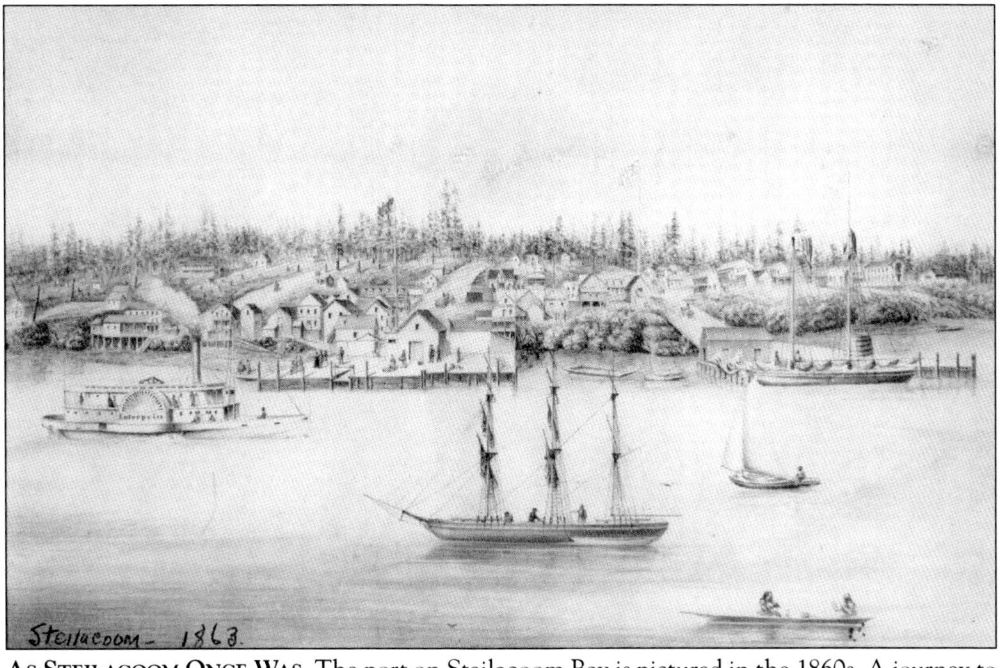

As Steilacoom Once Was. The port on Steilacoom Bay is pictured in the 1860s. A journey to Steilacoom presumably ended at Balch's Wharf (left center), the busiest port for the time. Phillip Keach built the wharf to the right at the end of Main Street. Several structures depicted in this lithograph currently stand and have been listed on the National Register of Historic Places.

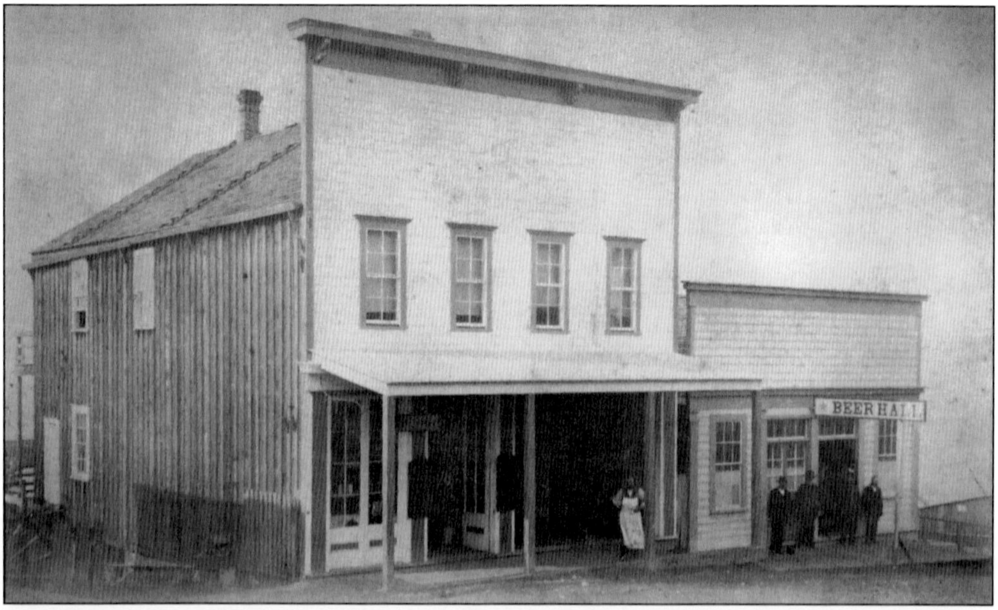

BEER HALL. George Weller built this structure in the 1850s for use as a butcher shop with living quarters upstairs. The beer hall was operated by Henry Rupp beginning in the 1880s through the 1890s. At the time this photograph was taken, the post office and a butcher shop occupied the larger building to the left of the beer hall.

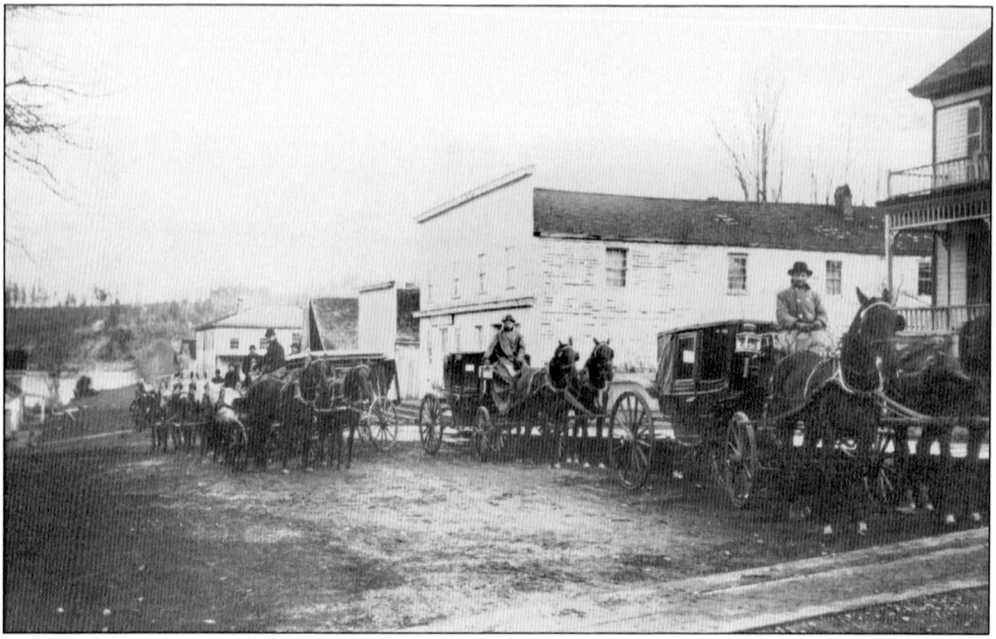

FUNERAL PROCESSIONAL. These somber rigs, a hearse and five carriages, were for the funeral of Henry P. Rupp, born 1870, who died in 1883. He was the son of Henry Rupp the saloon keeper.

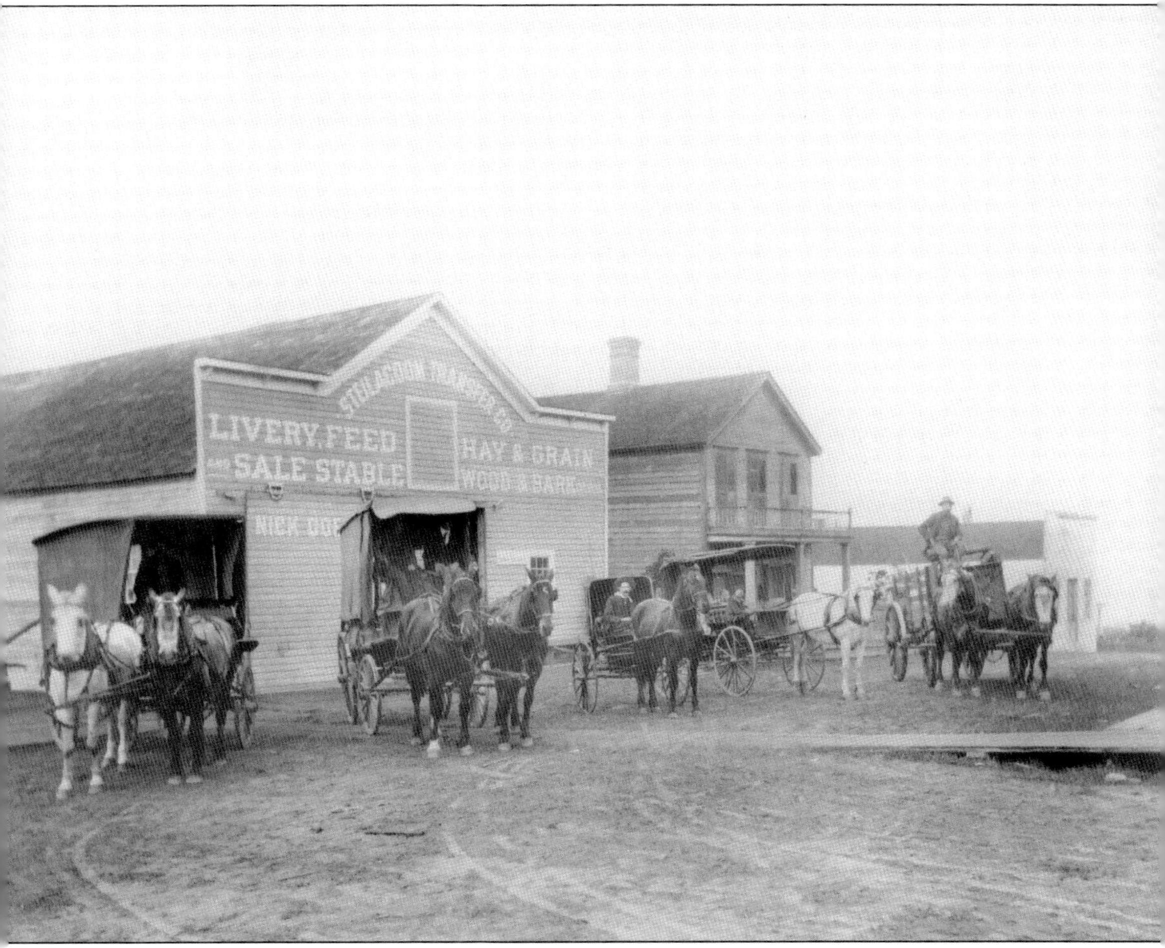

THE STEILACOOM TRANSFER COMPANY. Nick Doering, owner of the Steilacoom Transfer Company, can be seen on the far right. His sons are driving the other rigs pictured. Doering and his team were credited with grading Chambers Creek Road and Steilacoom Boulevard in addition to the roads in Steilacoom. The Steilacoom Transfer Company was located on the corner of Wilkes and Commercial Streets. The business later became the Steilacoom Fuel and Transfer Company, delivering coal and wood to Steilacoom homes. Doering is also credited with moving entire buildings with his mighty team of horses.

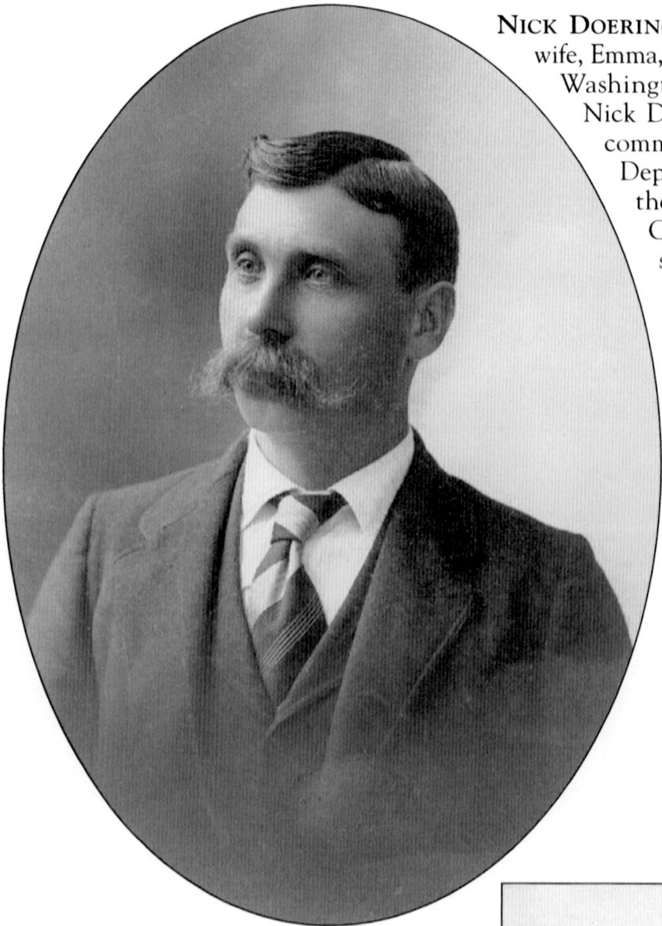

Nick Doering. Nick Doering married his wife, Emma, on November 11, 1889, the day Washington Territory became a state. Nick Doering was a supporter of his community, especially through the Depression; with his support and the donation of fuel, the Oberlin Church was able to stay open to serve the town.

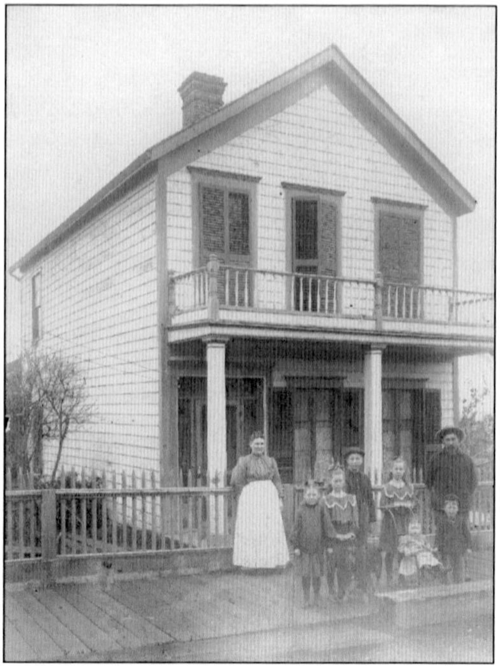

The Doering Family. The Doering home was moved from the water side of Commercial Street next to their livery stable farther down the street about 1911. Nick and Emma Doering are pictured with their children, from left to right, Inez, Daisy, Howard (in back), Viola, Matie (in carriage), and Earl.

LAND SURVEYOR. Pictured in 1895 is Stephen Judson with his wife, Edith, using his survey equipment. Judson was a surveyor in Pierce County.

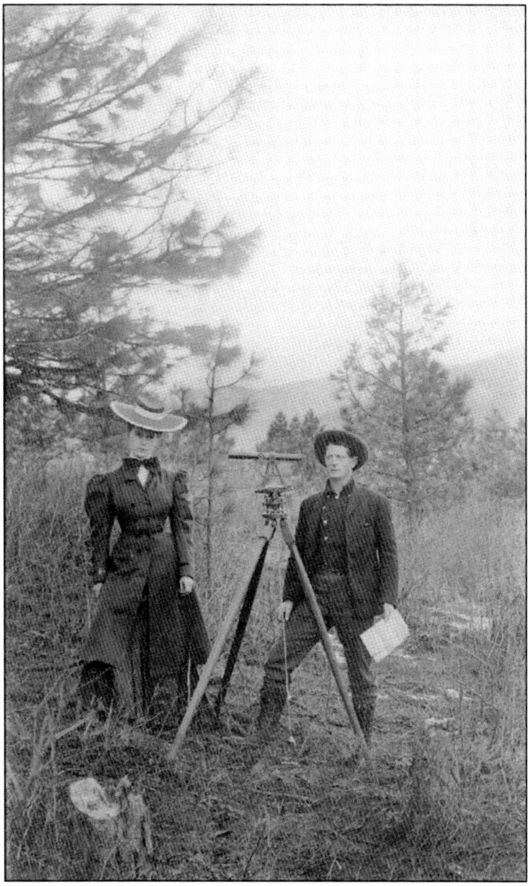

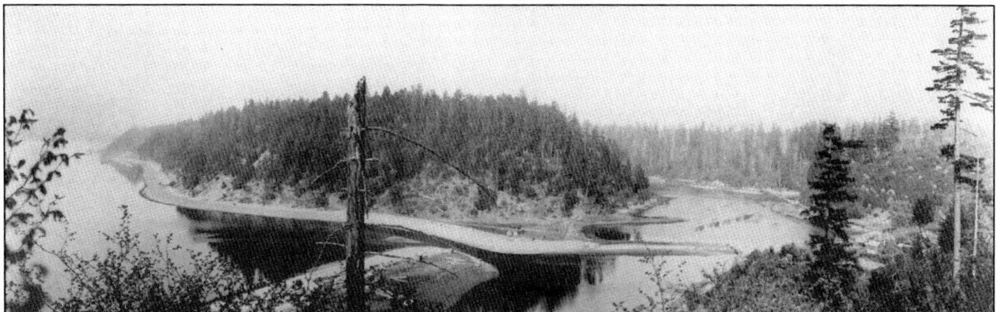

CHAMBERS BAY AND CREEK. When the Hudson Bay Company claimed this area for their subsidiary, the Puget Sound Agricultural Company, the creek was renamed for a short time as Heath Creek in honor of Joseph Heath, the lessor of the farm that eventually became Fort Steilacoom. By the late 1840s, Thomas McCutcheon Chambers settled on the land already occupied by Heath. Chambers received a letter from his friend Dr. William Tolmie that warned him of the consequences if he stayed on the land. The Hudson Bay Company officials paid Chambers a visit, and he introduced himself with his rifle resting on the fence. His strategy was successful because over the next few years he was appointed justice of the peace and then served as county commissioner once Pierce County was established. Chambers also opened three mills on what is now called Chambers Creek and Chambers Bay. He died in 1876 at the age of 81.

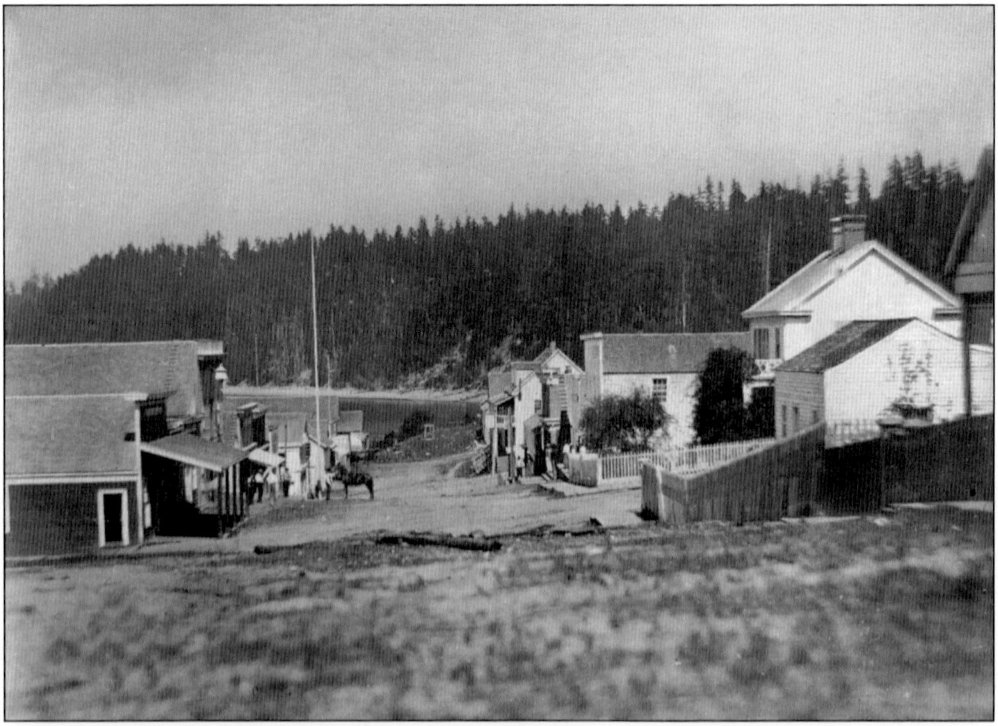

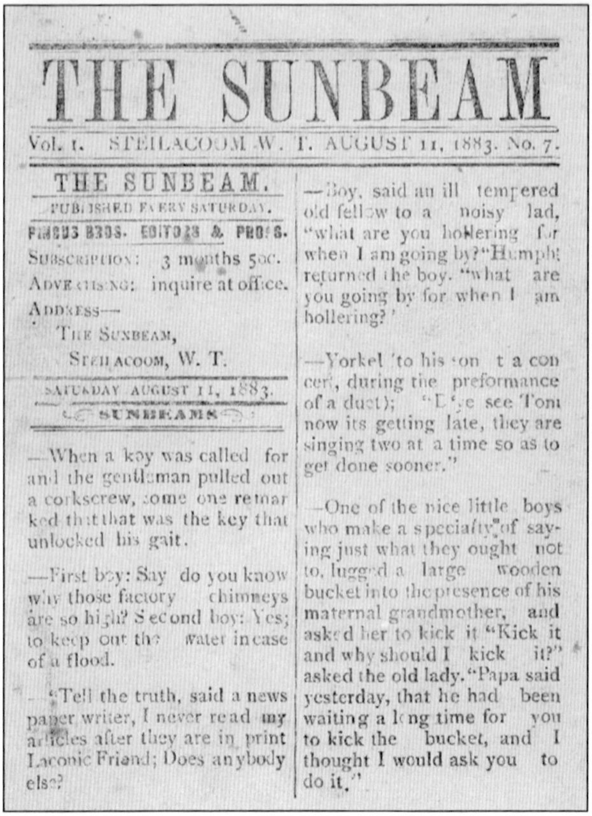

THE SUNBEAM

Vol. 1. STEILACOOM W. T. AUGUST 11, 1883. No. 7.

THE SUNBEAM.

PUBLISHED EVERY SATURDAY.

PROSCH BROS. EDITORS & PROPS.

SUBSCRIPTION: 3 months 50c.

ADVERTISING: inquire at office.

ADDRESS—

THE SUNBEAM,

STEILACOOM, W. T.

SATURDAY AUGUST 11, 1883.

SUNBEAMS

—When a key was called for and the gentleman pulled out a corkscrew, some one remarked that that was the key that unlocked his gait.

—First boy: Say do you know why those factory chimneys are so high? Second boy: Yes; to keep out the water in case of a flood.

—"Tell the truth, said a newspaper writer, I never read my articles after they are in print Laconic Friend; Does anybody else?

—Boy, said an ill tempered old fellow to a noisy lad, "what are you hollering for when I am going by?" "Humph! returned the boy. "what are you going by for when I am hollering?'

—Yorkel (to his son at a concert, during the preformance of a duet); "D'ye see Tom now its getting late, they are singing two at a time so as to get done sooner."

—One of the nice little boys who make a specialty of saying just what they ought not to, lugged a large wooden bucket into the presence of his maternal grandmother, and asked her to kick it "Kick it and why should I kick it?" asked the old lady. "Papa said yesterday, that he had been waiting a long time for you to kick the bucket, and I thought I would ask you to do it."

THE BUSIEST STREET IN THE TERRITORY. Pictured above is Commercial Avenue in the 1870s; the right side of the street was filled with saloons, shops, and restaurants. This was once the busiest street in the territory. By the dawn of the 20th century, a substantial amount of the structures had been abandoned and what wasn't abandoned was relocated to Lafayette Street, one block up the hill. Commercial Street now boasts an unobstructed view of the Puget Sound and Olympic Mountains.

THE *SUNBEAM*. The *Sunbeam* was one of the many newspapers printed in Steilacoom for the use of town promotion. Note the 1883 humor. Charles Prosch operated the second newspaper in Steilacoom beginning March 12, 1858, the *Puget Sound Herald*.

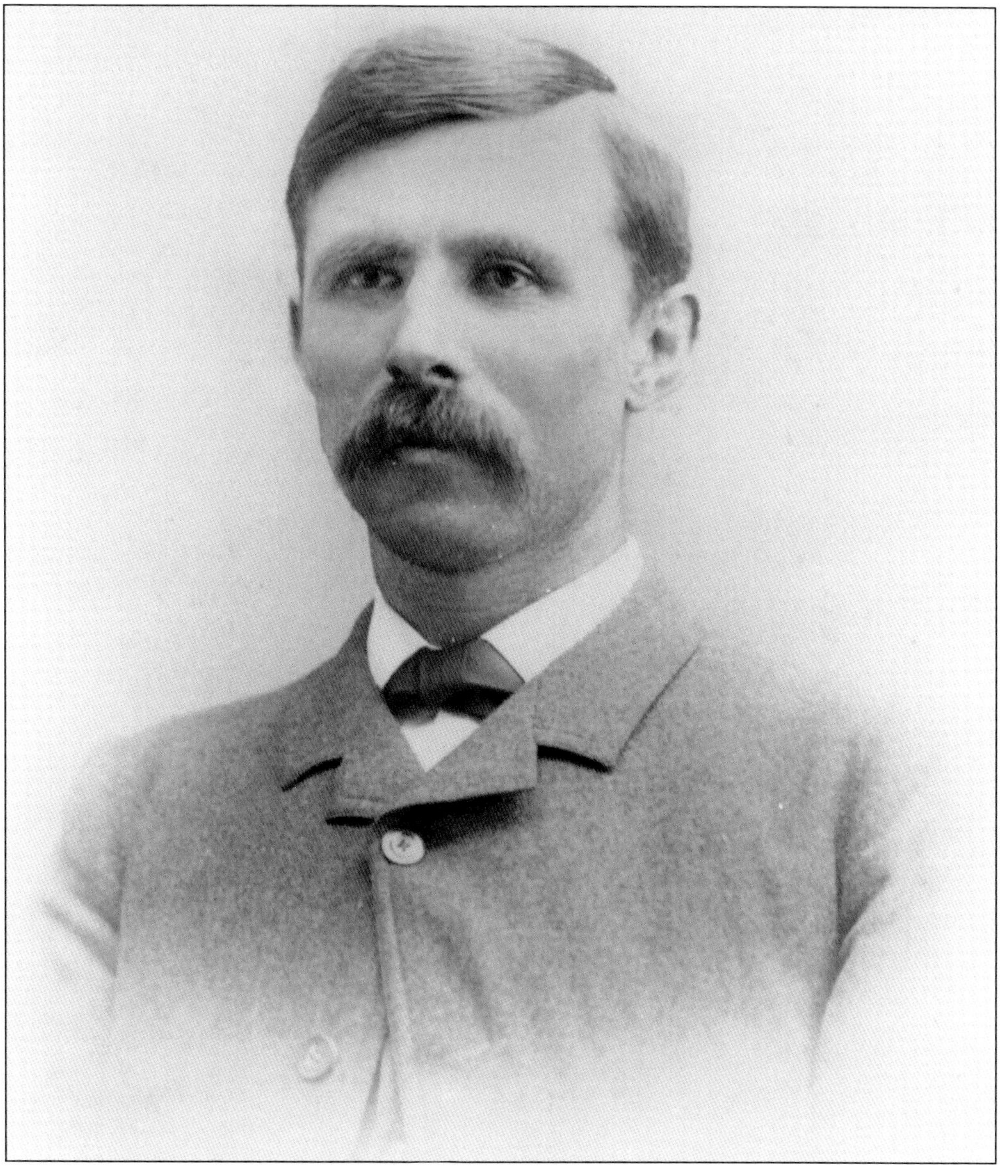

W. L. BAIR. Warren LeFevre Bair or "W. L." as he was known, was encouraged by his younger brother to move west to find opportunity, and that he did. He came to Steilacoom in April 1890, after a stop in Tacoma, and opened a drugstore on Commercial Street in January 1891. W. L. Bair's pioneer philosophy brought Steilacoom into the next century. He operated several successful businesses in town and designed and built the first water system. The water system was first installed at his second pharmacy location on Lafayette and Wilkes Streets. W. L. was also responsible for bringing telephone service to town; as home service evolved, he sold it to Bell Telephone, at which time he had 47 subscribers. The Bair Store was also the first in town to have electricity: W. L. plugged into the streetcar line that was right in front of his pharmacy. A good indication that the streetcar was nearing town was that the lights in the Bair Store would dim. W. P. Bonney, author of *History of Pierce County*, wrote about W. L., "He is held in the highest esteem by those who know him, and Steilacoom can boast of no better man or more enterprising citizen."

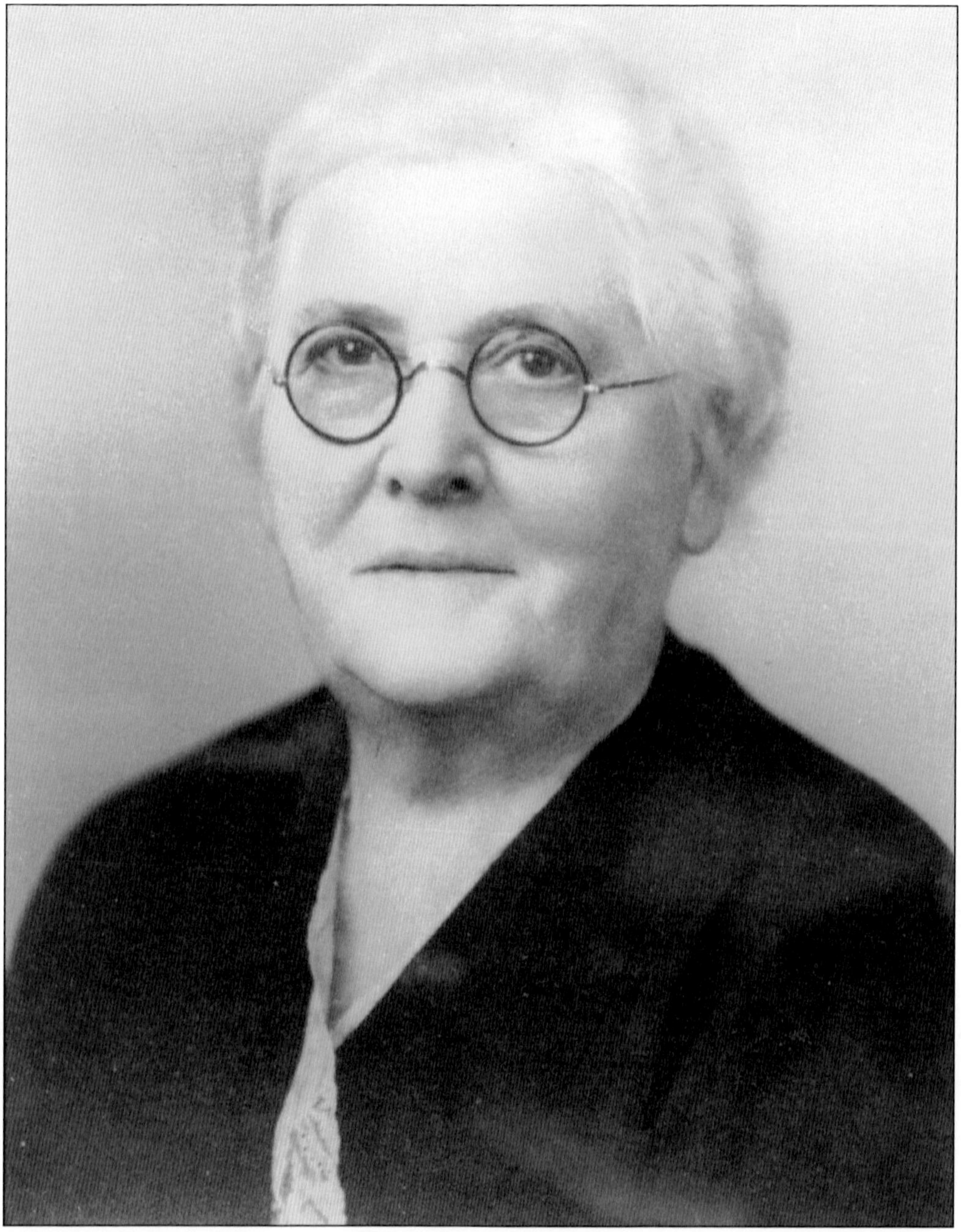

Grandma Bair. Hattie Godfrey Bair was the wife of W. L. Bair and an energetic supporter of life in Steilacoom. Without telling her husband, she sold most of their household belongings in Kansas and boarded the excursion train bound for Tacoma to join him out west. The arrival of the train was an event that the whole town of Tacoma showed up for as a welcome committee. Imagine his surprise when W. L. recognized his wife by the hat that she was wearing as she walked off the train! They moved from Tacoma and settled in Steilacoom. Hattie helped with day-to-day operations of several of her family's businesses. She was instrumental in organizing the Oberlin Church Ladies Aid and making ice cream for Masons at the lodge. Hattie Bair was known throughout the county for her cooking, and as she aged, she was called "Grandma" Bair.

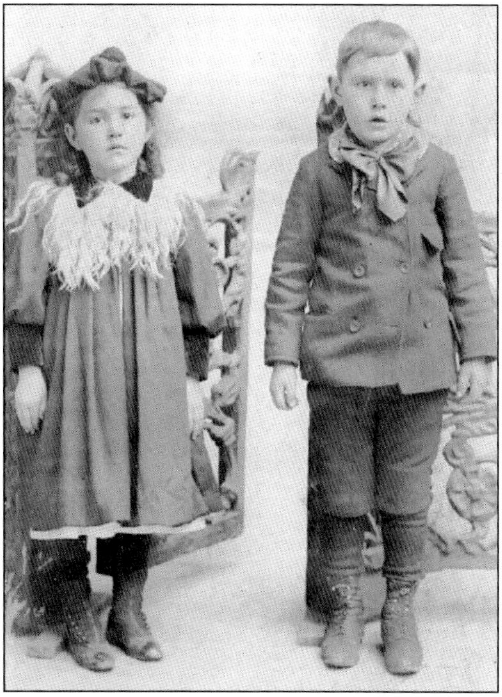

THE BAIR CHILDREN. Eudocia "Docia" Bair was born in Steilacoom in the house directly behind the drugstore when it was located on Commercial Street between Main and Balch Streets in 1892. Docia's older brother, Godfrey "Cub" Bair, was born in Tacoma in 1890 shortly after their mother's arrival west.

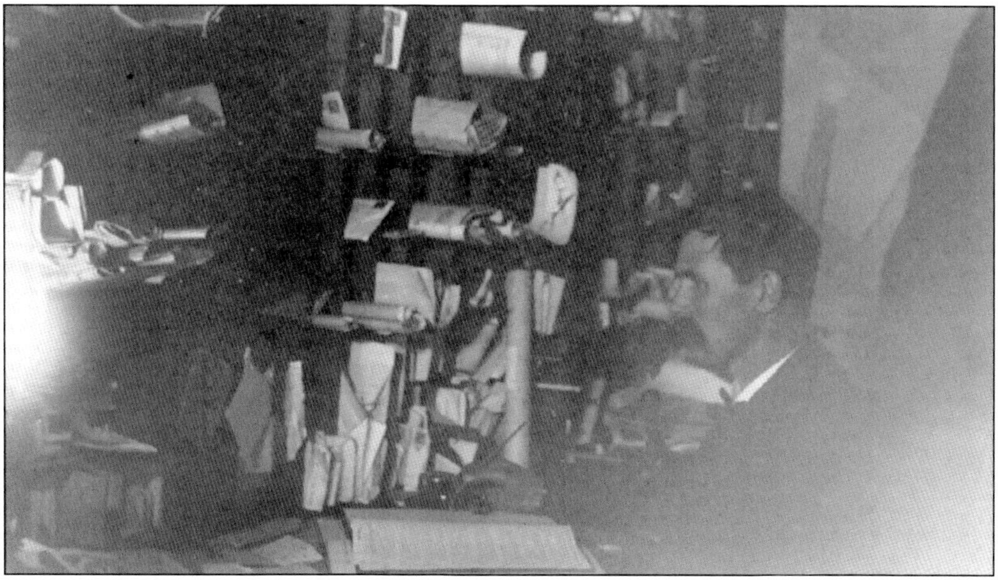

POSTMASTER BAIR. This photograph shows the interior of the post office when it was located next to the Bair Store on Lafayette Street. The postmaster was a position appointed by the president of the United States. W. L. Bair served as postmaster from 1893 to 1897 and for seven years under President Wilson. The position of postmaster changed with political party affiliation; if a Democratic president was in office, there would be a Democratic postmaster. In 1922, W. L.'s son-in-law, William "Bill" Leach, received his first appointment as postmaster when there was a Republican administration. Leach served under Presidents Harding, Coolidge, and Hoover. Eudocia Bair Leach served in the same position but was appointed by the Democratic president Franklin D. Roosevelt. They traded the title of postmaster for 37 years.

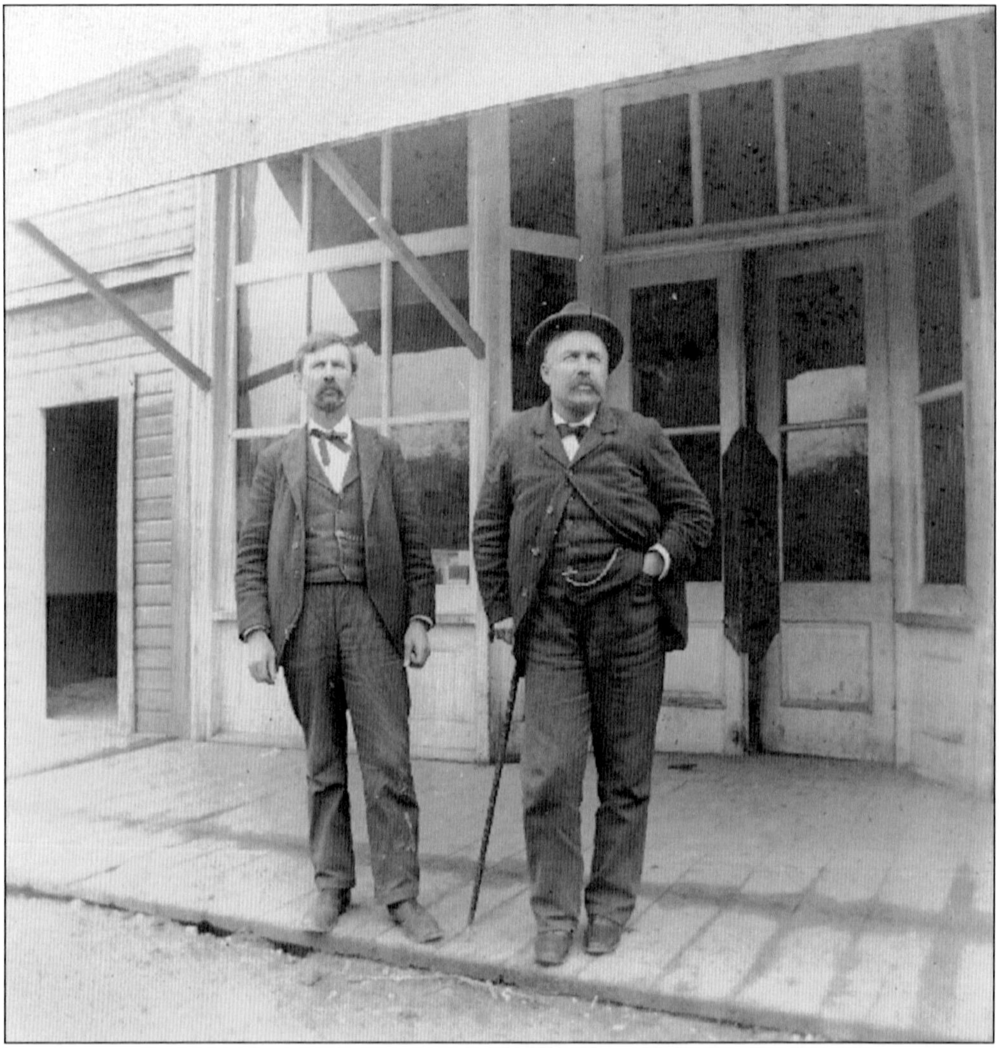

BAIR BROTHERS. W. L. Bair is pictured (left) with brother John in front of the Bair Store on Lafayette Street. Four of the five Bair children moved from the Midwest to the Northwest and lived out their lives in the town they helped develop.

Two

Congregation, Education, and Association

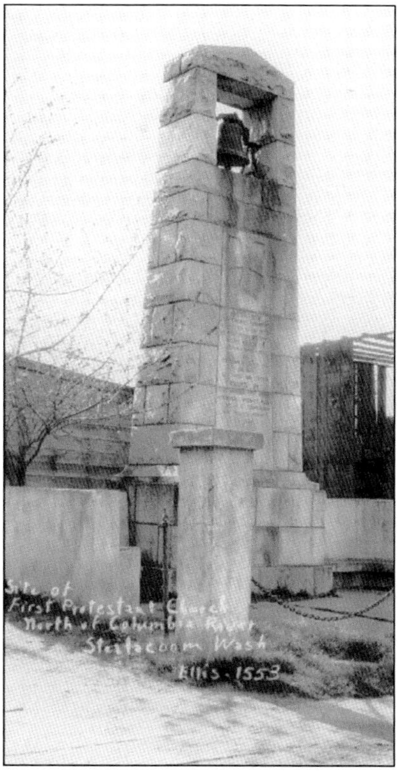

"The Bell Belongs in Steilacoom." This bell hung in the tower of the Methodist Episcopal church started by Reverend DeVore. Fund-raising began around town in 1856 for the purchase of the bell. The bell was delivered to Balch's Wharf in September 1858 for the price of $355, not including freight. It was mounted in the belfry, making it the first church bell in the territory. In the 1870s, a depression hit the region and the Methodist church didn't have the financial support it needed to continue in Steilacoom. Members of the Fern Hill congregation had just built a new church and knew of the bell that hung in the empty church. As a wagon pulled into town to haul it away, the would-be new owners were accosted by Nathanial Orr holding a pitchfork, E. R. Rogers, and W. H. Downey pounding his cane on the ground. The men explained that the church did indeed belong to the Methodists but that the bell belonged to the people of Steilacoom and the money to purchase it had been raised by Catholics and Protestants alike. With that explanation, the Fern Hill men turned around and went home. In 1908, the Washington State Historical Society, the Puget Sound Methodist Conference, and pioneer friends financed a stone monument so the town of Steilacoom could enjoy the bell. The bell was used to alert townspeople of emergencies.

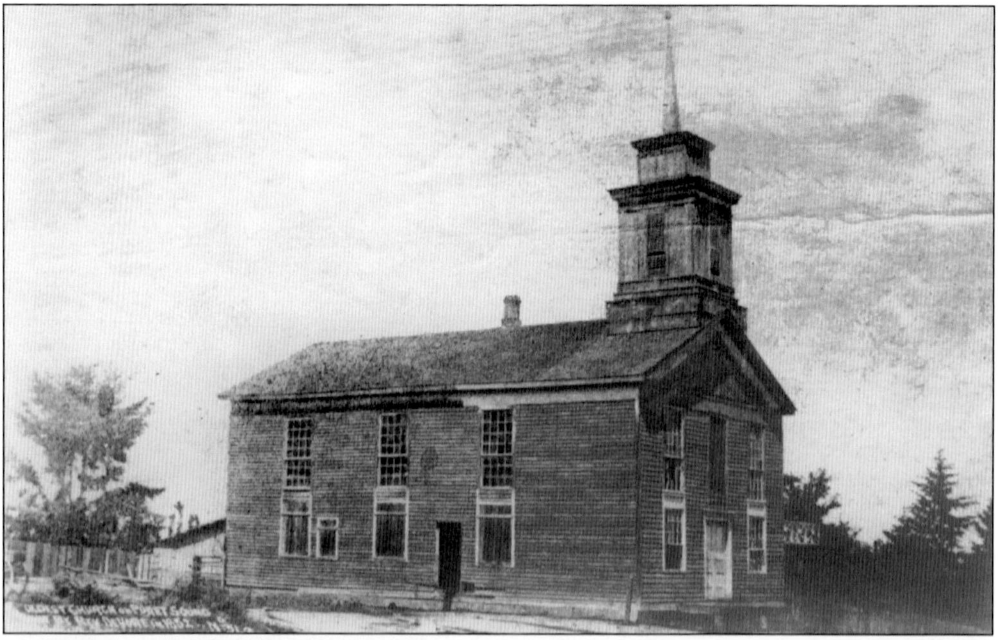

THE FIRST CHURCH IN THE WASHINGTON TERRITORY. The church built under the leadership of Reverend DeVore had to meet the needs of the town. The building was two stories; the first story served as a school, a library, and a meeting hall for political and social gatherings; the second story served as the church. The building was torn down in 1894, with a wooden bell tower erected nearby at the end of Wilkes Street.

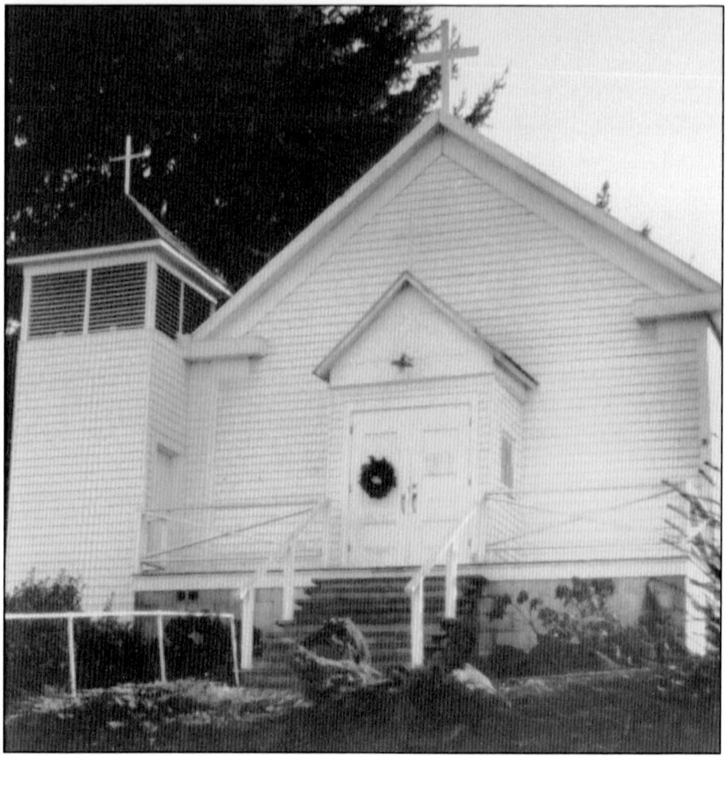

IMMACULATE CONCEPTION. This Catholic church was originally built in 1855 at Fort Steilacoom to accommodate the Irish Catholic soldiers. In an effort to meet the demand of the growing number of Catholic settlers in Steilacoom, the church was moved to the town in 1864. They disassembled the church board by board, moved it by wagon, and reconstructed the building at 1810 Nisqually Street. The Immaculate Conception church was placed on the National Register of Historic Places in 1974.

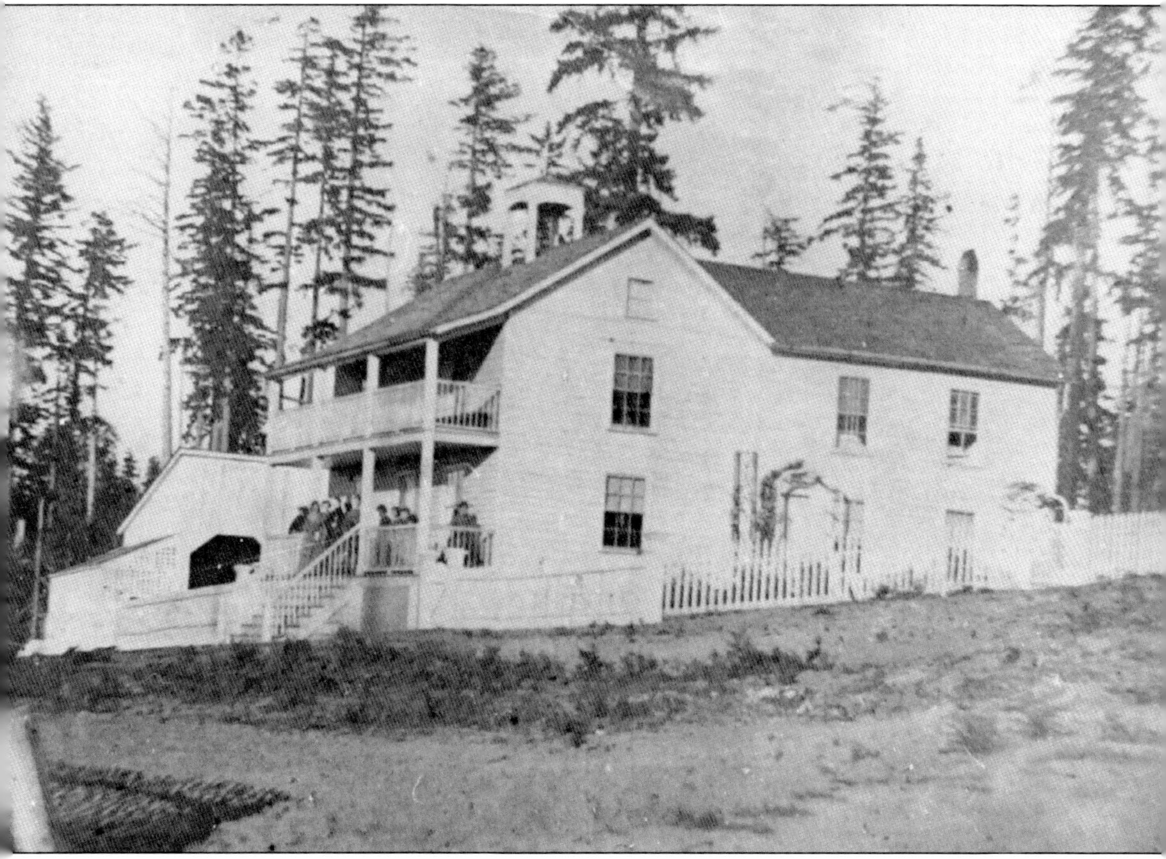

THE ACADEMY AND CONVENT. St. Joseph's Academy and Convent is pictured in 1865. The 1865–1866 school year had the largest enrollment at the school with seven boarders and 18 day students. The school was unique for the time because it offered a nine-month curriculum instead of the standard three months. In 1868, the troops left Fort Steilacoom, and the enrollment started to decline shortly after. The school officially closed in 1875. The Sisters of Providence left Steilacoom and started a school in Yakima.

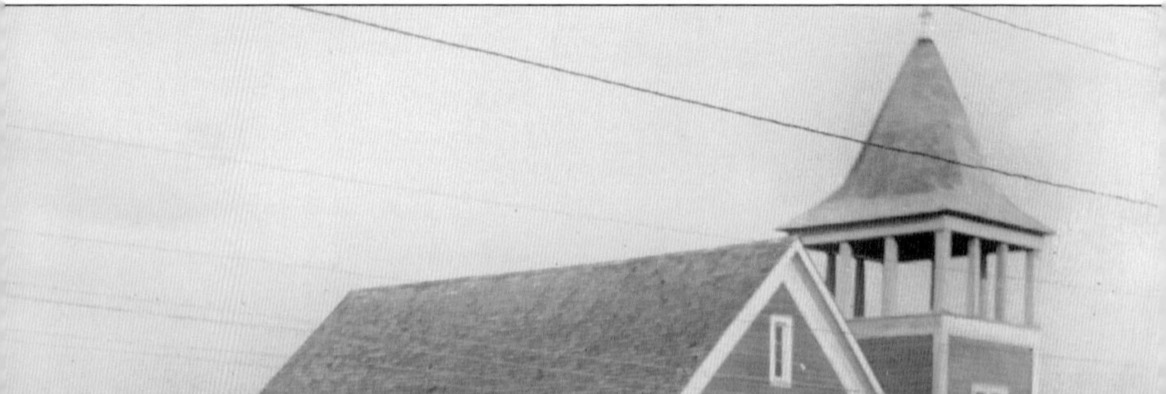

THE OBERLIN CONGREGATIONAL CHURCH. In 1883, John Flett and George Atkinson, home missionary superintendent of the Congregational Church, established Oberlin Congregational Church, the Steilacoom Academy, and the Lake View Congregational Church. The Reverend Arthur T. Burnell was hired to serve both churches and superintend the academy. He was ordained at the Lake View church on February 14, 1883, and the next month, the church in Steilacoom was organized. It was held in the former Presbyterian church, which had dissolved in 1876. Since Burnell and his wife, Mary, had both graduated from Oberlin College in Ohio, the name Oberlin was chosen and incorporation papers signed on April 27, 1883. In 1902, this church was built on the corner of Pacific and Lafayette Streets with timbers used from the old church. In 1961, the Oberlin congregation built a new church one block up at the corner of Pacific and Rainier Streets. The 1902 church is currently the Steilacoom Tribal Museum and Cultural Center.

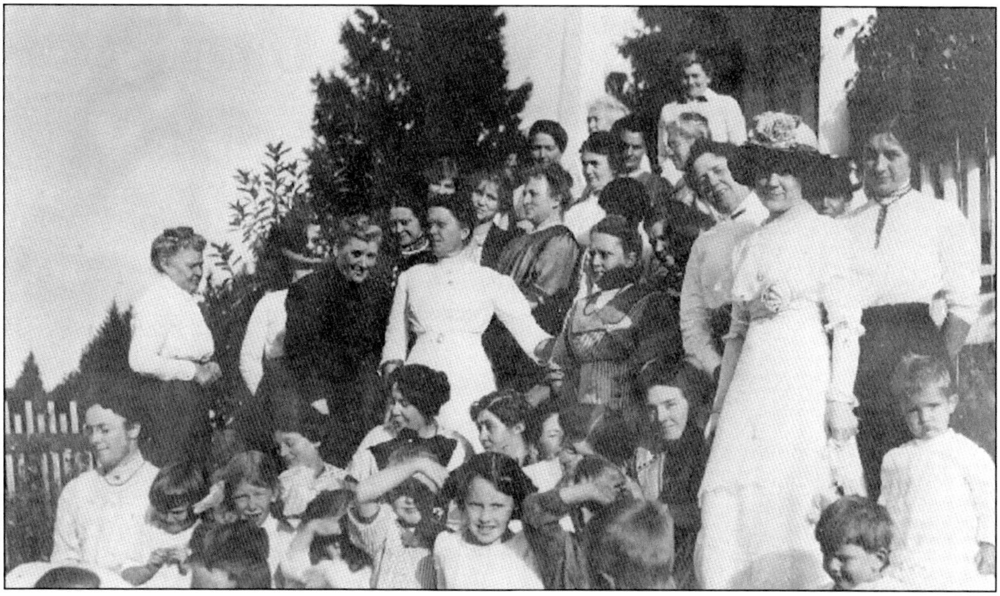

LADIES AID OF OBERLIN. Hattie Bair was the first president of the Ladies Aid Group, which she also helped organize. The ladies met in different homes of the members, and the children went everywhere with their mothers. Docia Bair as a child remarked that the meetings were "a real tea party for us children."

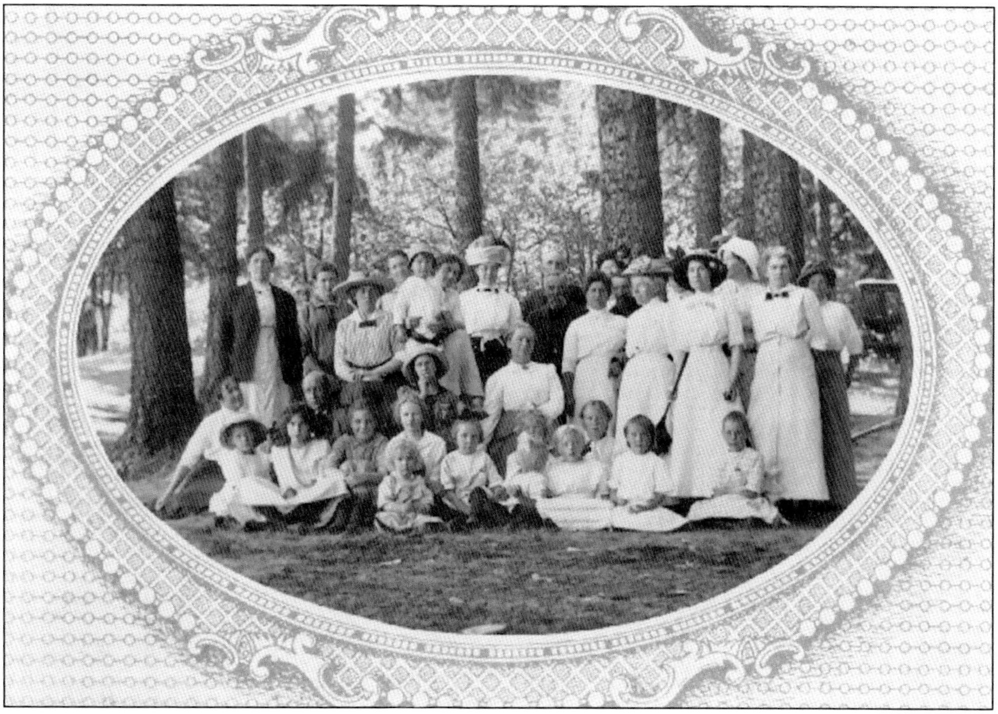

SUNDAY SCHOOL PICNIC. The Oberlin Congregational Church Sunday School Picnic was held at American Lake in the summer of 1913. The ladies in attendance were stylishly dressed. The Oberlin Congregational Church currently has a Sunday school program and remains active in the community.

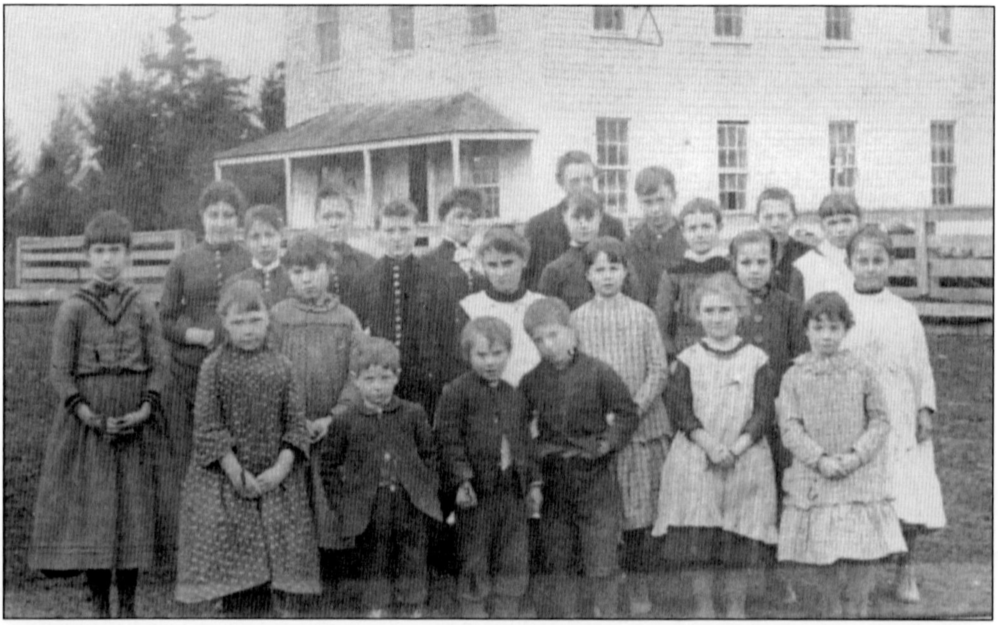

IN SESSION. The Steilacoom Academy, established in 1883, met at the old courthouse. Because it lacked a library, the Steilacoom Library was asked to loan their books. Tuition was advertised as $7 to $10 per term, with 75¢ for securing use of the library. The class of 1887 is, from left to right, the following: (first row) Eva Connick, John Judson, Glenn Orr, David Orr, Flora Downey, and Isabell Judson; (second row) Helen Serfling, Maude Dolman, Etta Downey, Janet Judson, Lena Eisenbeis, and Mattie Runquist; (third row) Kate Eisenbeis, Rose Rupp, Mamie Orr, Mary Judson, and June Burr; (fourth row) Louise Eisenbeis, Eliza Runquist, Fedelia Newberry (teacher), Nat Orr, Julius Dickens, and Frank Runquist.

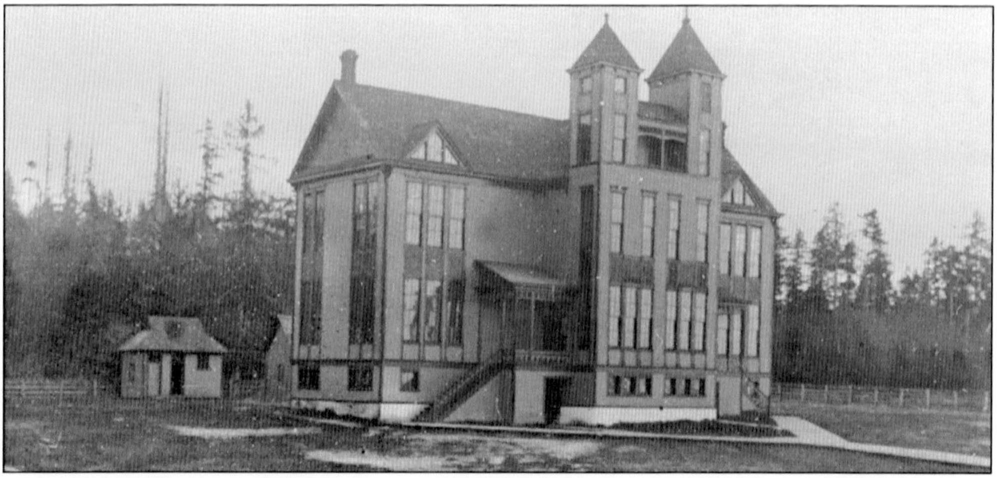

BUILDING APPROVED. In 1891, the school board bought a block of land on Nisqually Street for $2,000 and built a new school. The Panic of 1893 forced the school into deep debt, $20,000 plus interest. Two of the school's teachers, Annie Weller and Susie Runquist, offered to teach the children for free until there were funds available.

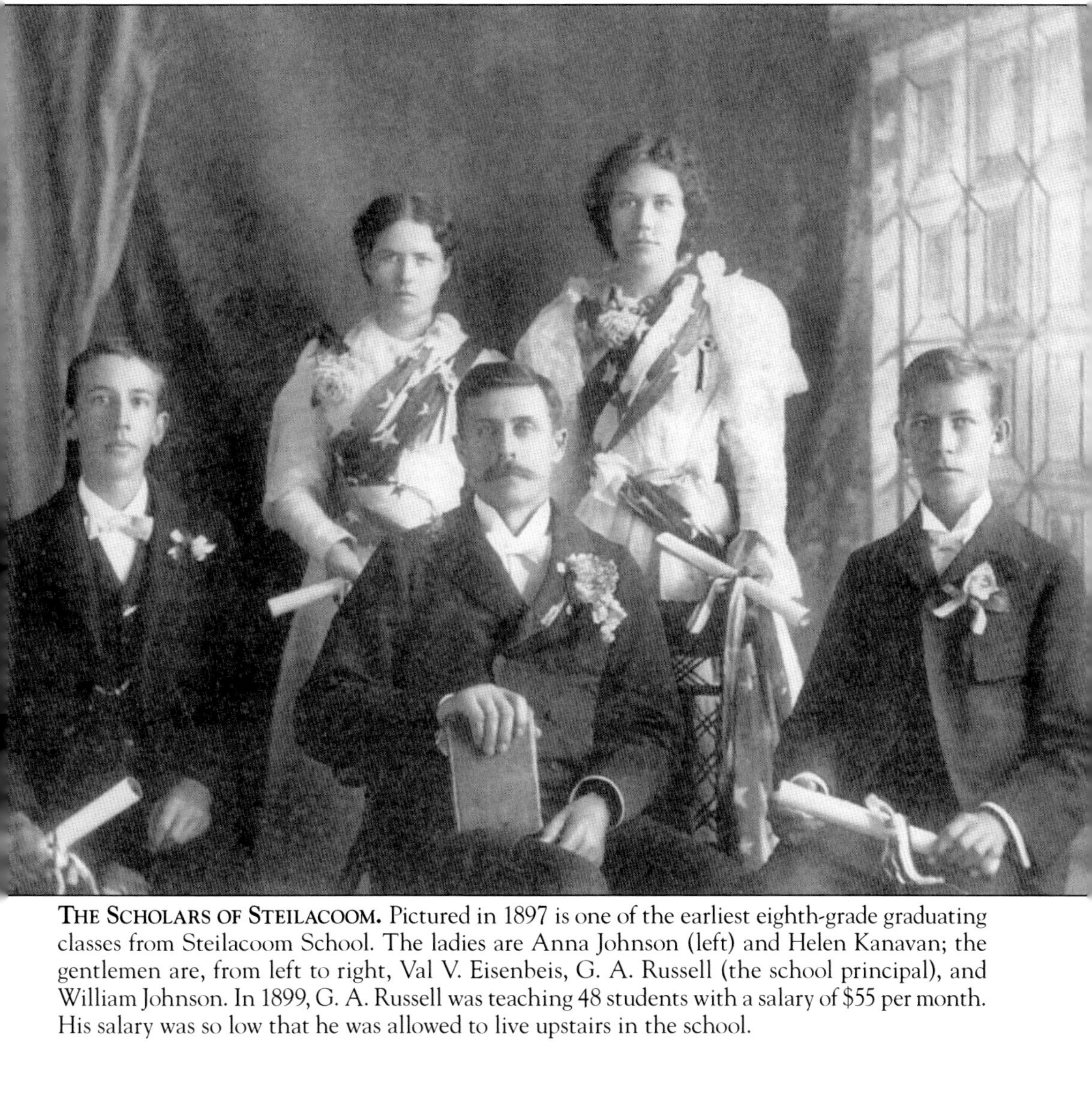

THE SCHOLARS OF STEILACOOM. Pictured in 1897 is one of the earliest eighth-grade graduating classes from Steilacoom School. The ladies are Anna Johnson (left) and Helen Kanavan; the gentlemen are, from left to right, Val V. Eisenbeis, G. A. Russell (the school principal), and William Johnson. In 1899, G. A. Russell was teaching 48 students with a salary of $55 per month. His salary was so low that he was allowed to live upstairs in the school.

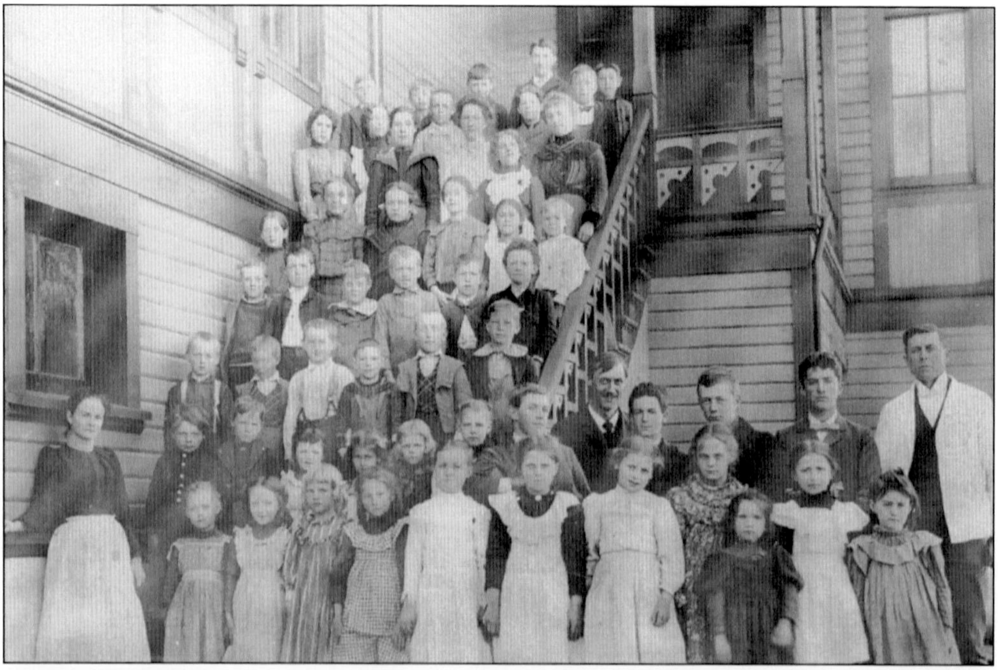

STEILACOOM SCHOOL. During the 1890s, the finances of the Steilacoom School District fluctuated. The teachers were paid accordingly. In 1893, Susie Runquist taught 53 first through fourth graders for a salary of $55 a month. By 1898, Lena Eisenbeis was teaching four grades for $30 a month.

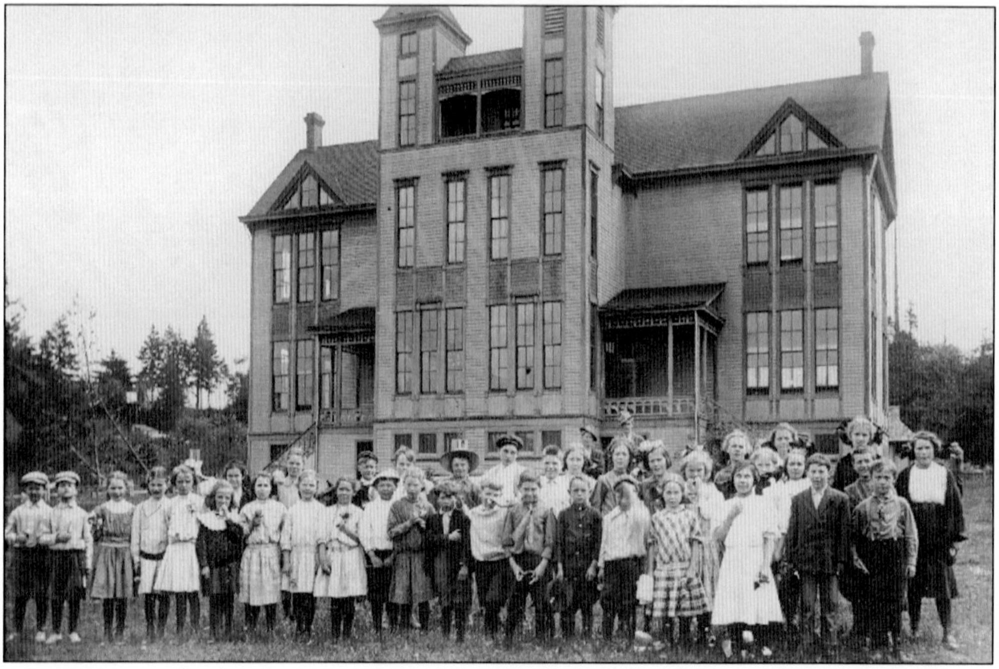

CLASSMATES. School was in session in the wooden structure on Nisqually Street from 1891 to 1917. In 1864, there were only three schools in Pierce County. As the population grew, the need to expand was evident. One of the downstairs classrooms was made into an auditorium, and that class was moved upstairs. Indoor plumbing was then installed in the basement.

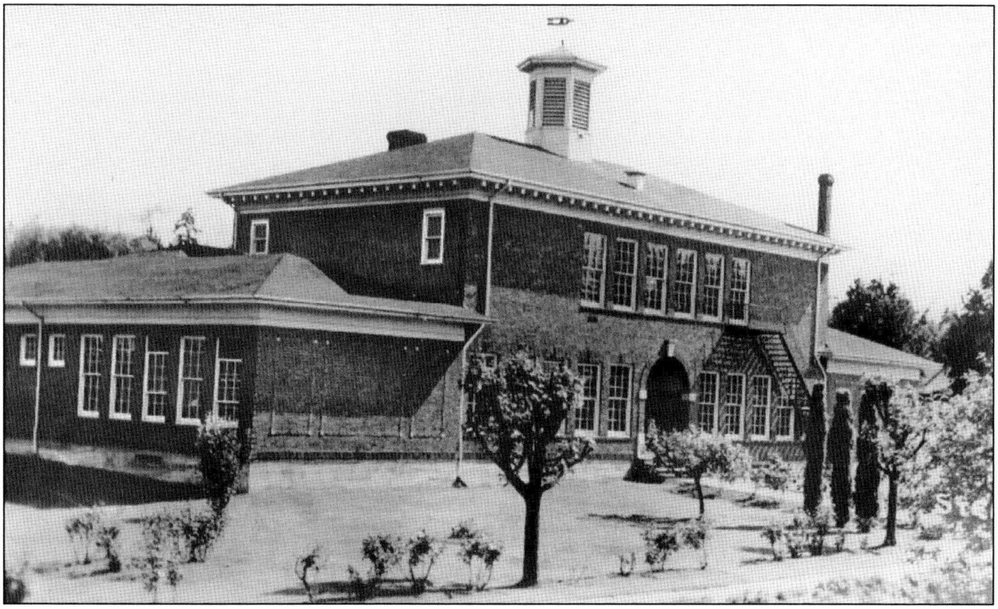

Pioneer School. In 1913, the town voted to build a brick school building costing $15,000. The school opened for the 1916–1917 school year, serving grades one through eight with three teachers: Eudocia Bair, Beatrice Bair, and Maud Burgna. Years later, in 1963, Cherrydale opened for primary education and the Steilacoom School was renamed Pioneer School.

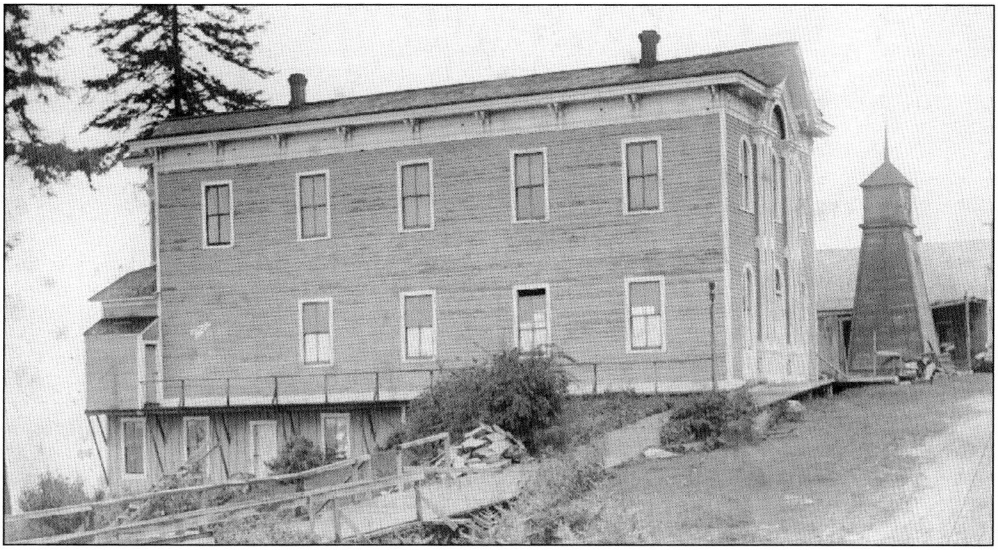

The Masonic Lodge. The Masons began making plans to build a lodge in 1861. Lafayette Balch donated the land, and a portion of the money for construction was loaned by one of the most suspiciously wealthy men in Pierce County, Charles Wren. The Masonic Lodge was moved from Commercial Street to Lafayette Street when the railroad purchased the property around 1910. Once the building was moved, it served as a grocery store for many years before a fire destroyed it in September 1939. The Masons rebuilt their lodge as a brick building four blocks south of the Lafayette location. As a result of dwindling membership, the Masons of Steilacoom eventually merged with another order. They officially moved out of town in 1994. The Masonic Cemetery is located in present-day Lakewood on Masonic Drive SW.

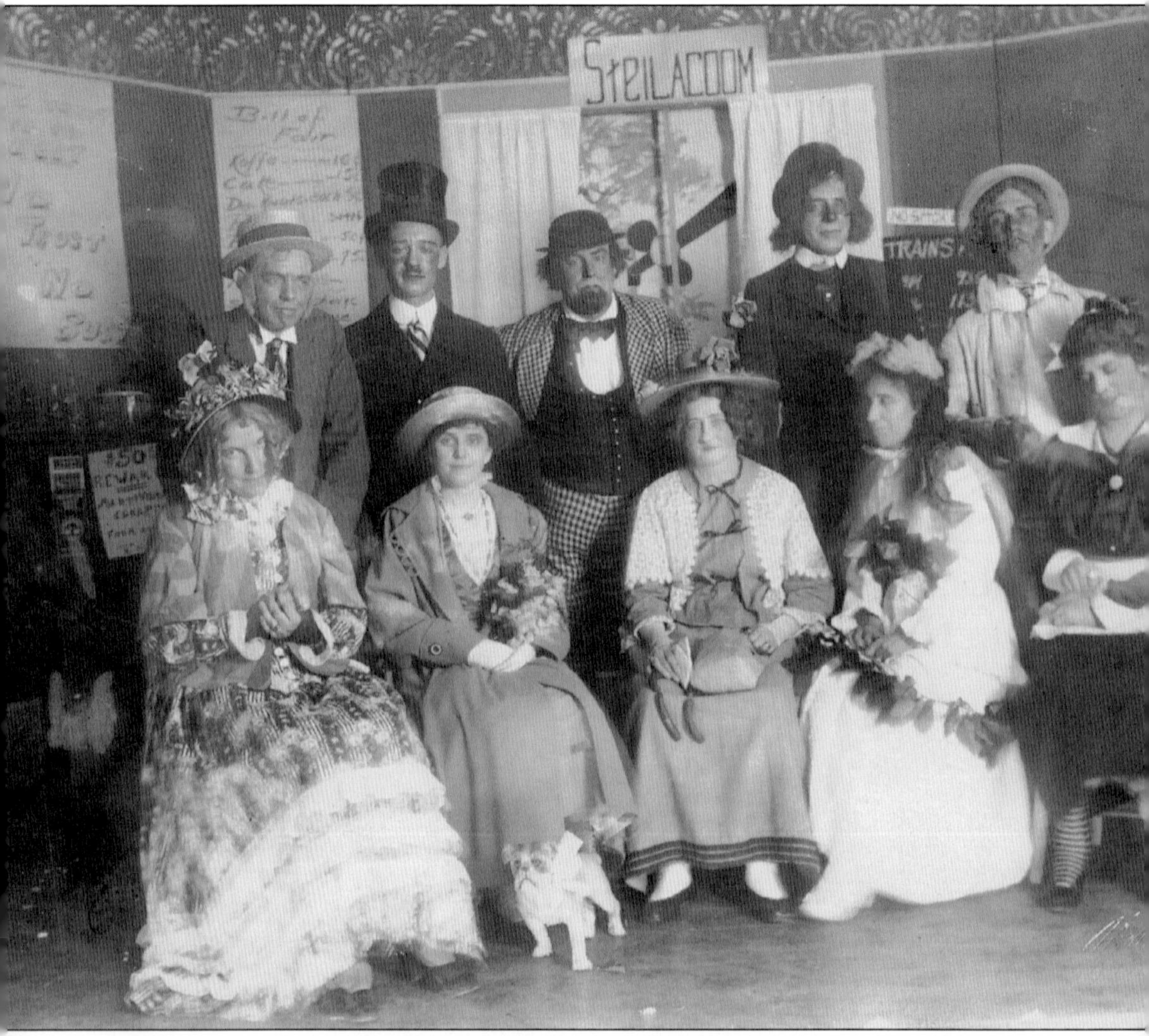

DRAMA CLUB. The Steilacoom Dramatic Club around 1917 was, from left to right, (first row) Birdeena Tuttle, Maud Burgna, Mary Garrigan, Dora Teevin, and Eudocia Bair; (second row) Bill Thompson, Nat Hatcher, Prof. Hiram Tuttle, Mrs. Steward, and Frank Callender.

STEILACOOM LIBRARY ASSOCIATION. The Steilacoom Library Association was incorporated in 1858 by the Washington Territorial Legislature. By March 1858, the constitution and bylaws had been adopted. The goal of the association was, according to the bylaws, "the diffusion of useful knowledge and sound morality." Membership was $5 per year and 25¢ per month. The library association reserved the right to revoke membership for "immoral or disreputable conduct." Books for the library were purchased from as far away as San Francisco and were also donated by townspeople and army officers leaving Fort Steilacoom.

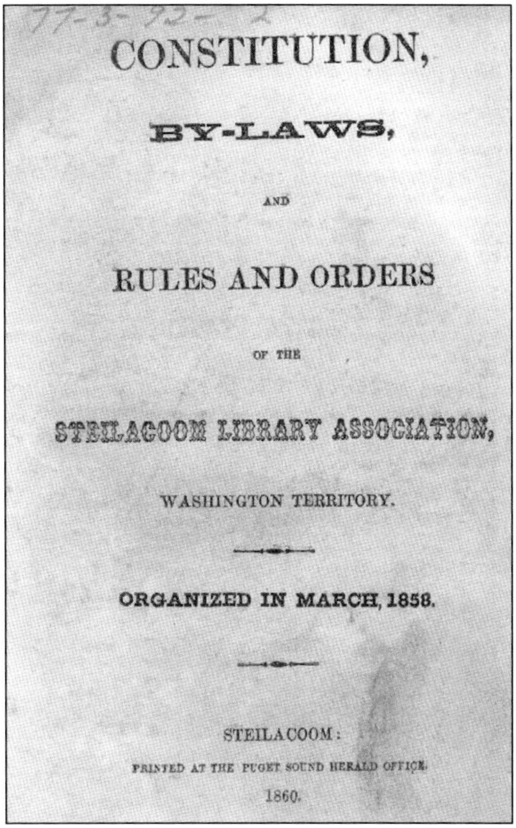

CONSTITUTION,

BY-LAWS,

AND

RULES AND ORDERS

OF THE

STEILACOOM LIBRARY ASSOCIATION,

WASHINGTON TERRITORY.

ORGANIZED IN MARCH, 1858.

STEILACOOM:

PRINTED AT THE PUGET SOUND HERALD OFFICE.

1860.

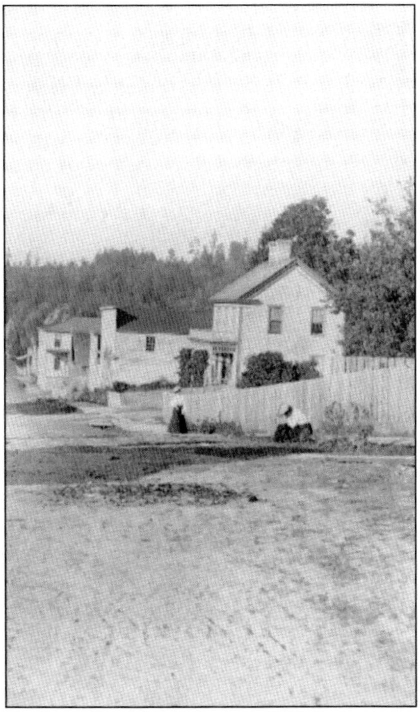

LIBRARY HOST HOME. The books of the Steilacoom Library Association were stored in many locations through the years. The first home on the right, the Philip Keach home, now known as Rolling Hill, was a host home for the books. The library association had three goals in mind: "first, by establishing a library, secondly, a reading room and thirdly, by procuring public lectures, essays and establishing debates." The first debate topic was "Riches are better for the development of character than poverty." The association was not without scandal. A young boy saw men boxing up the books and heading to the wharf. The boy immediately told his mother, who was able to get in touch with E. R. Rogers, who in turn rallied a group of concerned citizens carrying rifles and went to the wharf to rescue the books. The books were then stored at the McCaw and Rogers Store. As people died or moved away, the library association didn't meet with regular frequency. When E. R. Rogers relocated his business in the 1890s, the books were left behind in the old brick building. The books were recovered in 1900 after renewed interest in the library association. The books remain in Steilacoom. (Courtesy of the Davidson family collection.)

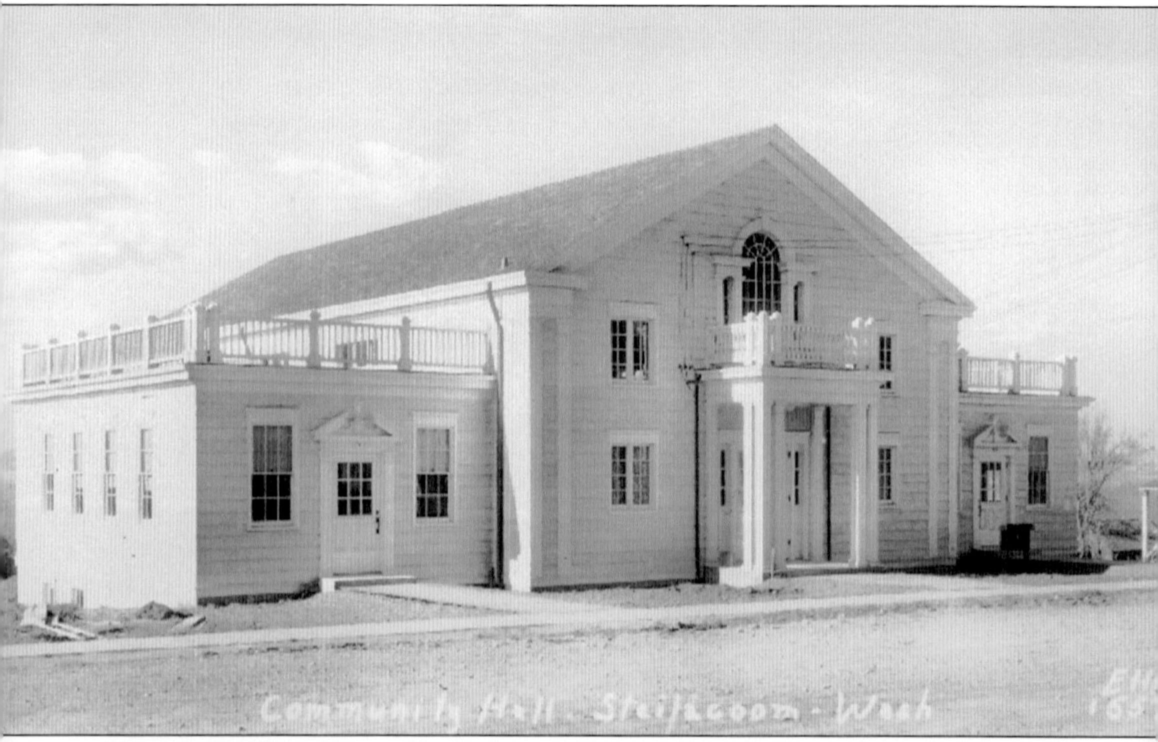

STEILACOOM TOWN HALL. The Steilacoom Town Hall was built in 1930 at the beginning of the Depression. The Steilacoom Library Association, the chamber of commerce, and the tennis club spearheaded the building project. Dr. Charles Taylor offered four lots in the center of town for a municipal building. With that donation, the town council moved forward and a bond issue of $7,000 was submitted and passed by the voters in March 1930. In October of that year, the building was officially dedicated. It has been used for Steilacoom Town Council meetings and has housed the library and meeting rooms.

Three

Business Boomed and Then Relocated

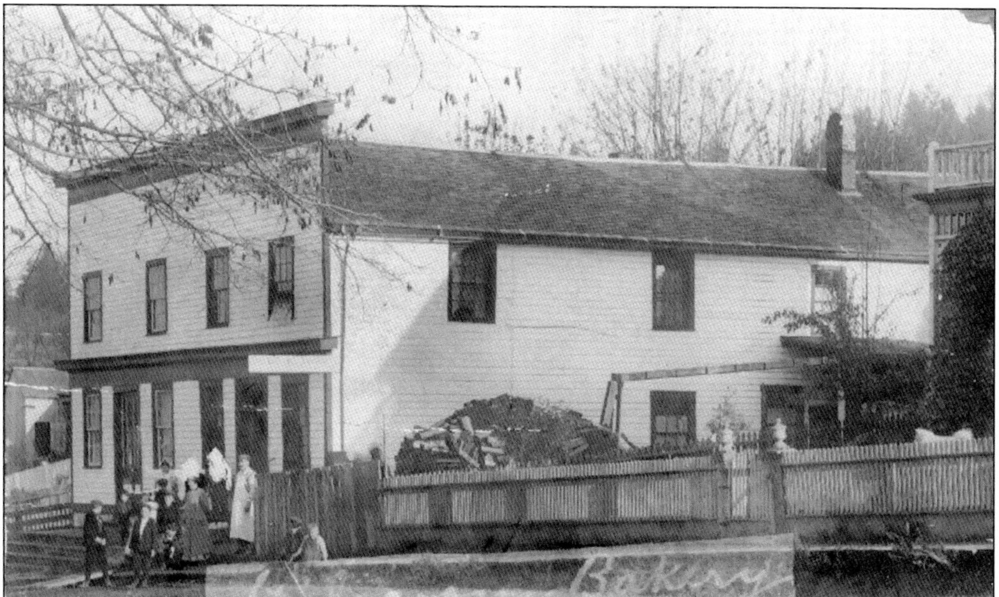

The Steilacoom Bakery. Fred Eisenbeis and the Eisenbeis family, pictured in 1885, were the town bakers. Their home was next door to their bakery. The Eisenbeises were early settlers in Steilacoom. The Steilacoom Bakery was located in the first business district in Steilacoom. Commercial Street was one of the busiest streets in the territory.

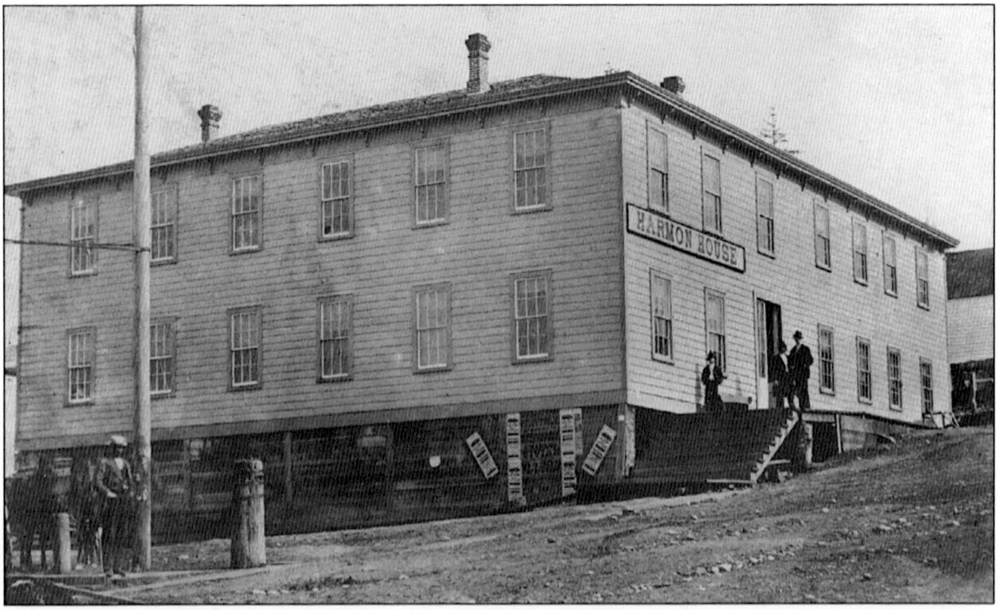

THE HARMON HOUSE. The hotel was advertised in the *Puget Sound Express* on December 3, 1875: "Having been newly built and furnished in a superb manner, this hotel is now open for the reception of guests. Having leased this magnificent house for a term of years, it will be my sole object to please. The finest rooms and the best table on Puget Sound, at moderate prices to suit the times. All those seeking pleasure and comfort will find it to their interest to give me a call. The hotel is situated at the corner of Balch and Commercial Streets, near the steamer landings, and a daily stage to and from Lakeview Station, on the line of the Northern Pacific Railroad, conveys passengers to and from this hotel. W. H. Mastin, Proprietor."

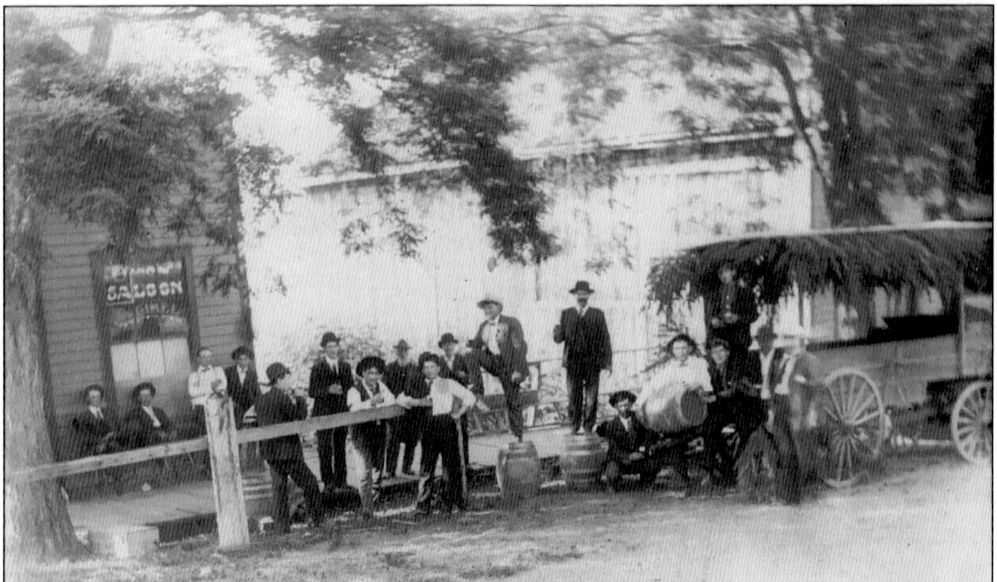

THE UNION SALOON. Locals pose for a picture in front of the Union Saloon, located on Commercial Street. The building was moved one block up to Lafayette Street when the railroad came through c. 1912.

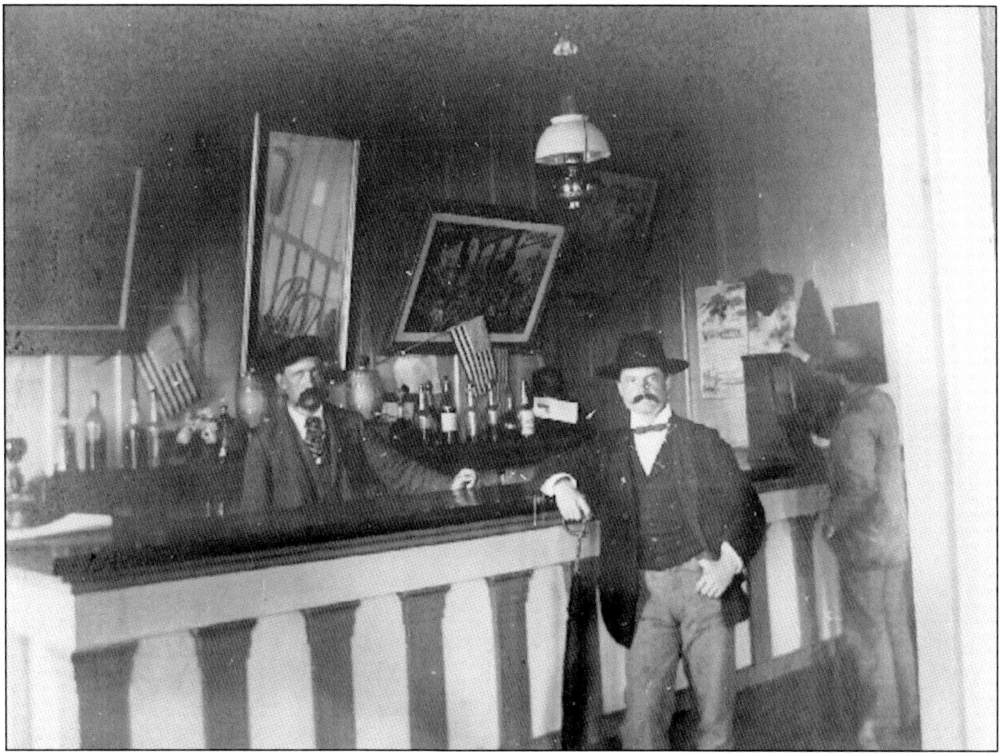

SALOON KEEPER. Here is a rare glimpse into the interior of a building around 1900. Jack Blythe is the saloon keeper behind the counter, but the names of the other patrons and the name of the saloon remain unknown.

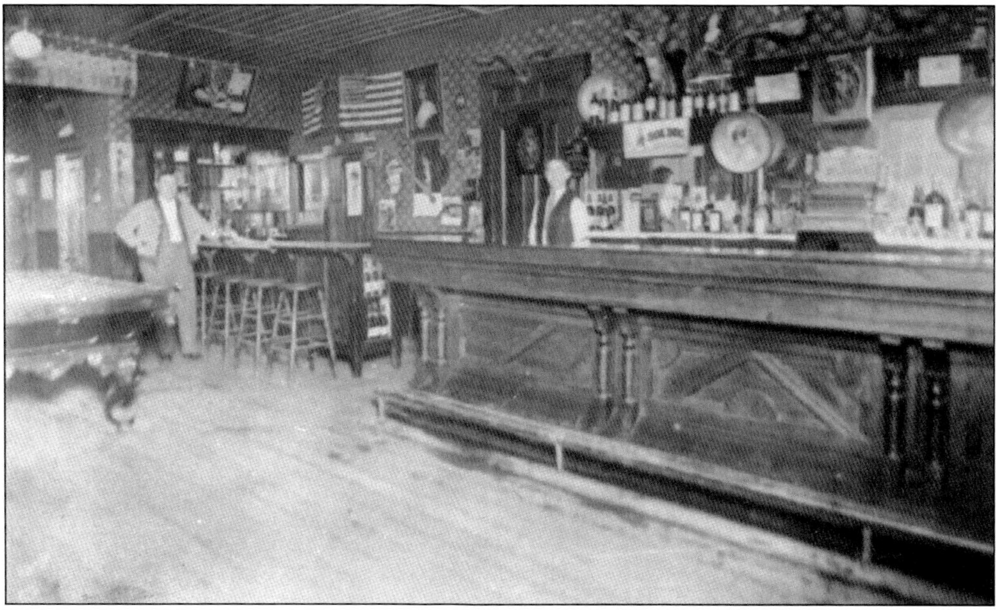

INTERIOR OF A SALOON. This picture was taken of the interior of the Scheisz Saloon after the building was relocated to the corner of Main and Lafayette Streets. The occupants' identities are not known.

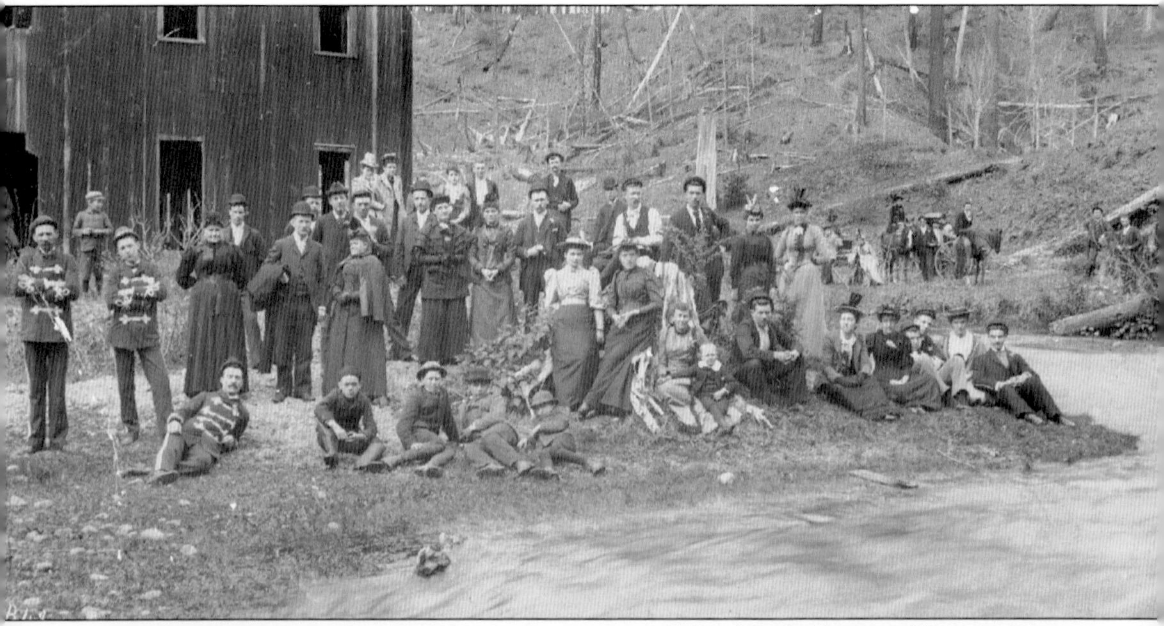

CHAMBERS MILLS. Pictured here is a picnic near one of the three mills owned by Judge Thomas Chambers. The gristmill, lumber mill, and flour mill were located half a mile north of Steilacoom on Chambers Creek. In 1859, the demand for flour was such that neighboring farmers asked Chambers to expand his mill and he consented. A four-story mill was built, and the machinery came from California. In 1895, when this picture was taken, the mills were no longer in operation. The mills are gone, but a marker on the bank of the creek commemorates the site where the Chambers enterprise once stood.

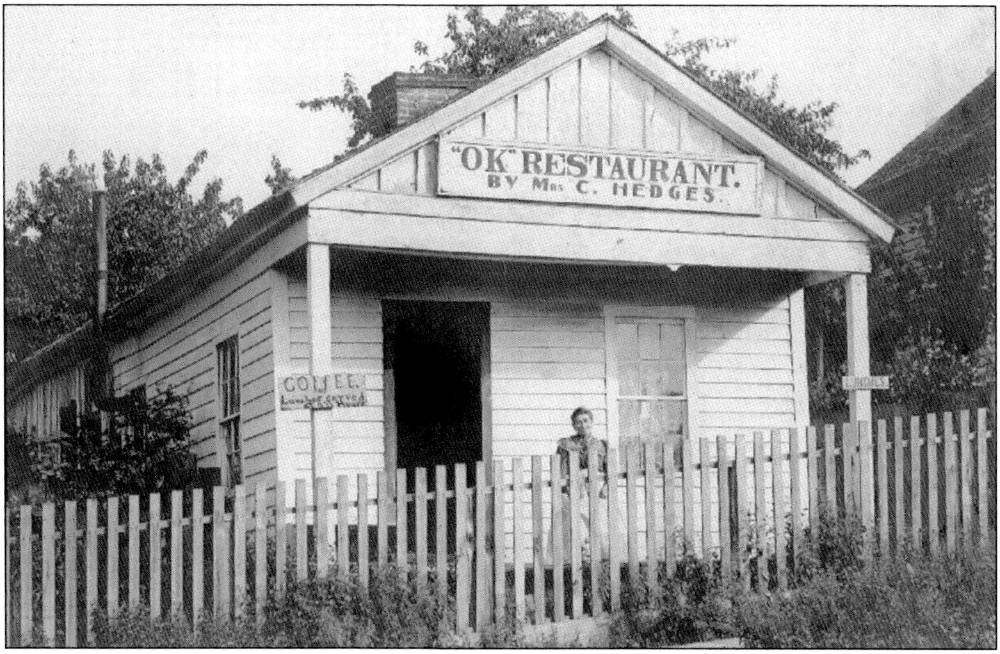

The O. K. Restaurant. Catherine Hedges, proprietress of the O. K. Restaurant, was in business around 1900. Hedges was widowed, and since there were very few career opportunities for women to support themselves and their children, she opened a restaurant.

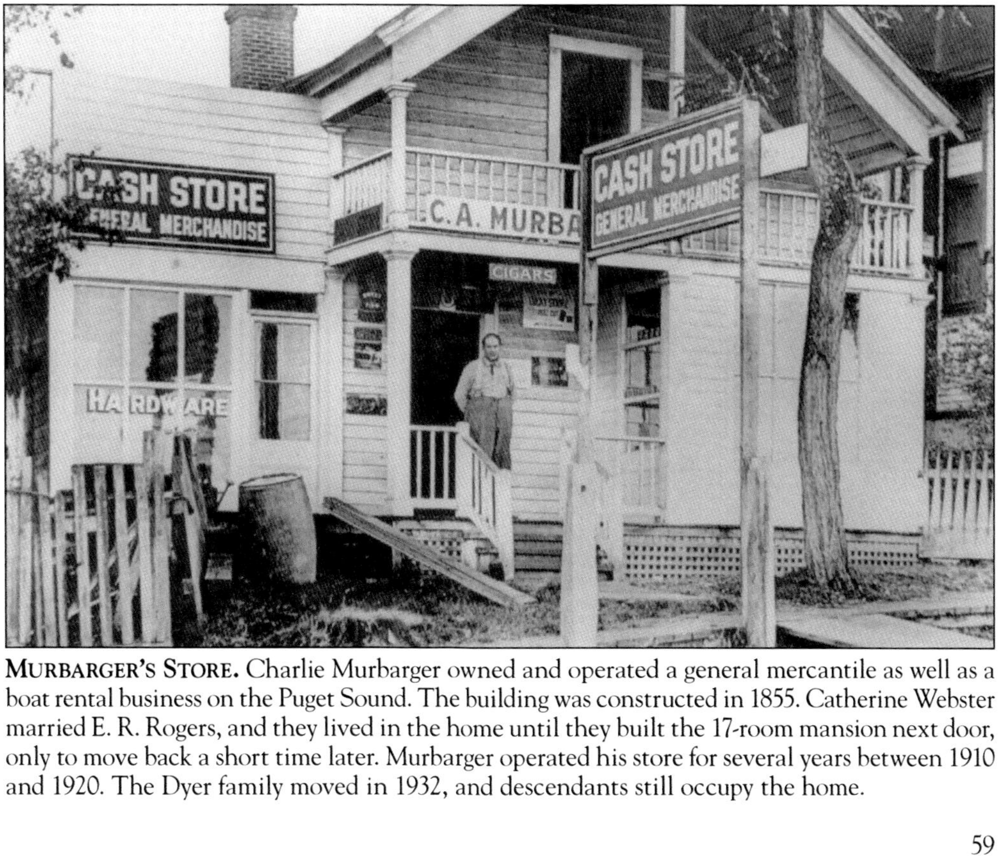

Murbarger's Store. Charlie Murbarger owned and operated a general mercantile as well as a boat rental business on the Puget Sound. The building was constructed in 1855. Catherine Webster married E. R. Rogers, and they lived in the home until they built the 17-room mansion next door, only to move back a short time later. Murbarger operated his store for several years between 1910 and 1920. The Dyer family moved in 1932, and descendants still occupy the home.

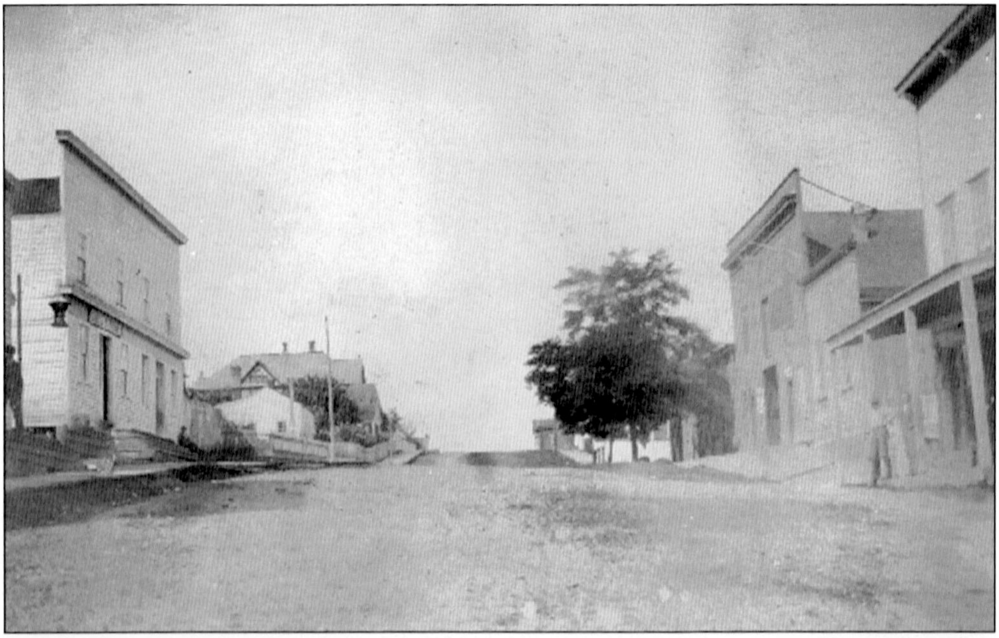

COMMERCIAL STREET. By 1912, the railroad had purchased all of the beachfront to build the railway. The land was used for the right-of-way for the tracks. This photograph is near the intersection of Puyallup and Commercial Streets. Puyallup Street no longer ends on Commercial, and the hill has disappeared to the bulkhead that supports the railroad tracks.

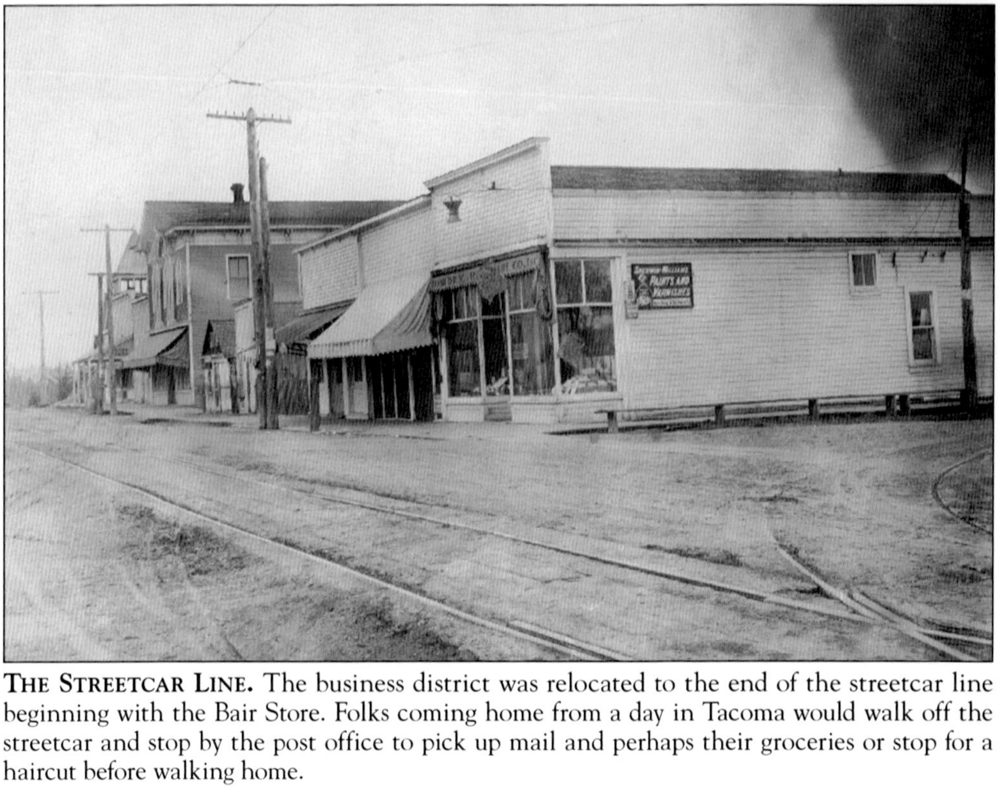

THE STREETCAR LINE. The business district was relocated to the end of the streetcar line beginning with the Bair Store. Folks coming home from a day in Tacoma would walk off the streetcar and stop by the post office to pick up mail and perhaps their groceries or stop for a haircut before walking home.

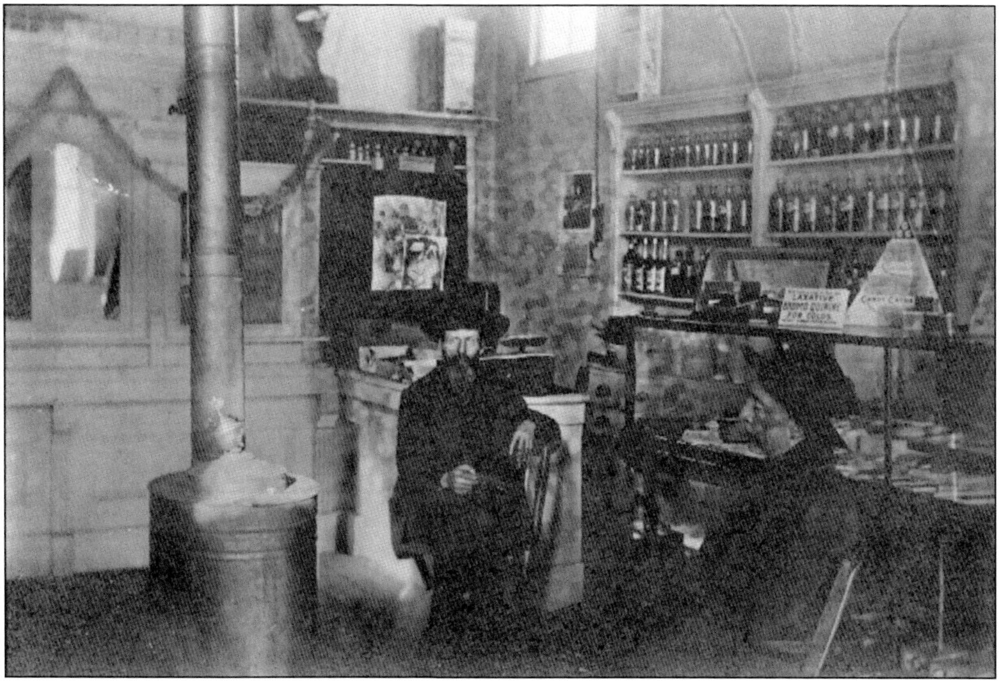

INTERIOR OF BAIR DRUG. Fred Doyne (left) and Omar K. Cheney are seen inside the Bair Store seated by the potbellied stove. The store was the prime location as the town's informal gathering spot.

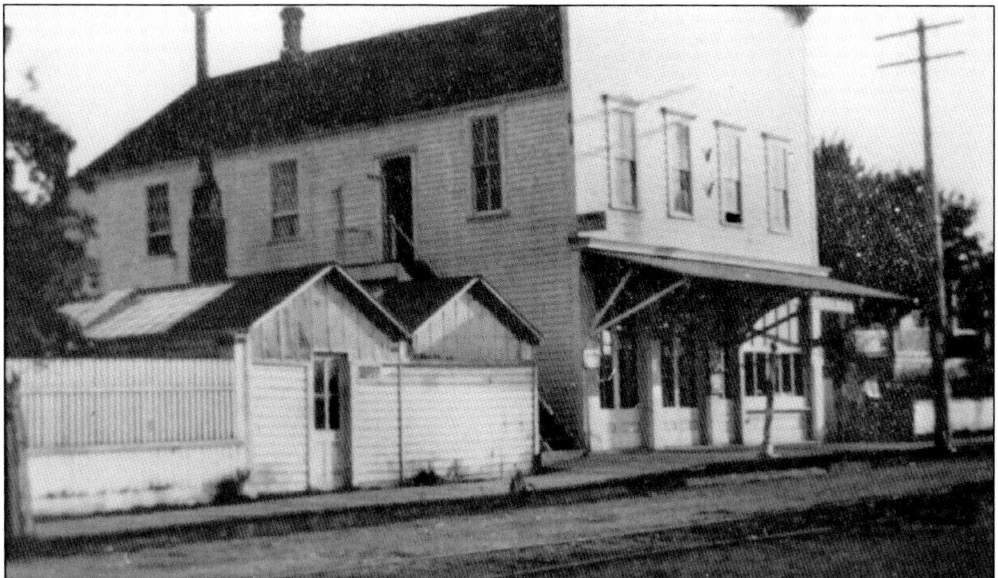

O'DONNELL BUILDING. The building owned by William O'Donnell served many purposes, beginning possibly as a livery stable in the 1860s, then as a boardinghouse, saloon, pool hall, and as a meeting place for a group of Pentecostals on the second floor. They surprised residents with their singing and music at the dock and baptismal immersions at the beach. The building was razed, and Jake Smith built a new grocery store on the site in 1938.

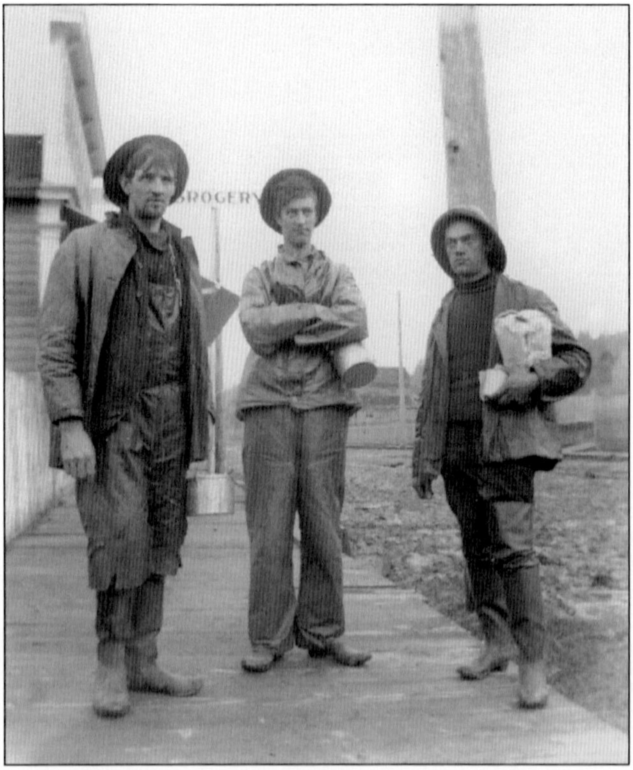

TEMPORARY RESIDENTS OF STEILACOOM. In 1900, some 300 fishermen were casting their nets from the beaches of Steilacoom. After Steilacoom was no longer a commercial town, many of the waterfront buildings were abandoned. The abandonment provided temporary housing for visiting fisherman. The salmon fishing season began in August and ended in January. On December 15, 1900, the *Tacoma Evening News* reported that "the biggest purse-seine haul thus far this season at Steilacoom was 1,540 salmon, which were sold within three hours after the net was set for $385. . . . The biggest beach seine haul . . . was 404 salmon which netted the crew of five men $101 pin money. The haul was made in a little more than 35 minutes."

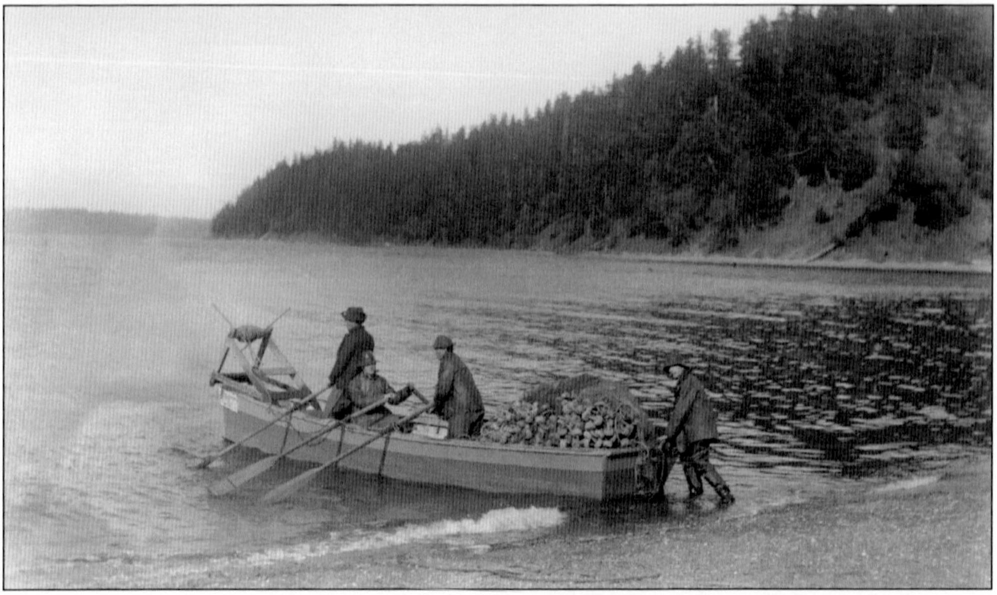

FISHING BOAT. The man launching the boat at the mouth of Chambers Creek most likely stood on the beach holding the shore ends of two ropes while the other men cast the seine and a net with corks and sinkers. The fisherman would row the boat quickly away from shore to drop the net into the deep water and then quickly row to shore where they would pull in the seine. This type of fishing is no longer a legal method of fishing for salmon, but the mouth of Chambers Creek remains a lucrative fishing spot for sport fisherman and the Native American people.

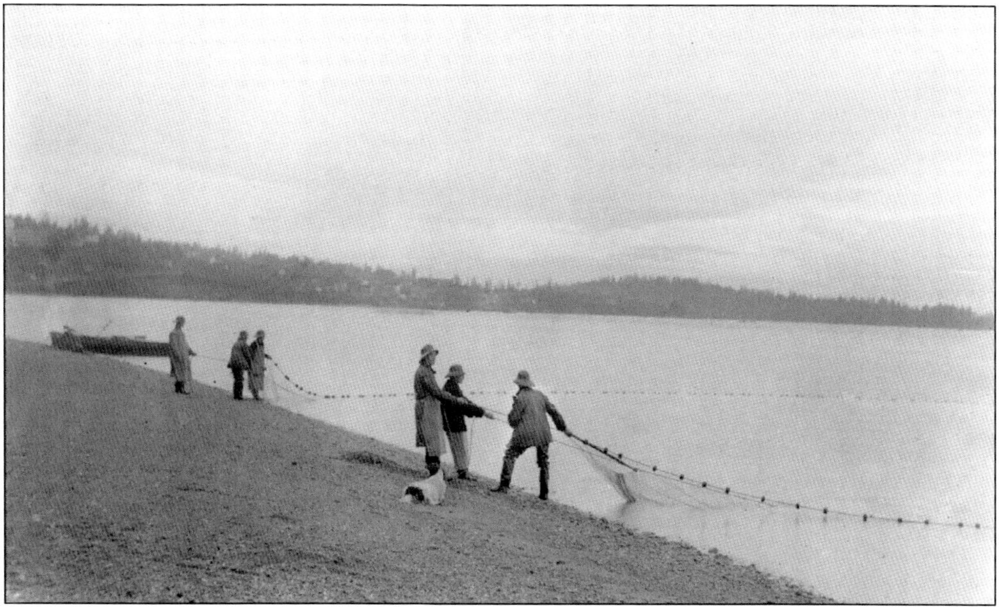

Fishing on Silver Beach. Outfitted for fall and winter weather on the Puget Sound, this team of commercial fisherman may have sold their catch to one of the cannery steamers anchored in the bay. The going rate was 25¢ per pound with no size requirements.

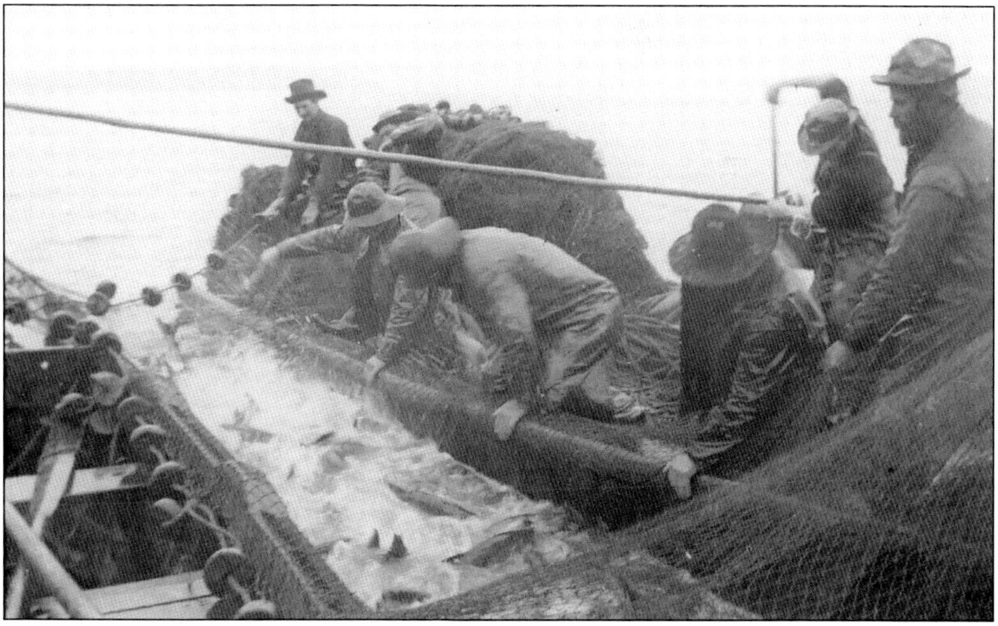

The World Represented. Steilacoom John had the reputation of being the most expert fisherman on the Puget Sound. He was known as one who could spear salmon. He and his wife, Annie, had been fishing the waters for 60 years. However, the majority of the commercial fishermen were not local; they were from places all over the world. Lands represented were Norway, Sweden, Finland, Greece, France, and Austria. August through December, Steilacoom was host to those who earned a living fishing.

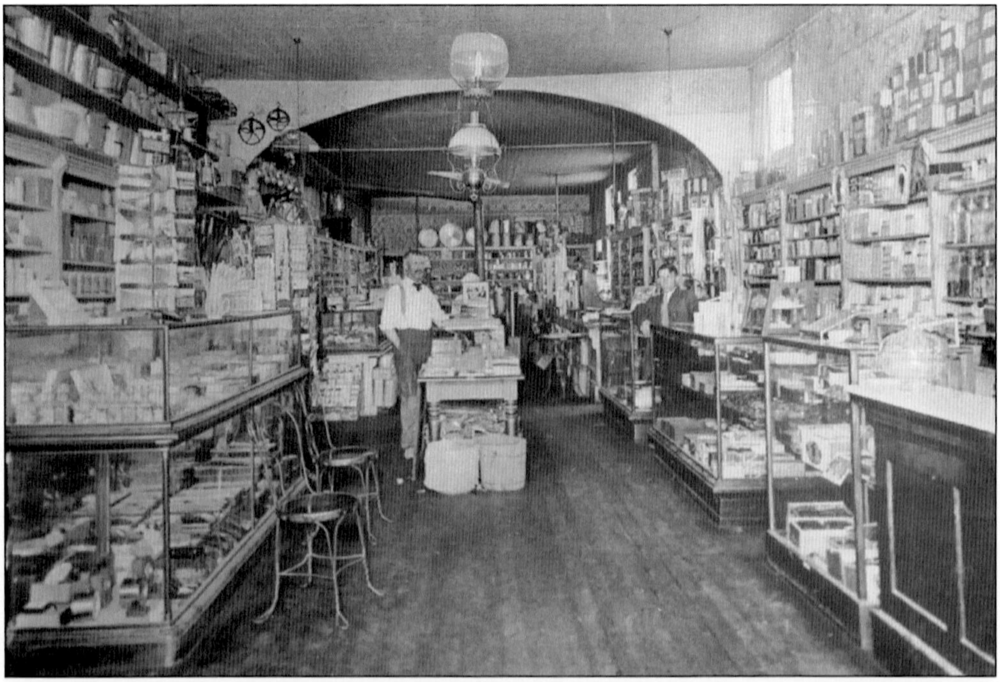

BAIR THE DRUGGIST. W. L. Bair (left) and "Shorty" Bair are behind the counter inside the store after 1908. The store was built in 1895 on Lafayette Street to take advantage of the foot traffic from the new streetcar line. The Bair Store was the first commercial building on Lafayette Street, where it can still be seen today.

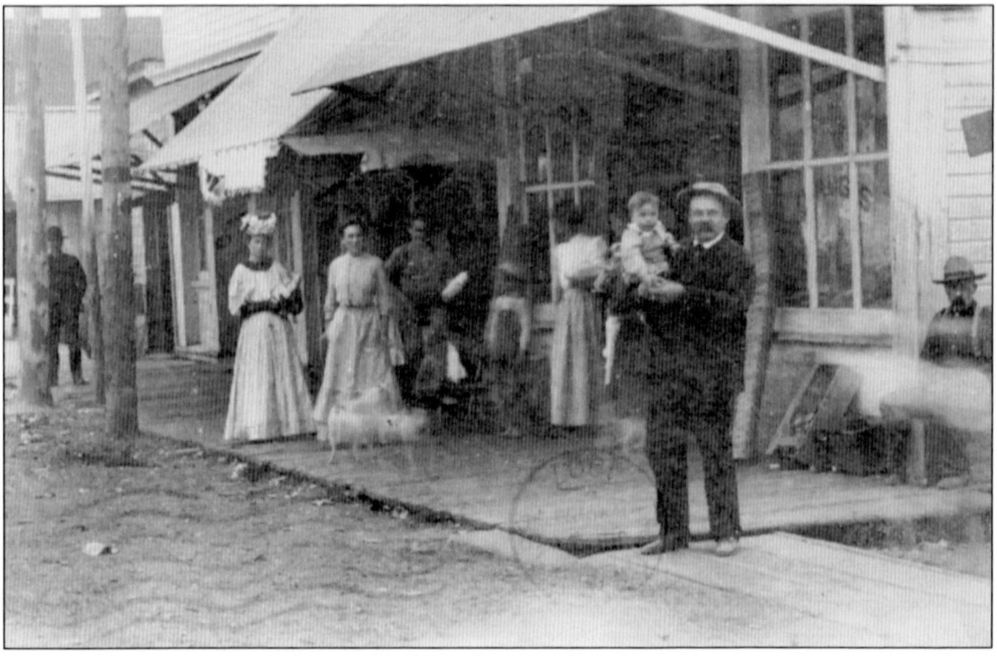

SOCIAL CENTER. A postcard, most likely made at the Bair Store, shows patrons posing in front of the entrance on the corner of Lafayette and Wilkes Streets. The postmark reads 1907. By 1907, the store was unofficially the social center of town.

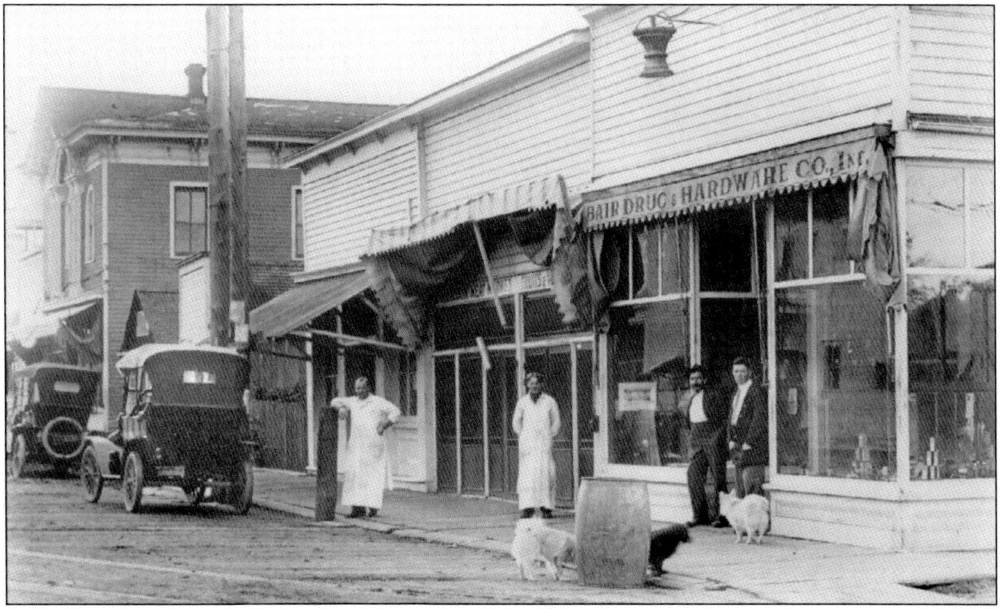

THE MAIN CORNER. The Steilacoom Meat Market and a fruit and vegetable stand are next to the newly renamed Bair Drug and Hardware Company. The store added hardware to its name because W. L. purchased the surplus of hardware from the E. R. Rogers estate in 1906. The men in the white aprons are most likely the butchers for the Steilacoom Meat Market.

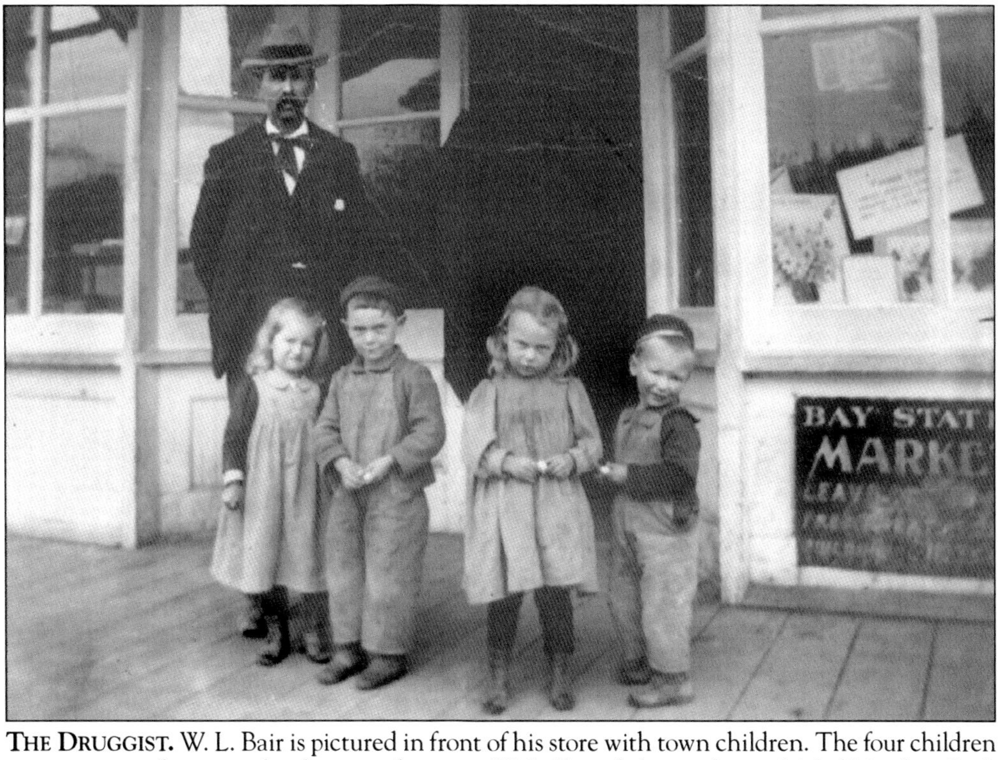

THE DRUGGIST. W. L. Bair is pictured in front of his store with town children. The four children were cousins of one another but no relation to W. L. From left to right are Mabel Hatcher, Stub Atwood, Pearl Atwood, and Nat Hatcher.

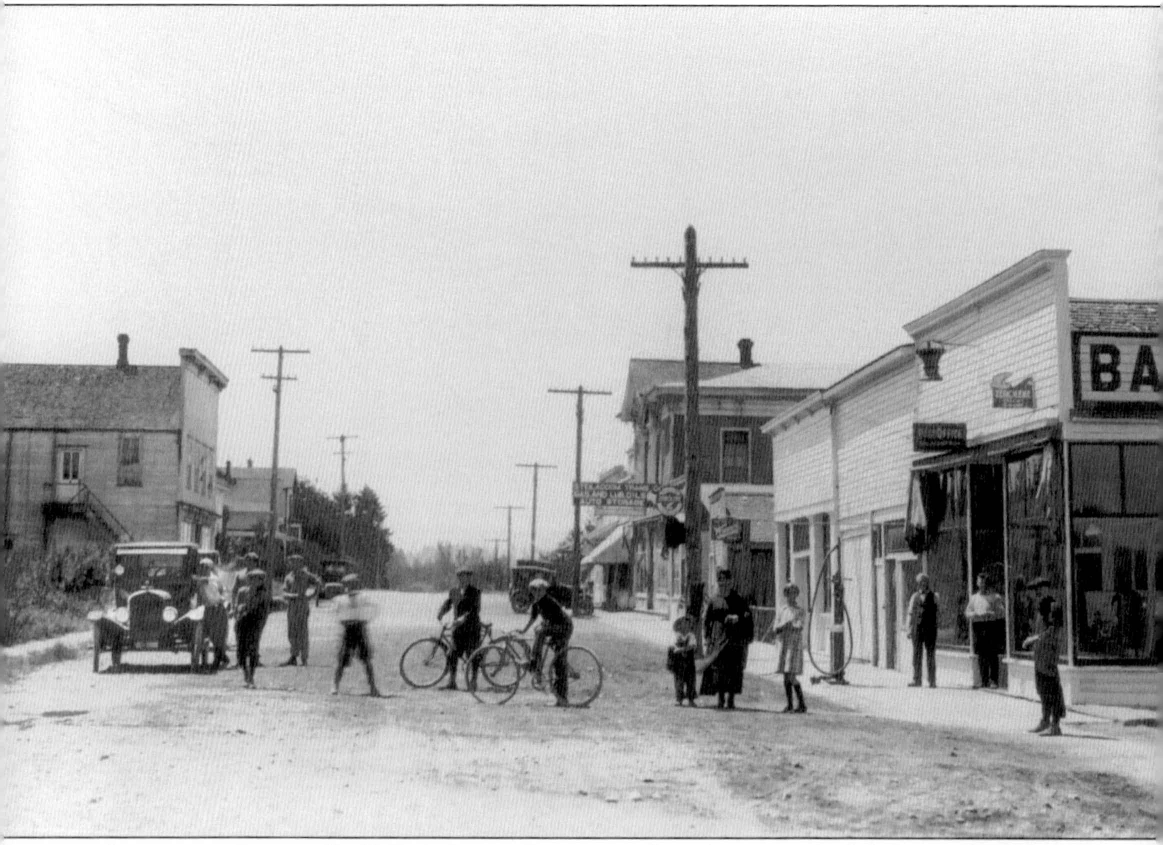

LAFAYETTE STREET. By 1920, Lafayette Street was the only commercial district in Steilacoom. When this photograph was taken, the permanent transformation to small town was complete. The Bair Store is on the corner of Wilkes and Lafayette Streets, with the post office next door, and farther on is the old Masonic Lodge, which housed a butcher shop, a pool hall, and a grocery.

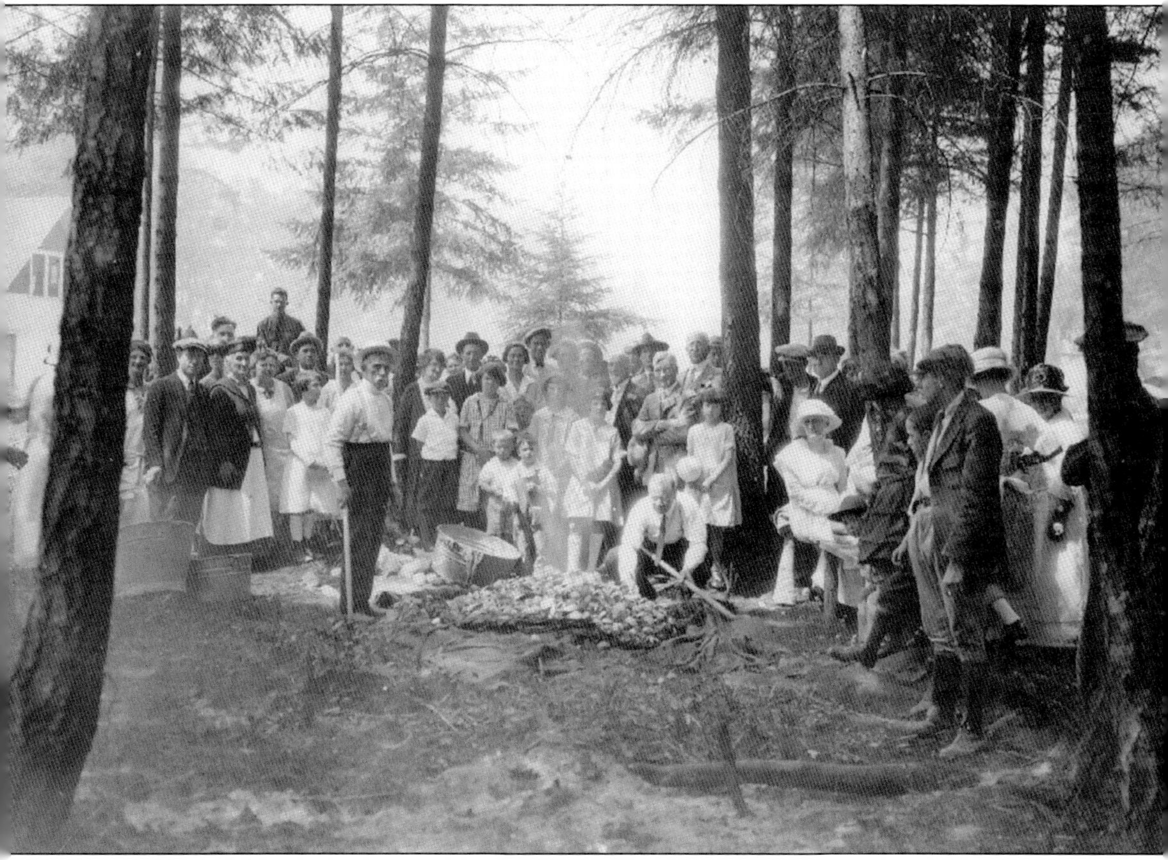

CLAMBAKE. In 1924, clambake festivities were held to commemorate Steilacoom's first year with an official chamber of commerce. The event took place at Garrigan's Park. Capt. Neil Henly, president of the chamber, is standing holding a rake.

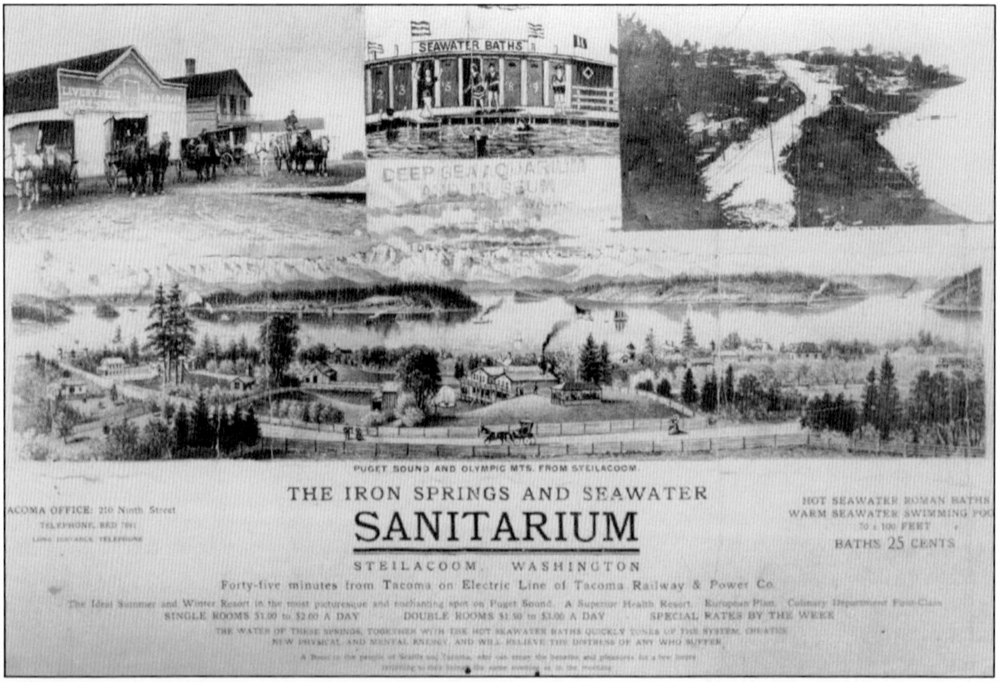

RELAX AT IRON SPRINGS. After Tacoma was chosen as the terminus for the transcontinental railroad, the business environment in Steilacoom changed from industry to hospitality. In 1891, with the introduction of the streetcar, Steilacoom became a vacation destination. Ed and W. L. Bair worked together to remodel the old brewery to become the Iron Springs Sanitarium, a place to relax and recuperate by the healing waters of the iron springs. Evidently the neighbors were not pleased with having a "sanitarium," so the name was changed to the Iron Springs Hotel.

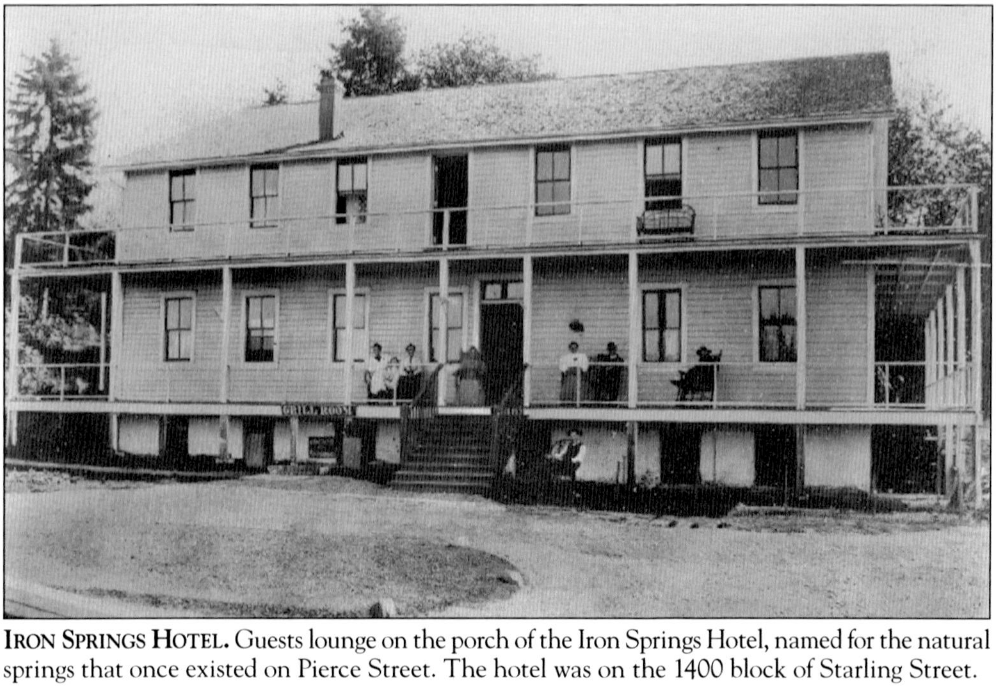

IRON SPRINGS HOTEL. Guests lounge on the porch of the Iron Springs Hotel, named for the natural springs that once existed on Pierce Street. The hotel was on the 1400 block of Starling Street.

LEISURE TIME ON THE HOTEL GROUNDS. Here we see tourists enjoying their time at Iron Springs. Young "Cub" Bair was the pump operator who would bring the saltwater uphill to the pool. His work would have to be done at high tide and at night when the streetcar was not running because he used the electricity from the streetcar lines. The hotel was turned over to Ed Bair, who sold it to Felix Bravin as a chicken dinner place. When Bravin took it over in the days of Prohibition, it was believed that the main business was bootlegging.

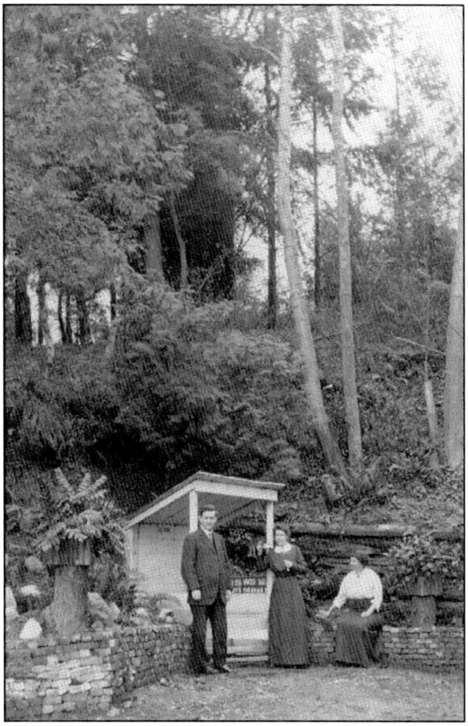

A RESORT FOR ALL SEASONS. The menu of service does not make mention of the family-style chicken dinners Hattie Bair would serve on Sunday. For 50¢, guest enjoyed dinner that included chicken, biscuits, gravy, salad, vegetables, and pie. People would take the "electric" for the scenic ride and Hattie's delicious home cooking. According to Docia Bair Leach, the surveyors for the Northern Pacific Railroad lived at the hotel for a long time.

The Ideal Summer and Winter Resort....

In the most picturesque and enchanted spot on Puget Sound, where Nature has provided all that tends to the health and pleasure of man: The bubbling springs; the rippling brooks; the mighty forests; the calm, placid waters of Puget Sound—fanned by the balmy breeze of the great Pacific—where winter is unknown; likewise the tropical heat of summer. It is indeed *one of Nature's most healthful and pleasure resorts,* where the afflicted are cured, the convalescent and delicate restored and the pleasure seeker delighted.

A PLEASURE RESORT unsurpassed. Here are beautiful drives and promenades through virgin forests and natural parks; hunting, fishing, sailing, rowing, bathing, etc., together with a large, warm sea water swimming pool or natatorium, where one can enjoy the invigorating luxury of a plunge in the waters of the briny deep. An excellent, safe and comfortable place to learn to swim.

The Iron Springs

Iron being the best tonic, blood purifier and blood maker, nature through these springs provides the most effective and pleasant method of obtaining desired results by toning up the system, creating new physical and mental energy and thus restoring convalescents and over-worked, ailing or aged people.

Sea Water

The tonic, curative and antiseptic effect of sea water are well known to have saved and prolonged the lives of mankind from time immemorial.

Mud Baths

Nature has still further provided this favored spot with *a large deposit of a very superior quality of medicinal clay,* which is administered as "Mud Baths," thus making a combination of disease-destroying and health giving elements superior to any health resort in the known world.

When your doctor fails, come out and get cured

HISTORY

The collections of "The Deep Sea Aquarium" were started in 1880 by a young man who landed in San Francisco from the school of mines of Denver, Colorado, on his way to Alaska to look over the mining situation. There being no regular passenger vessels running up the coast he was in a quandary how to proceed when a man came into the lobby of his hotel and asked, "Is there anyone here who would like to make a trip to the Arctic Ocean on a whaler?" The young man asked, "Does the vessel stop at Sitka, Alaska on its way north?" "Oh yes!" said the man. "Alright," said the young fellow.

Well, the vessel did not stop anywhere but continued into the Arctic Ocean. The young fellow was glad it did not stop for as soon as he got his "sea legs" and his stomach became settled he enjoyed the trip very much. He became very much interested in the life of the sea, from the whale down, and there began the collection of what is now a most interesting and educational display, "The Deep Sea Aquarium." The principle features of the exhibit are explained to guests. Though not as young as he used to be, the old time whaler is still on the job.

In order to keep up the display and feed "The Monster" an admission fee of twenty-five cents for adults, fifteen cents for children ten years and older, is charged. Children under ten, free. School classes, including teacher, fifteen cents each. No one can afford to miss seeing this display.

E. E. Bair—THE MONSTER

AQUARIUM HISTORY. Capt. Ed Bair came from Kansas and spent time on the sea, which is where he developed a love for collecting specimens from the deep sea and beaches. His aquarium began in the Iron Springs Hotel and then moved to a house and finally ended up at Saltar's Point. For a quarter, one would receive a tour and a lecture that explained his collection. It is believed that he gave himself the title of "Captain," perhaps to establish credibility as a resource on the sea. The tour of the aquarium culminated with the story of the "most terrible, most horrible monster known to man." With that, he would swing open the door to expose a moonshine still. Bair's aquarium was in business during Prohibition.

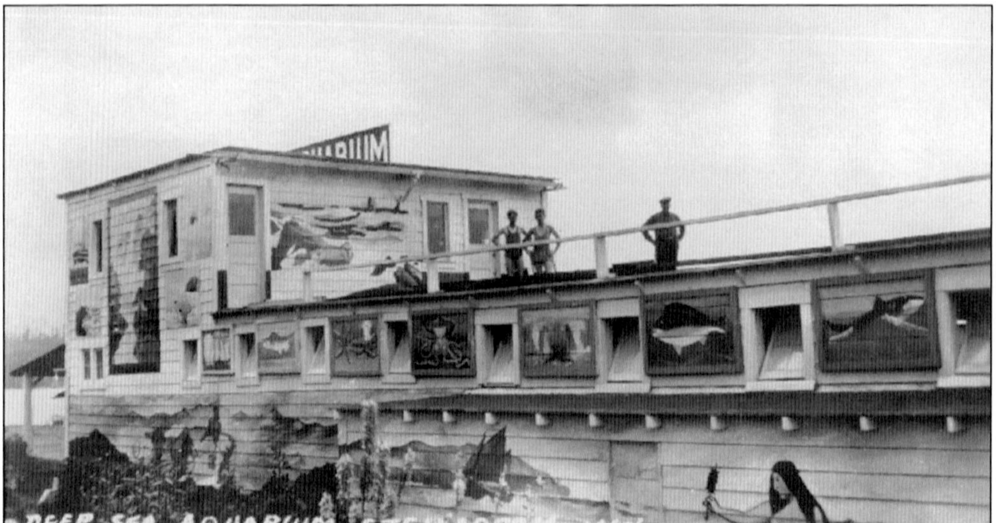

DEEP SEA AQUARIUM. A patient of Western State Hospital painted the exterior of the aquarium, which was located on Saltar's Point; the museum was filled with pickled sea creatures and shells. The Deep Sea Aquarium had no living specimens within the structure; however, there may have been a seal that lived in a cage near the porch and played in the water with the ebb and flow of the tide. When the Deep Sea Aquarium closed, the treasures belonging to Ed Bair were donated to the University of Washington.

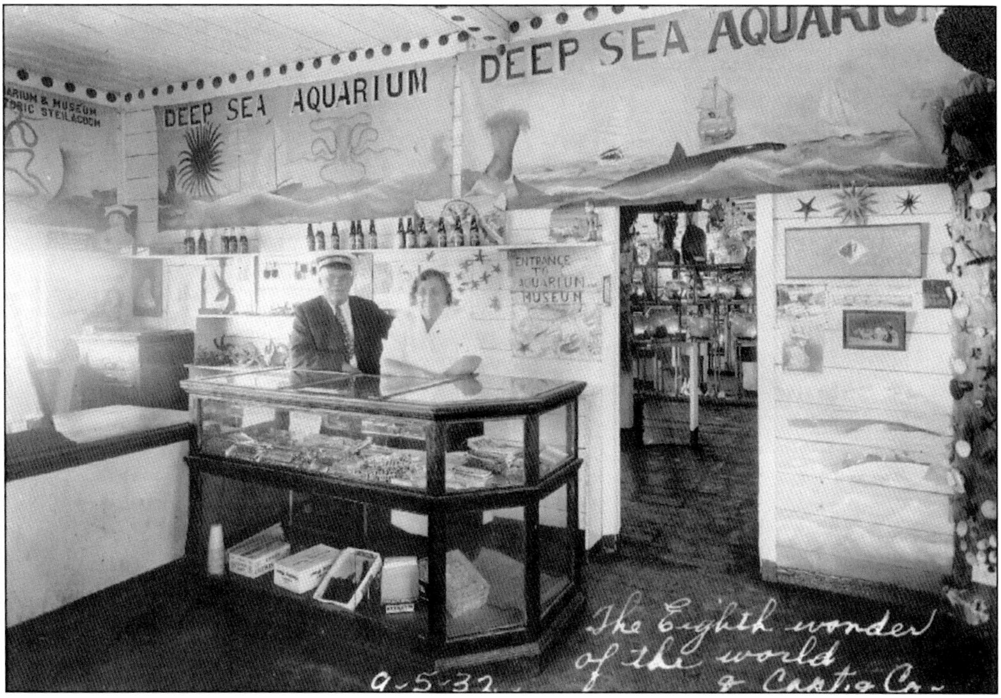

The Eighth Wonder of the World. Proprietor Edward Bair and employee Nina Egan work the counter at the aquarium. The Deep Sea Aquarium was in operation from 1919 to 1940. The building was torn down in 1940 after the death of Ed Bair.

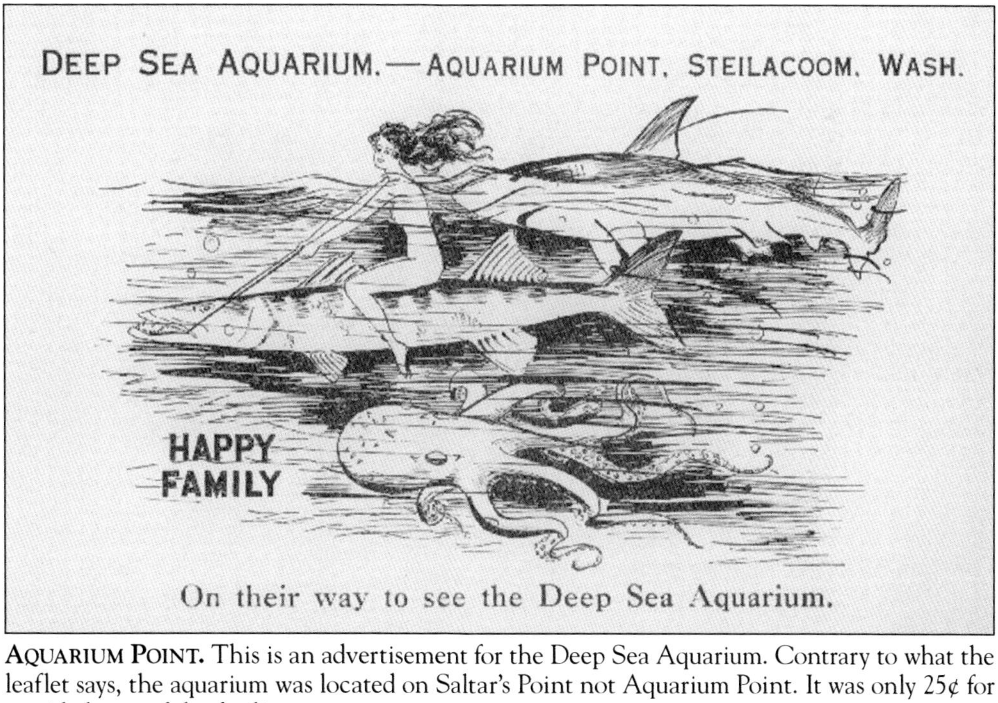

Aquarium Point. This is an advertisement for the Deep Sea Aquarium. Contrary to what the leaflet says, the aquarium was located on Saltar's Point not Aquarium Point. It was only 25¢ for a guided tour of the facility.

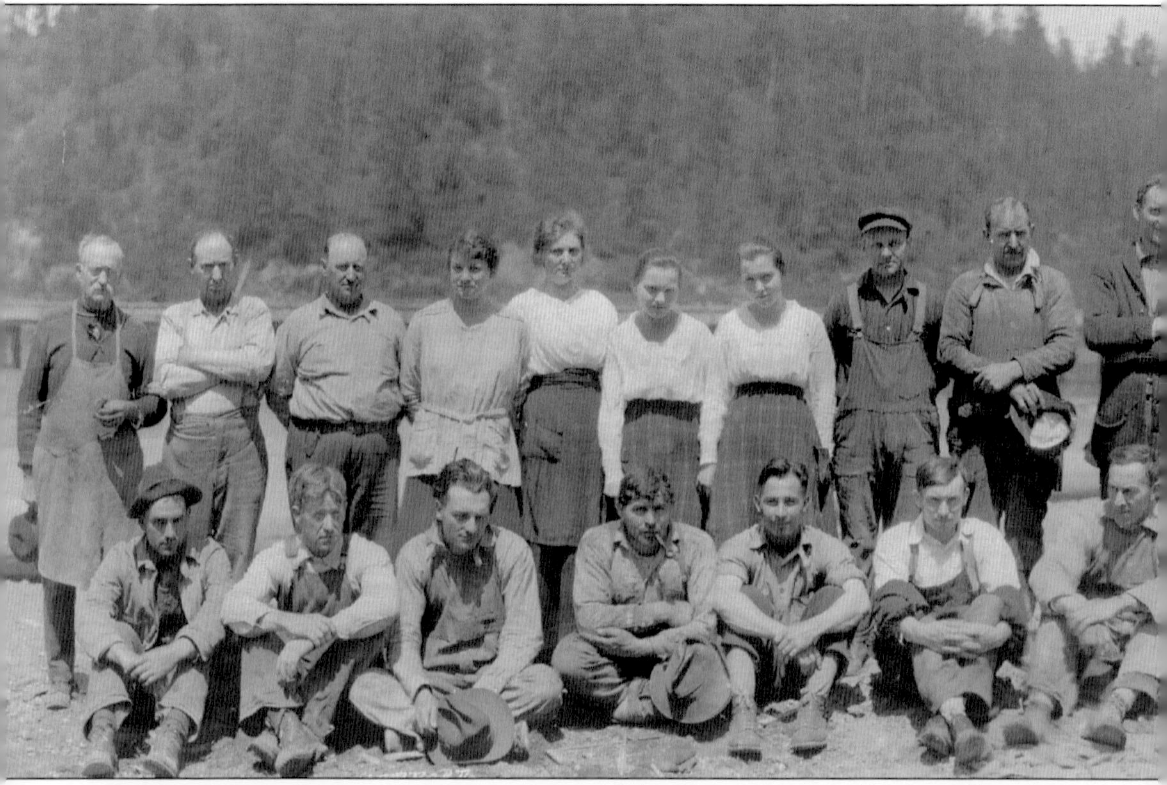

The Paper Mill. Pictured here are employees of the Cascade Paper Mill. The mill opened in 1919 on Chambers Creek Road, just outside of town. The mill closed during the Depression

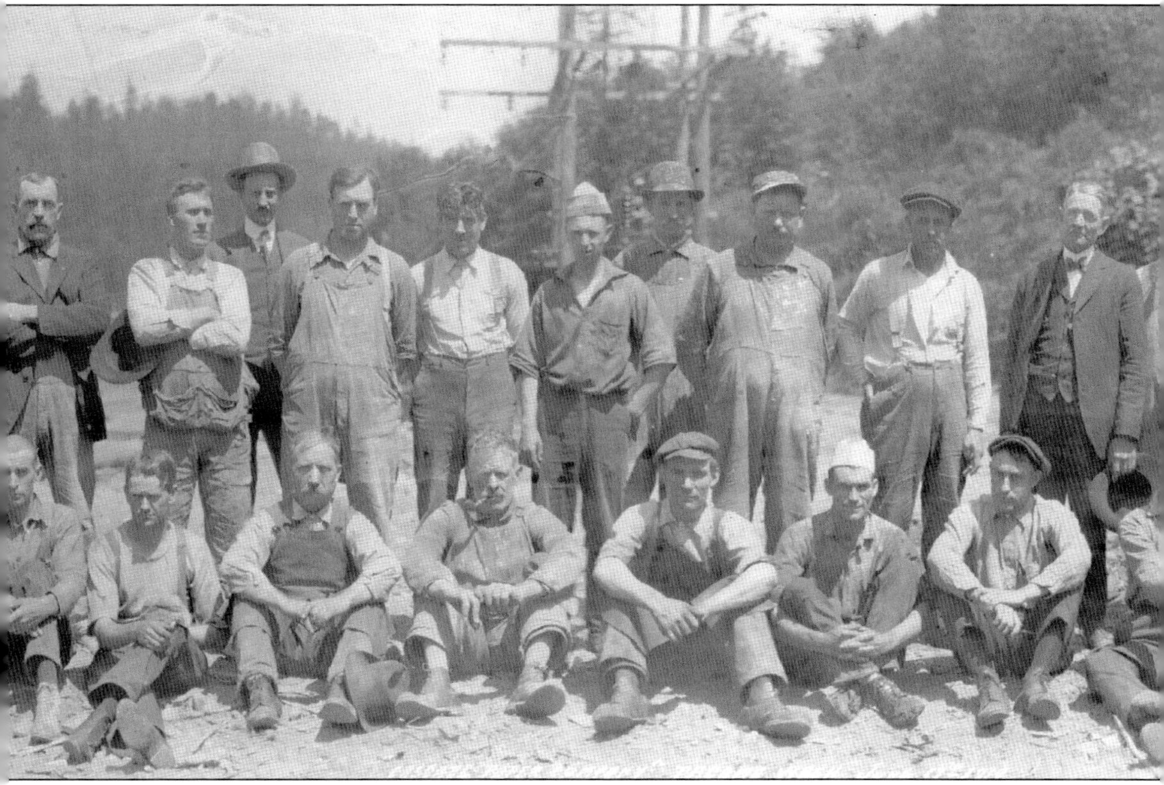

and reopened for business in 1937. The last paper product to be manufactured on the site was newsprint. The mill closed permanently in 2000.

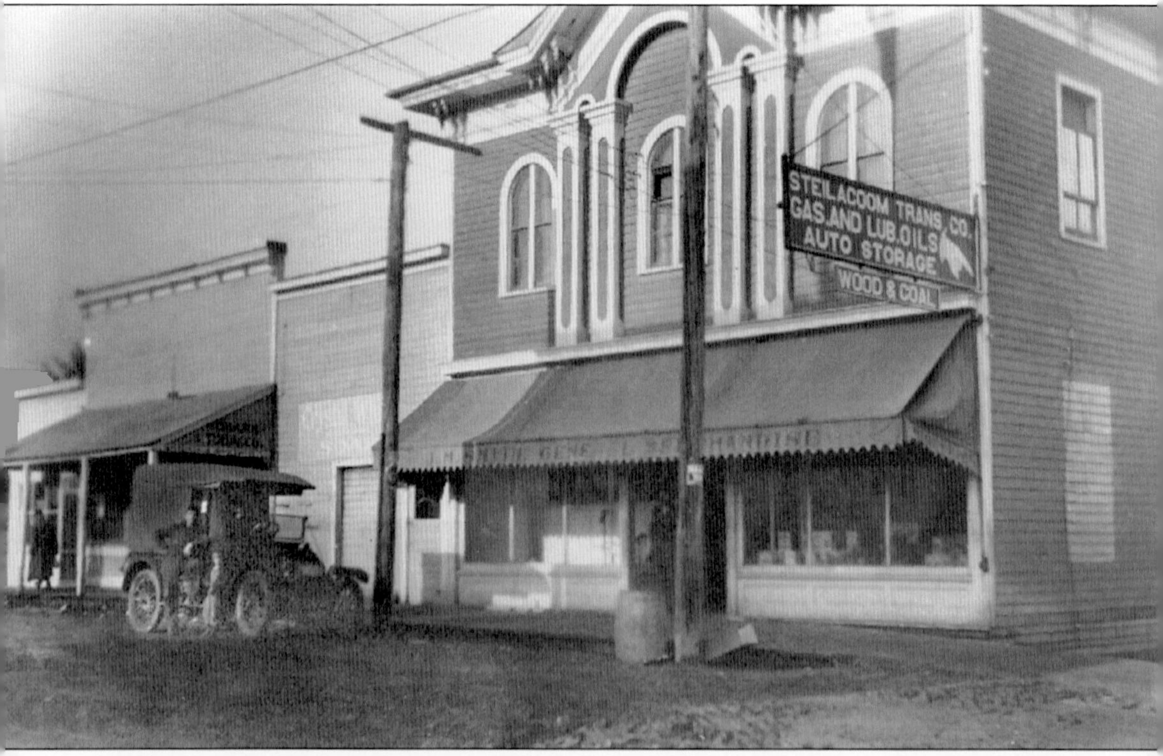

MASONIC LODGE RELOCATES. Nick Doering moved the wooden hall to Lafayette Street when the Northern Pacific Railroad purchased the water side of Commercial Street. The building was one of the last structures to be relocated. It was used as a grocery store and pool hall with meeting rooms upstairs. In 1939, it burned to the ground and took the store, pool hall, soda fountain, butcher, and barbershop with it.

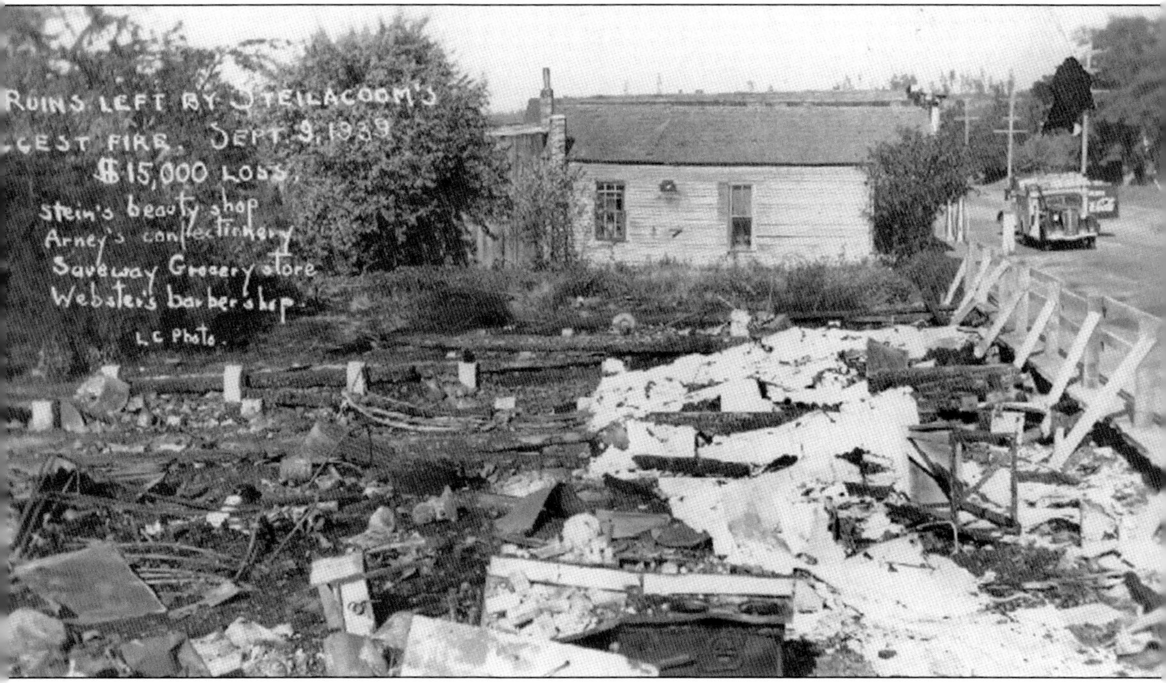

THE FIRE OF 1939. The fire hit the Steilacoom business district on September 9 and destroyed three buildings with damage estimated at $15,000. Jim Lester and other poker players were in the middle of their game at Arnie's Confectionery when smoke came through the walls. The alarm sounded, and the monument bell rang. Every available person helped to put out the fire. Lynn Scholes was credited with saving the Bair Store by standing on the roof with a hose. Firefighters from Tacoma and Fort Lewis did not arrive in time to save the buildings, but the fire was prevented from spreading. One of the buildings lost that night was the old Masonic Lodge, built in the 1860s. The block was left vacant except for the Bair Store until 1951, when the post office was built on the site, now occupied by Key Bank.

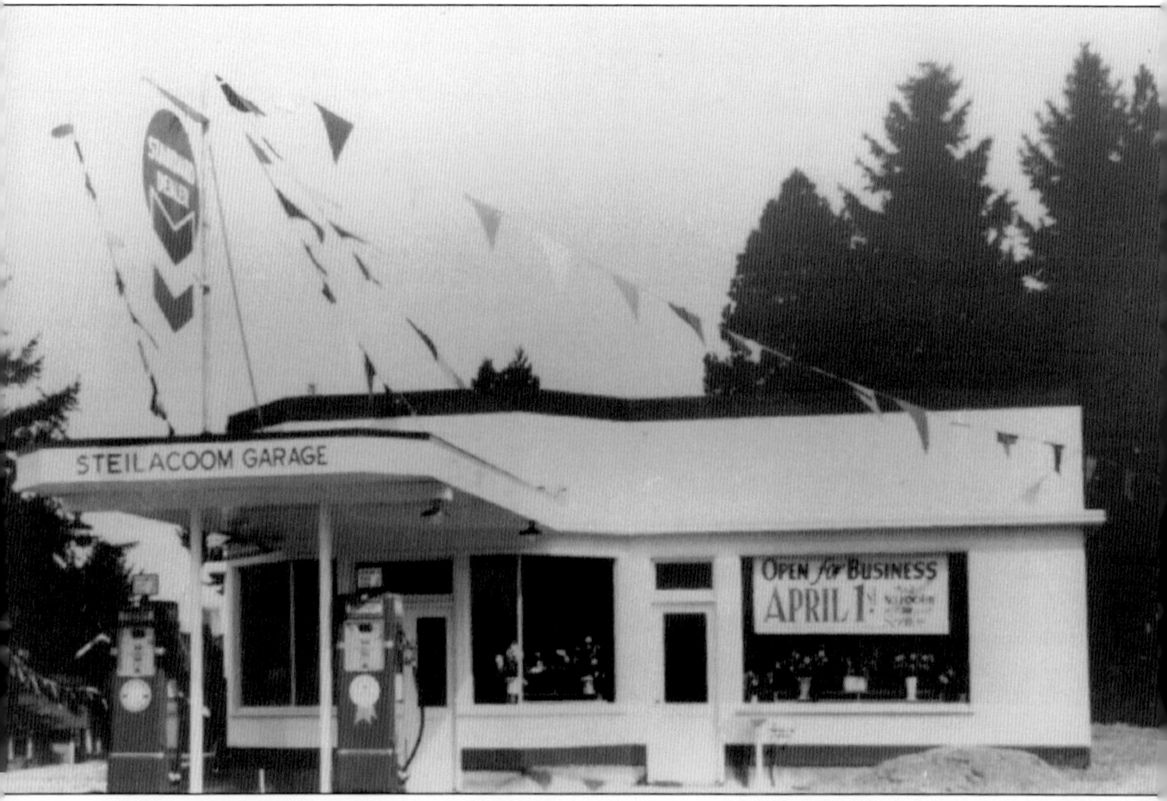

GRAND OPENING. On March 21, 1942, George Kuper opened his Steilacoom Garage on the corner of Rainier and Union Streets. There was a dance in celebration of the grand opening. The *Lakewood Log* reported the garage was "the first commercial structure in Steilacoom to be equipped with a neat Ladies Lavatory." Currently this building is used by Espresso by the Bay, a drive-through coffee shop. The lavatory is still open.

Four

Moving People From Here to There

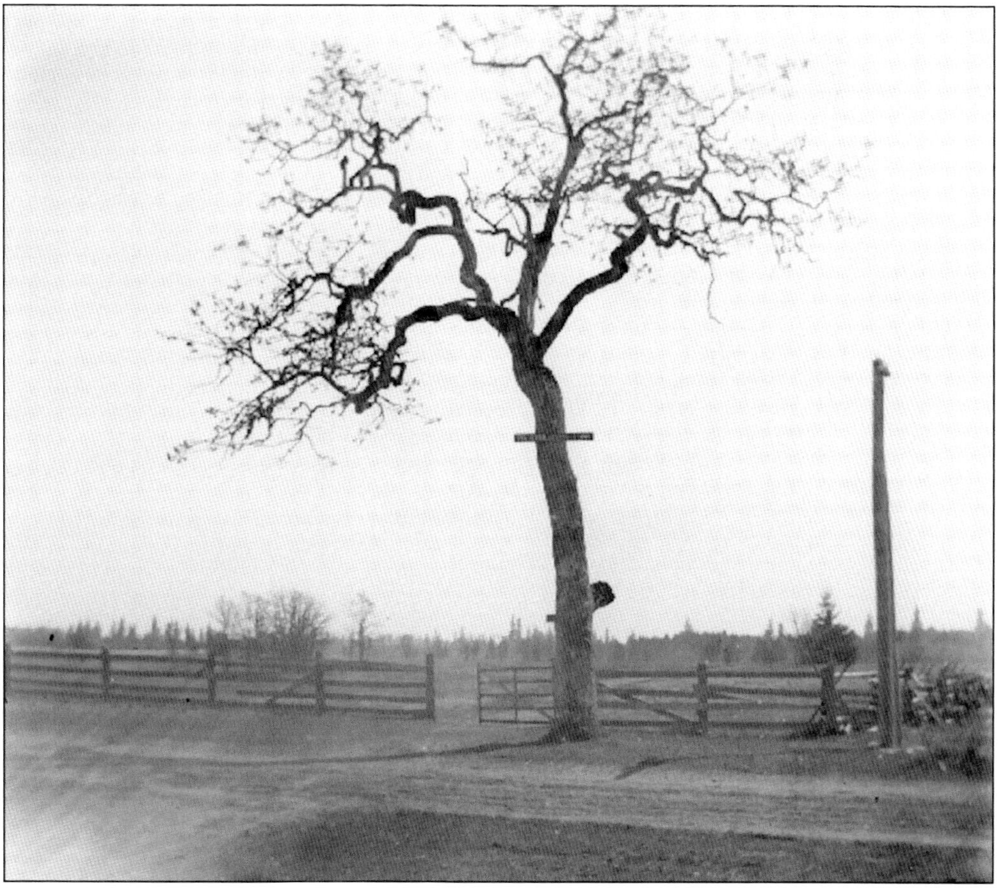

Three Mile Tree. This tree was probably three miles from Steilacoom toward Tacoma. The exact location of the tree is unknown today; however, it is a perfect example of what a "road sign" may have looked like. The sign posted on this old tree could have been used as a guide for horses and motor vehicles alike.

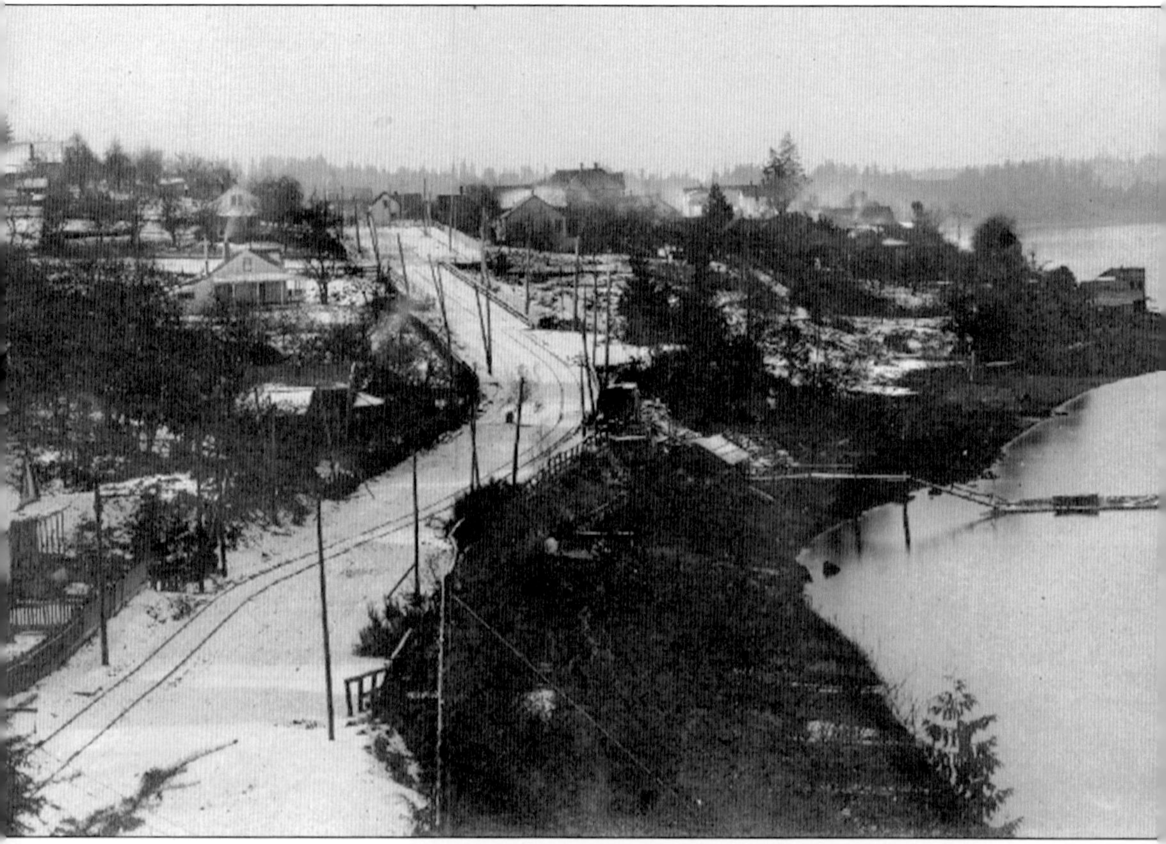

THE FIRST STREETCAR LINE. This view in 1900 is of the Steilacoom-Tacoma streetcar line. The track stretched nearly 15 miles; it was quite rare to have a streetcar serving more than a five-mile area. In 1906, Tacoma High School (now Stadium) opened, and Steilacoom students would ride the streetcar daily to attend high school. The line discontinued service when the Northern Pacific Railroad was built.

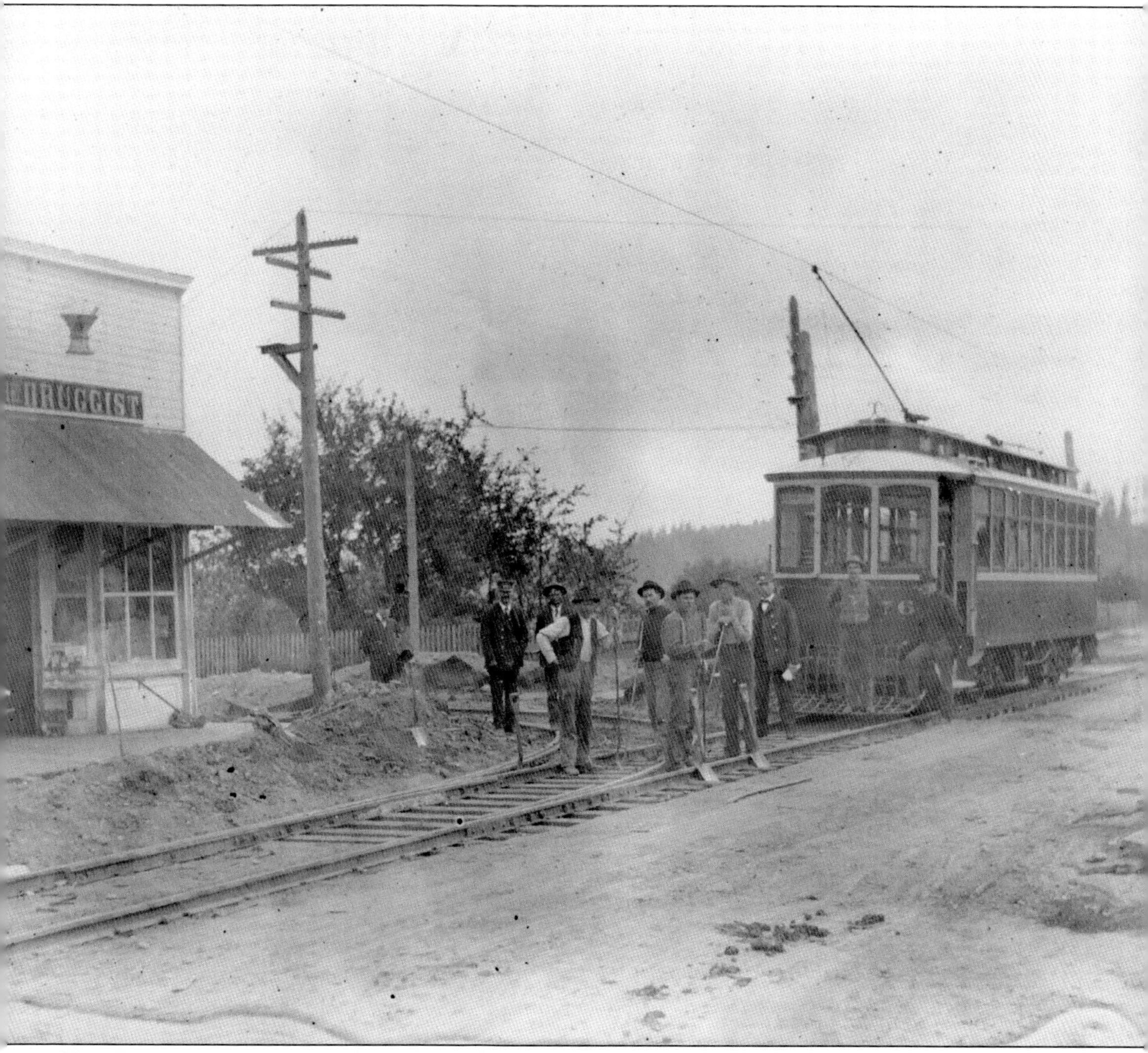

THE END OF THE LINE. Steilacoom Trolley car No. 76 is stopped at the wye in front of the Bair Store on Lafayette Street around 1895. The wye was built so streetcars could turn around quickly and easily for the return trip to Tacoma.

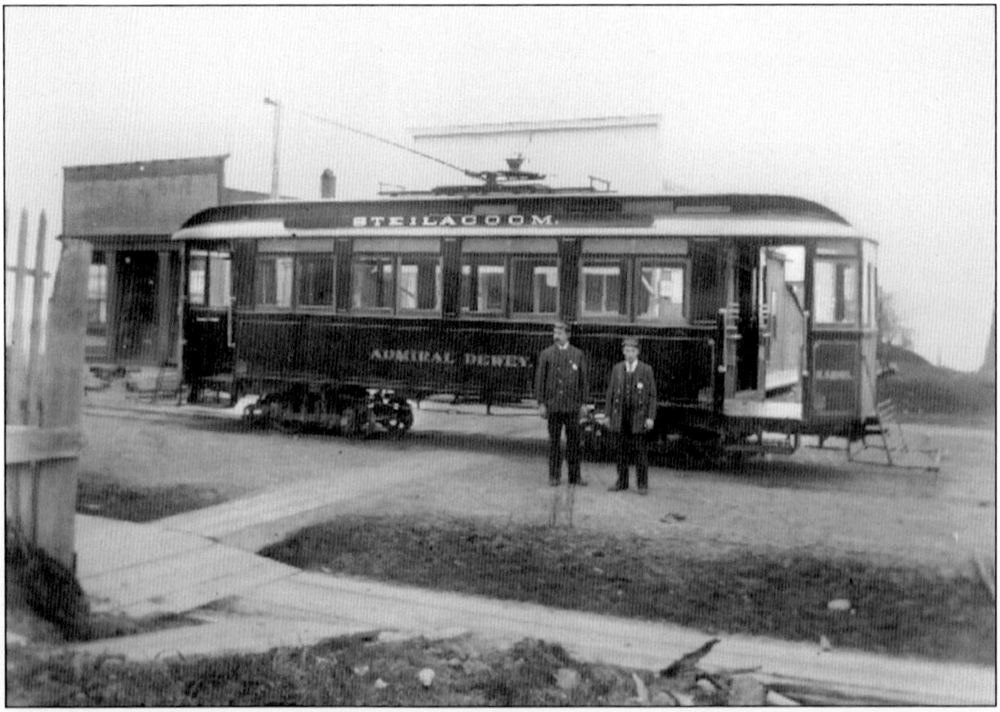

THE *ADMIRAL DEWEY*. In 1893, the *Admiral Dewey* streetcar was delivering passengers and the U.S. mail to Steilacoom. The streetcar was a modern marvel and made it possible for those who worked and lived in Steilacoom to commute to Tacoma for work and come home to Steilacoom every night. The Tacoma and Steilacoom Railway Company was indeed one of the first interurban streetcar lines.

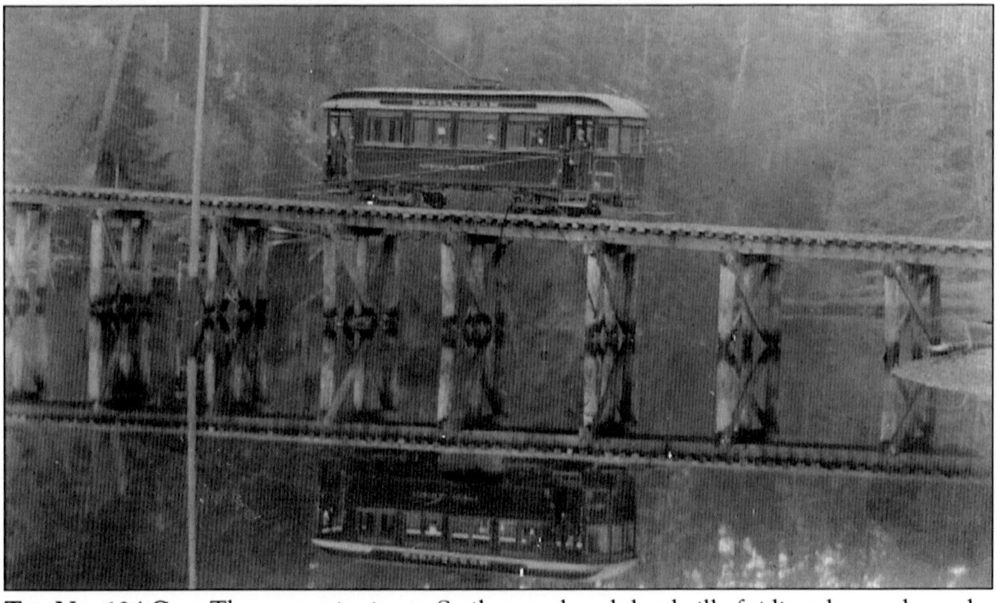

THE NO. 104 CAR. Those vacationing to Steilacoom loved the thrill of riding the car down the hill, through the trees, and across the wooden bridge at Chambers Creek, to be welcomed by the calming waters and pristine beaches on the Puget Sound.

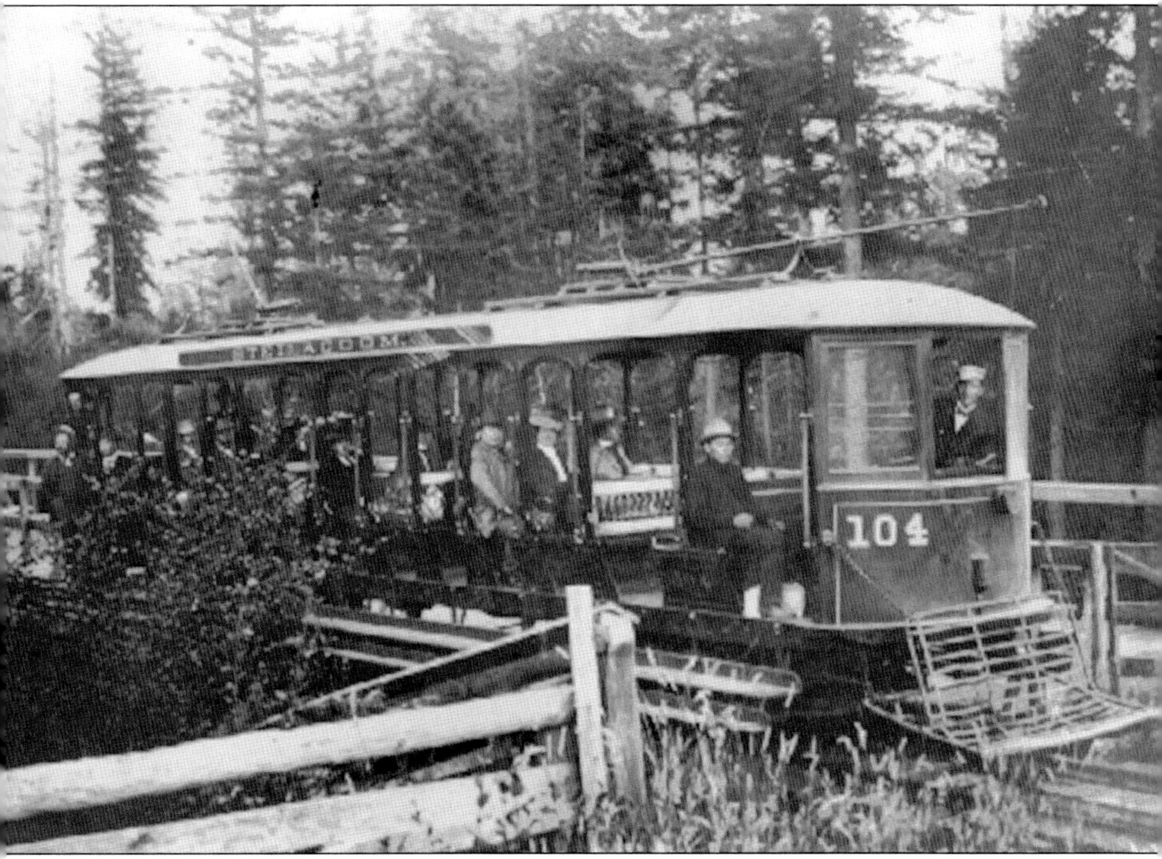

The Commuter Car. Here the Steilacoom car No. 104 makes one of several trips a day between Steilacoom and Tacoma in 1892. The Tacoma and Steilacoom Railway Company had the following schedule, according the *Tacoma Daily Ledger*: leaving Tacoma at Eleventh Street at 6:30 a.m., 8:00 a.m., 9:30 a.m., 11:00 a.m., 12:30 p.m., 2:00 p.m., 3:30 p.m., 5:00 p.m., and 6:00 p.m.

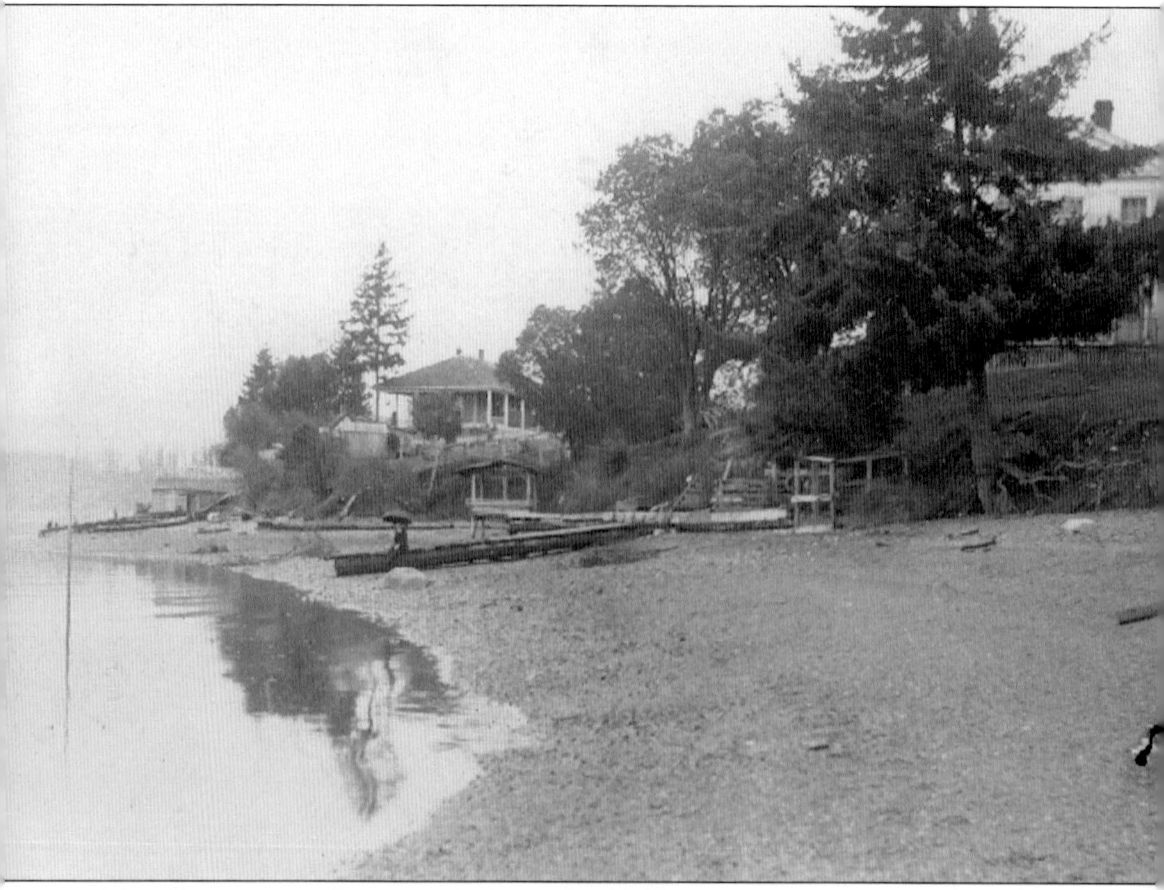

MAKE ROOM FOR THE RAILROAD. On June 6, 1910, Ordinance No. 85 was passed by the Steilacoom Town Council, granting the Northern Pacific Railroad the right to construct the railroad across Steilacoom. Property along the waterfront was purchased for $5,000 a lot, including half of the business section along Commercial Street. Rock used for riprap was barged in from the San Juan Islands, cottages were torn down, some buildings were moved, and the shoreline began to change. Capt. John Saltar's home was one of the casualties of the railroad.

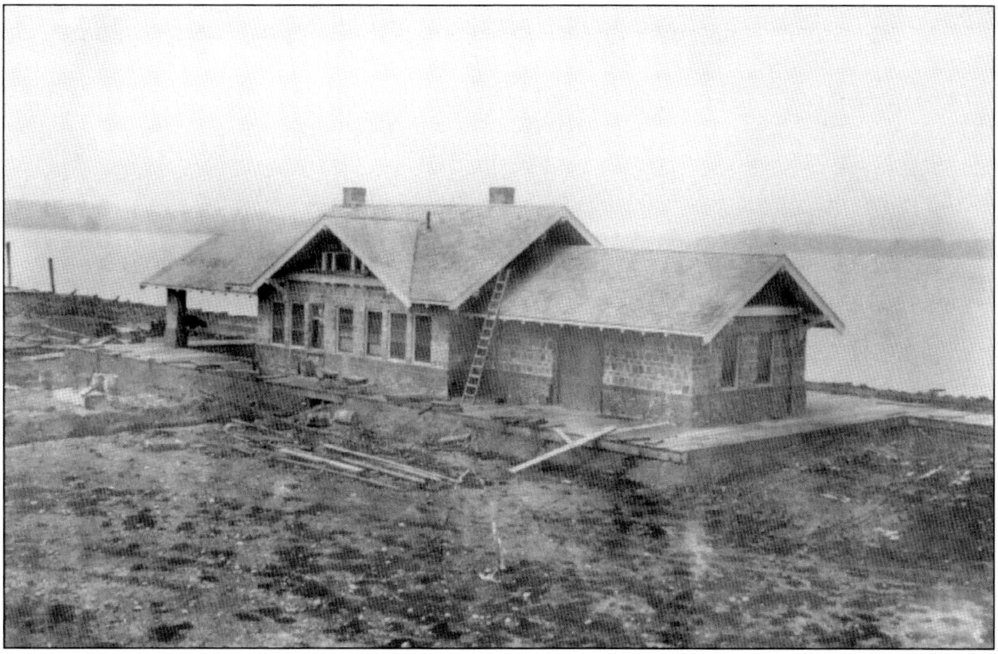

Building a Depot. Construction of the Steilacoom Depot began in 1913 after clearing a waterfront orchard. The depot was constructed just north of the ferry terminal. In the distance are McNeil and Anderson Islands. The first train came through on December 15, 1914. The opening was such an exciting occasion that the schoolchildren came down to the depot to sing a song especially written for the event.

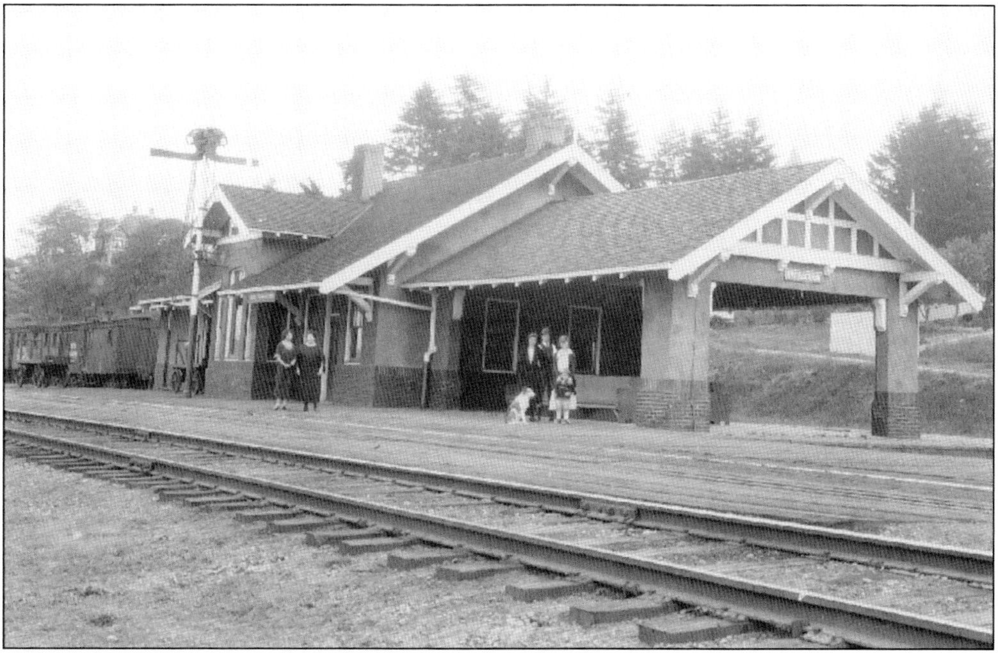

Ready for Travelers. Here we see the Steilacoom train depot along the Northern Pacific Railroad line in 1920. Puget Sound is to the left of the tracks. The train made regular stops to the Steilacoom Depot, affording residents speedy travel to Tacoma, Seattle, and Portland.

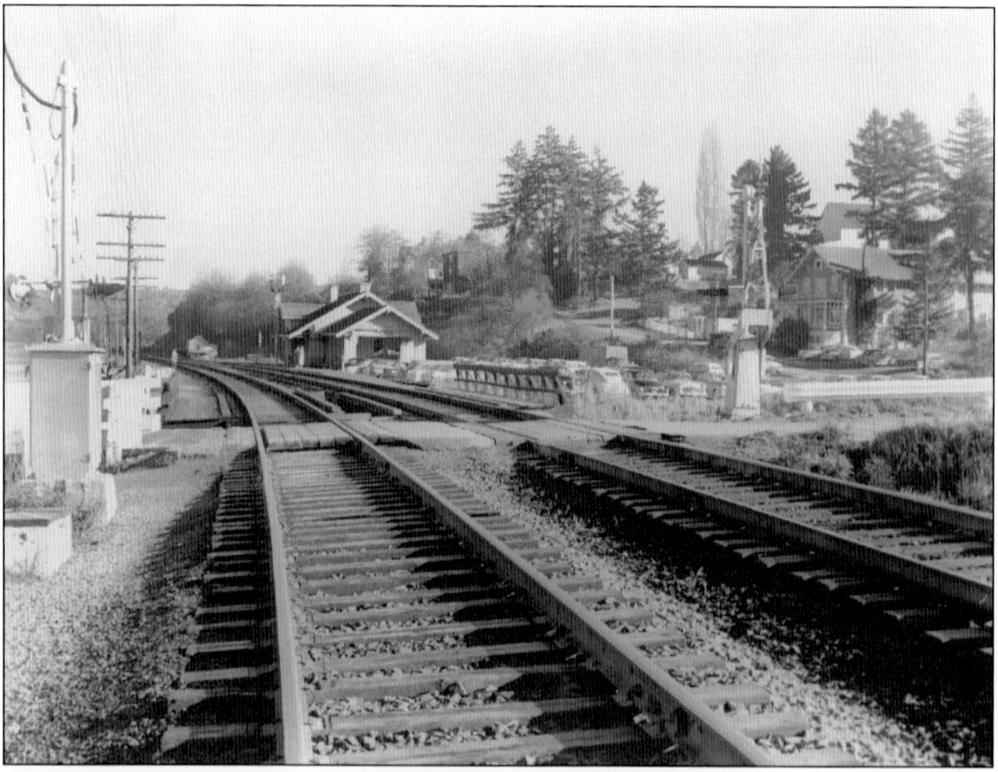

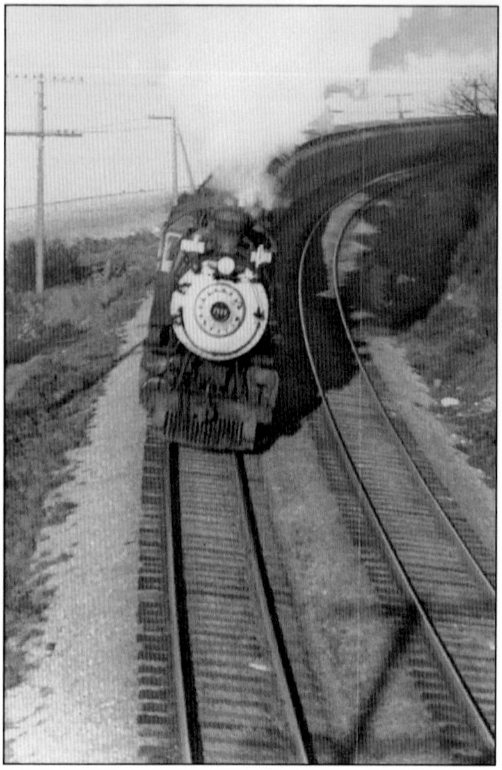

FROM WEST TACOMA. This is the completed train depot at Union and Commercial Streets. These tracks carry passengers and products north and south from British Columbia to Southern California.

STEAM LOCOMOTIVE. Here we see the locomotive passing through Steilacoom from West Tacoma en route south. Dr. Charles Taylor and his family took a vacation to Long Beach, California, boarding the train in Steilacoom in the 1920s. The doctor had his car shipped to California by boat so the family would have transportation when they arrived.

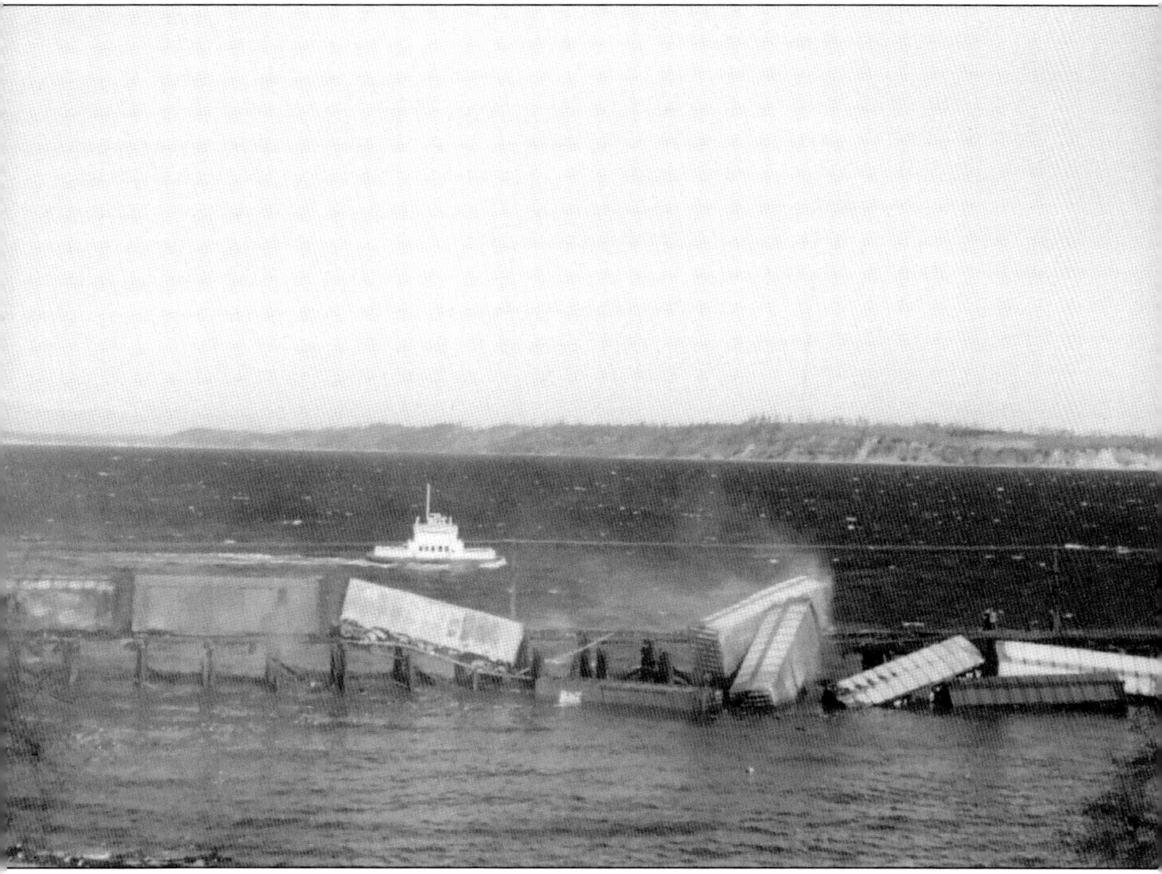

TRAIN WRECK. In March 1954, Milton Davidson, a college student at the time, captured this once-in-a-lifetime picture of a train derailment from the wooden trestle that caught fire. The Davidson family has been the proud owner of the Phillip Keach home since the 1930s; the home is now named Rolling Hill.

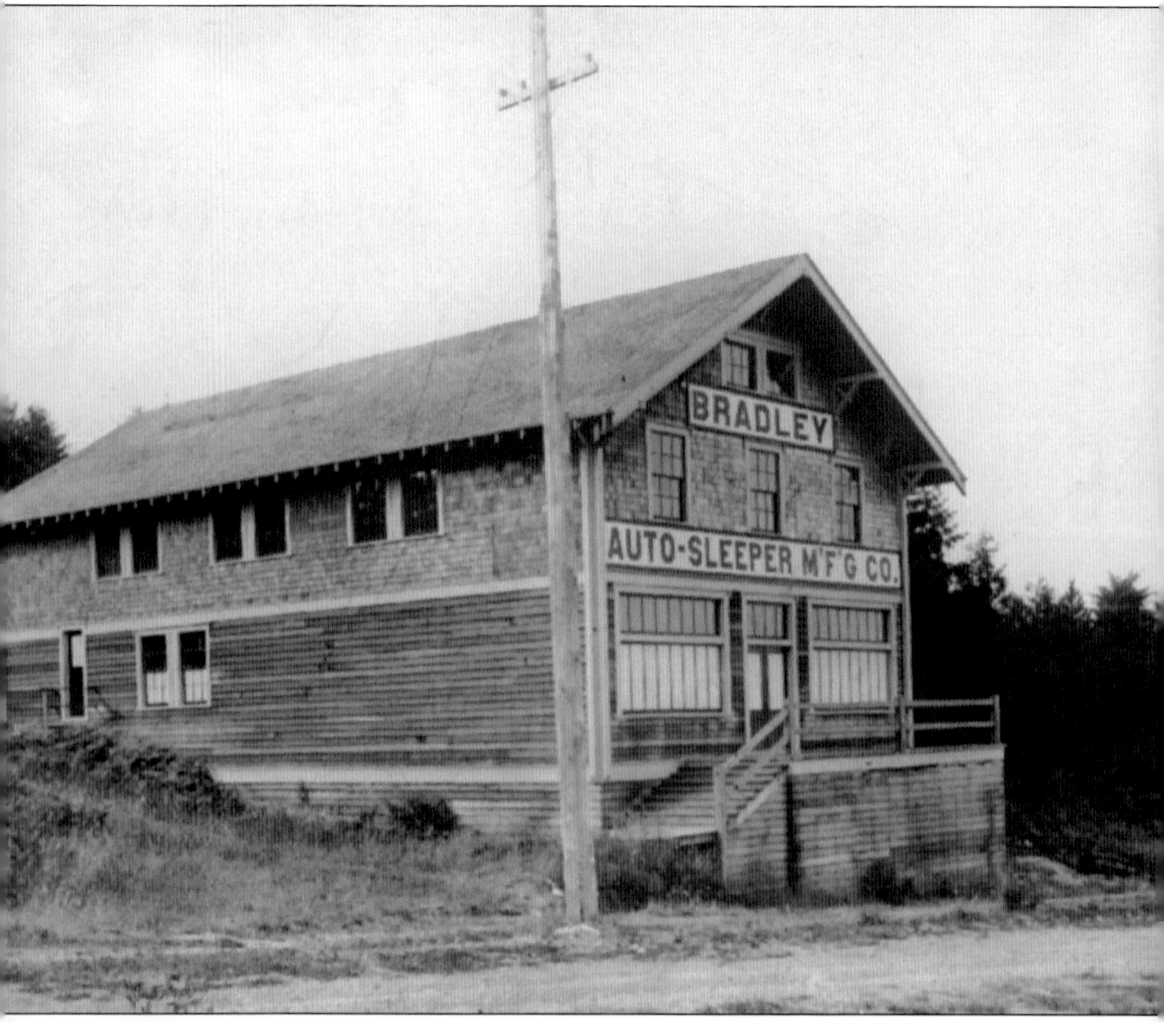

RAILROAD HOTEL. The Bradley Auto-Sleeper Manufacturing Company made mattresses. The building was originally a hotel operated by the railroad. The building is directly across the street from the depot and currently operates as the Soundview Apartments.

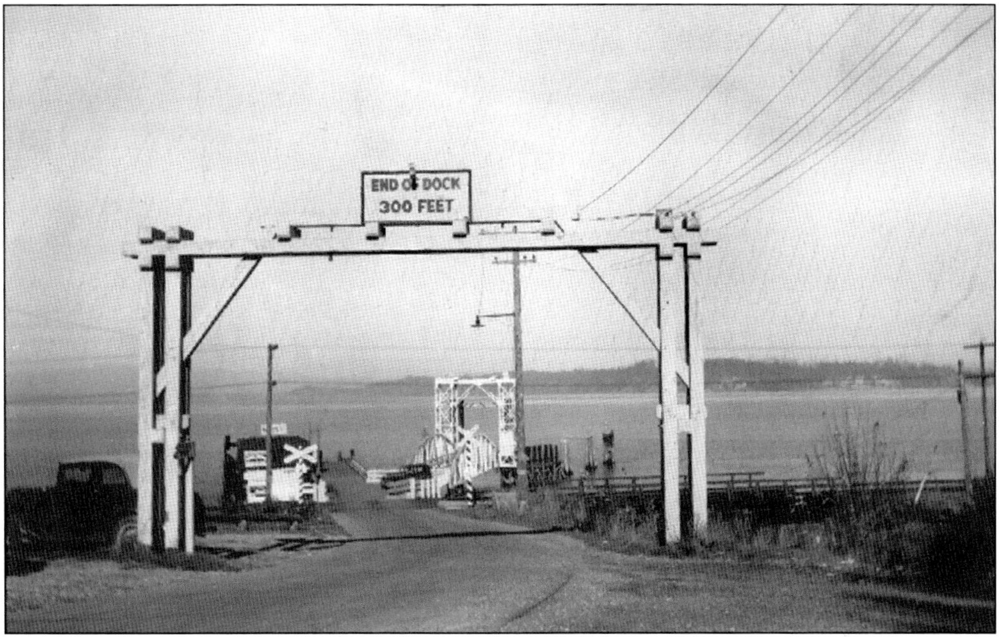

FERRY DOCK. The ferry landing is located at the end of Union Avenue. McNeil Island prison ferry traffic as well as the Anderson, Ketron, and Longbranch ferries have used the dock. To the right under the bridge is the boat launch. The bridge was a popular place for town boys to carry out "truth or dare"—one would be dared to stand under the bridge and stare upward at a passing train. The dock was also home to the Dock Lunch, a small restaurant that catered to ferry passengers and penitentiary workers.

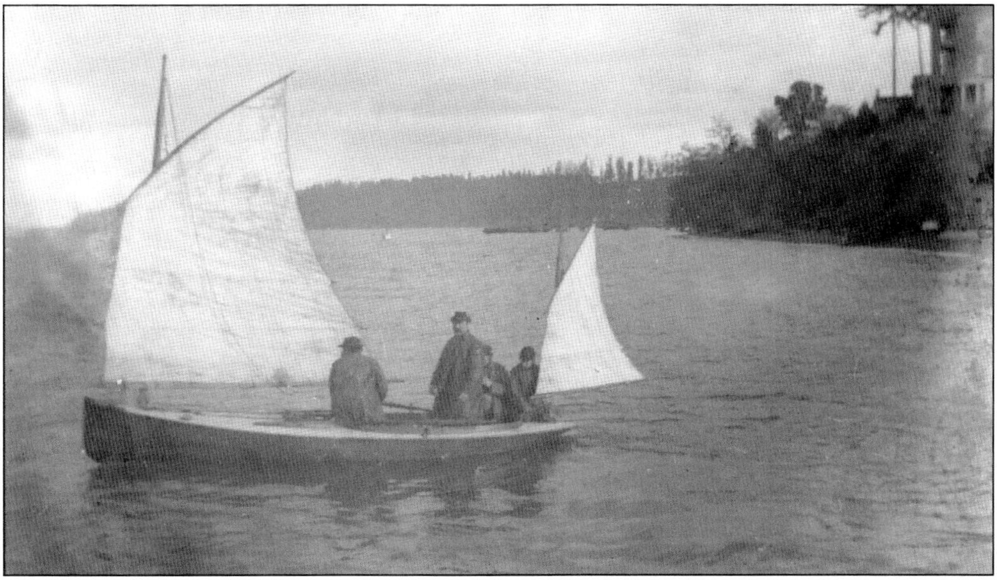

THE PEN BOAT. McNeil Island residents received their parcels and correspondence courtesy of the mail boat traveling between Steilacoom and McNeil Islands. This photograph was taken around 1890. Many Steilacoom residents worked at the penitentiary, including Neil Henly, who built the first sailboat that would take deliveries to the island. One of the present-day passenger ferries that transports workers to the prison is named in honor of Capt. Neil Henly.

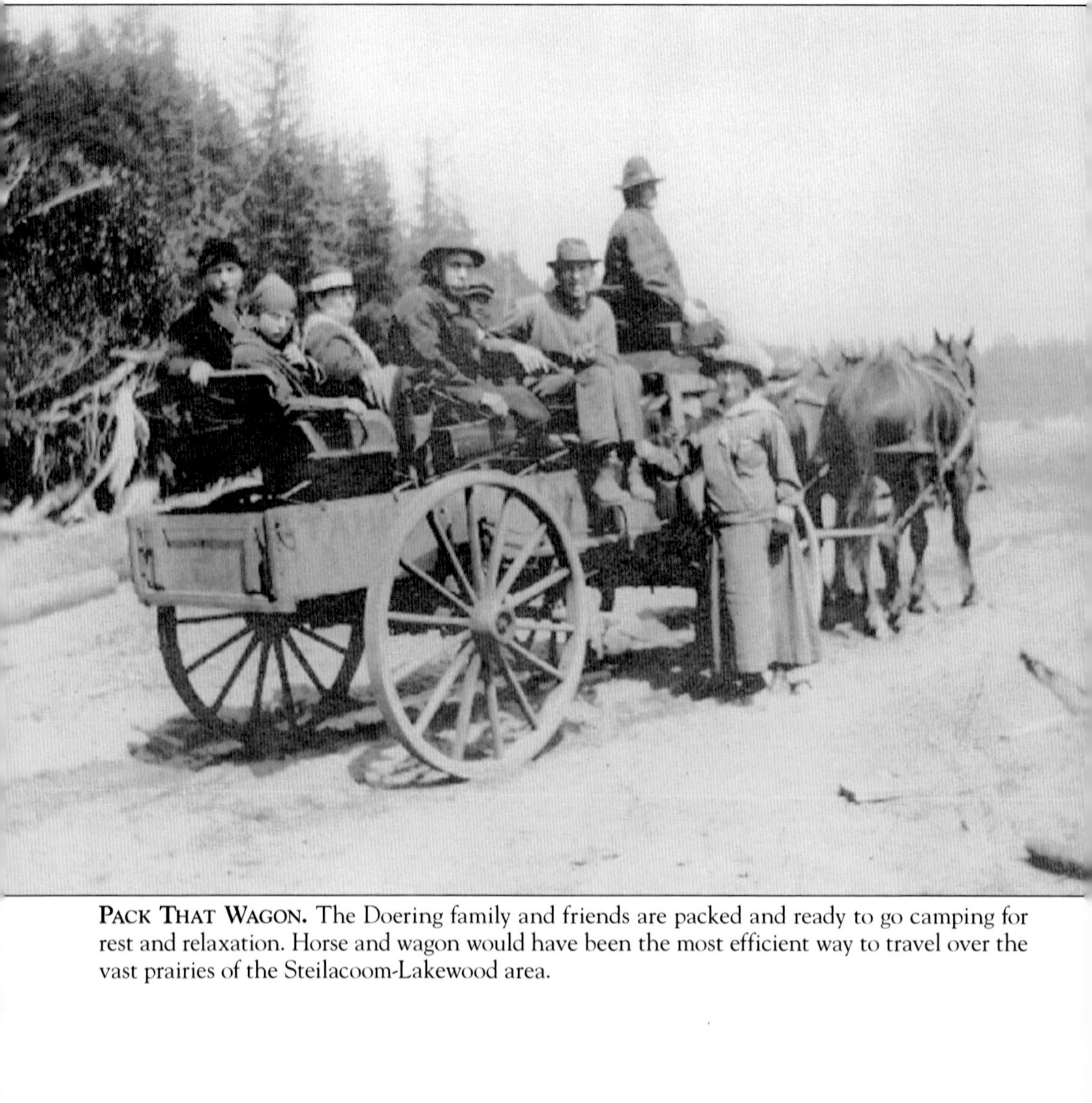

PACK THAT WAGON. The Doering family and friends are packed and ready to go camping for rest and relaxation. Horse and wagon would have been the most efficient way to travel over the vast prairies of the Steilacoom-Lakewood area.

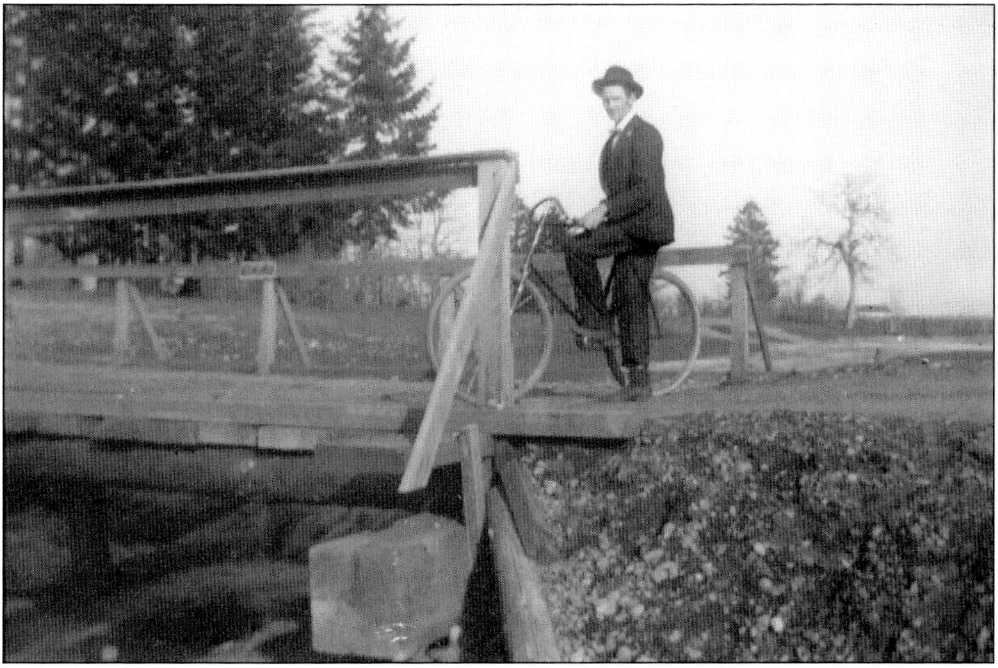

Over the Bridge. Steilacoom has many ravines that empty into the Puget Sound. The bridges were built of local lumber, and some of the trees were so large that one plank from a tree would suffice for a walking bridge. Modern materials have replaced the wooden bridges.

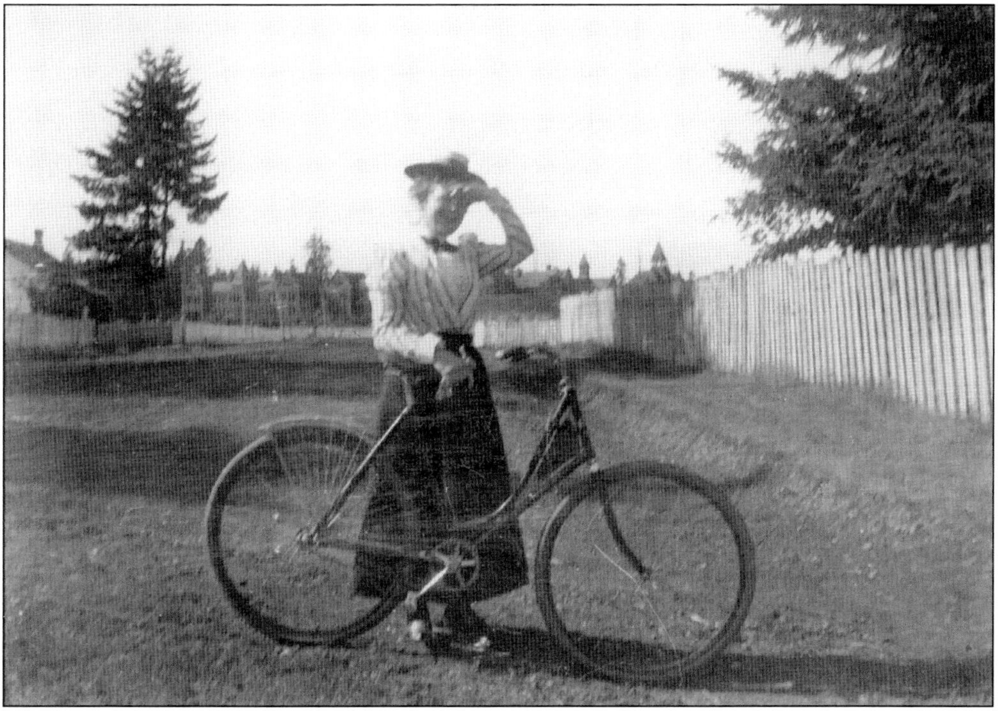

Woman with Bike. This woman pauses to pose for a photographer during a ride down what could be Steilacoom Boulevard or Military Road with Western State Hospital in the background.

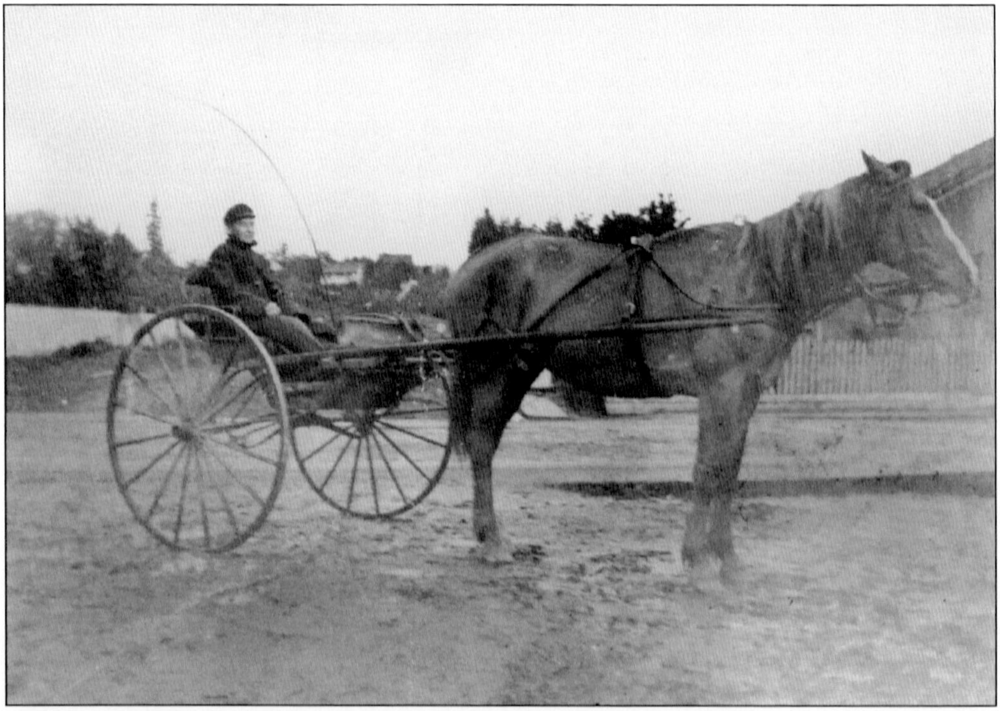

HORSE AND BUGGY. The days of the horse and buggy in the town of Steilacoom lasted for over 50 years. Pictured in 1889 with his horse and buggy is Martin Andrews at the corner of Wilkes and Lafayette Streets.

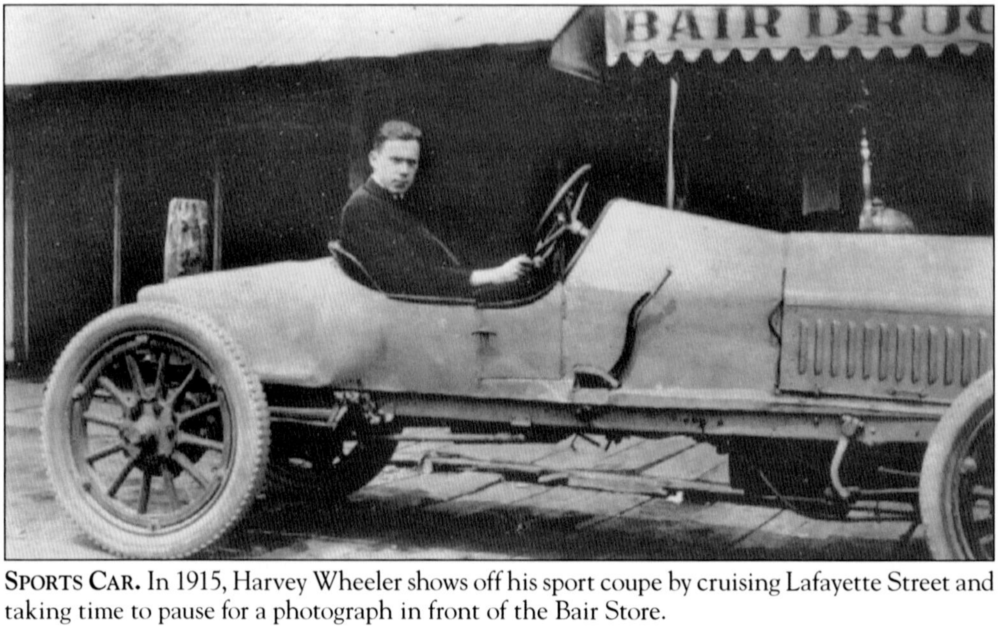

SPORTS CAR. In 1915, Harvey Wheeler shows off his sport coupe by cruising Lafayette Street and taking time to pause for a photograph in front of the Bair Store.

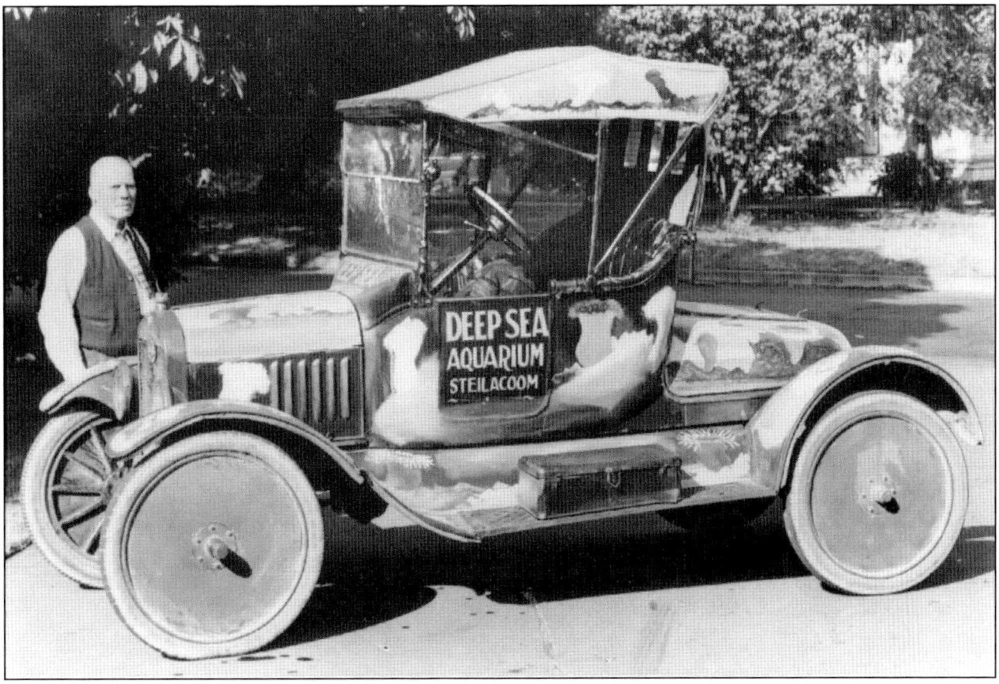

THE COMPANY CAR. Ed Bair, owner of the Deep Sea Aquarium, advertised his business on his car. Always the promoter, he had brightly colored signs posted throughout the western states.

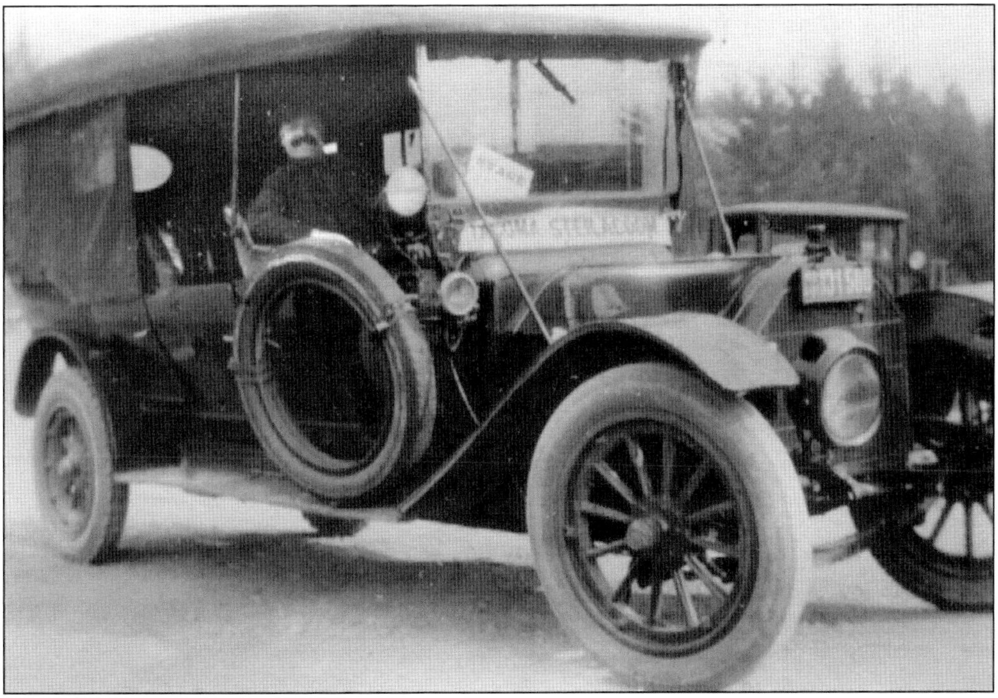

THE STEILACOOM-TACOMA STAGE. This was one of the first motorcar taxis serving travelers between Tacoma and Steilacoom. The driver pictured here was waiting to transport his passengers in a touring car from the 1920s.

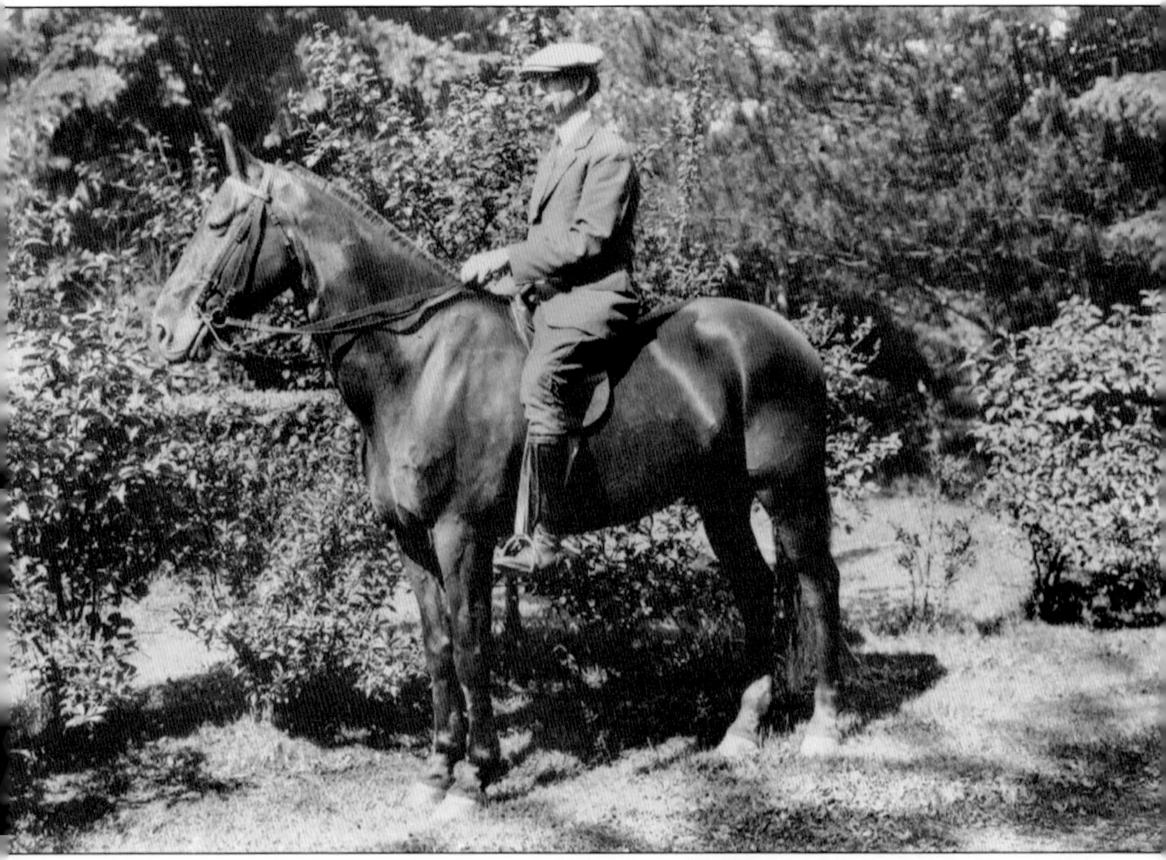

HORSEBACK. Willis E. Morris was the mayor of the town of Steilacoom for many terms. He regularly trotted around town on horseback. His first term as mayor was in 1925. He brought Steilacoom through the Depression with charisma and style. Mayor Morris was the choir director, president of the chamber of commerce, and the president of Pacific Iron and Steelworks in Tacoma.

Five

Recreation and Relaxation

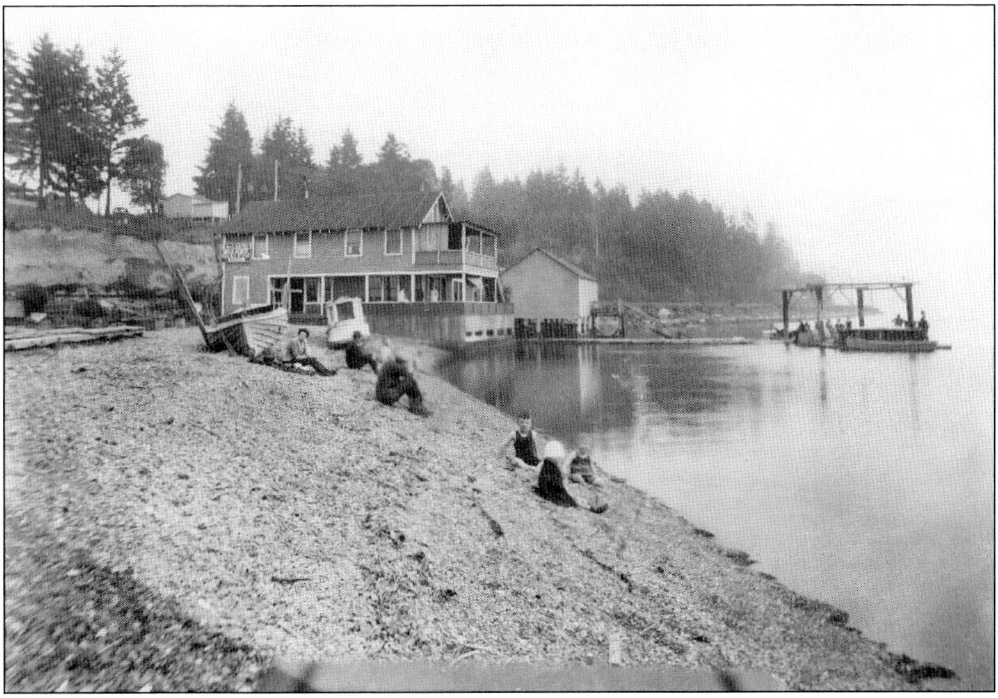

Green's Boathouse. Pictured in the 1920s, Green's served as a boardinghouse and a boathouse on Saltar's Point. Mamie and Charley Green built a boardinghouse near where the marina is today. The family lived upstairs, and the main floor was for boarders. The building was appropriately named the Soundview Inn. The Greens' rowboats were painted green, of course. The boats were available for rental for paddling the Puget Sound. Like in so many towns without modern fire equipment, the building was lost to fire.

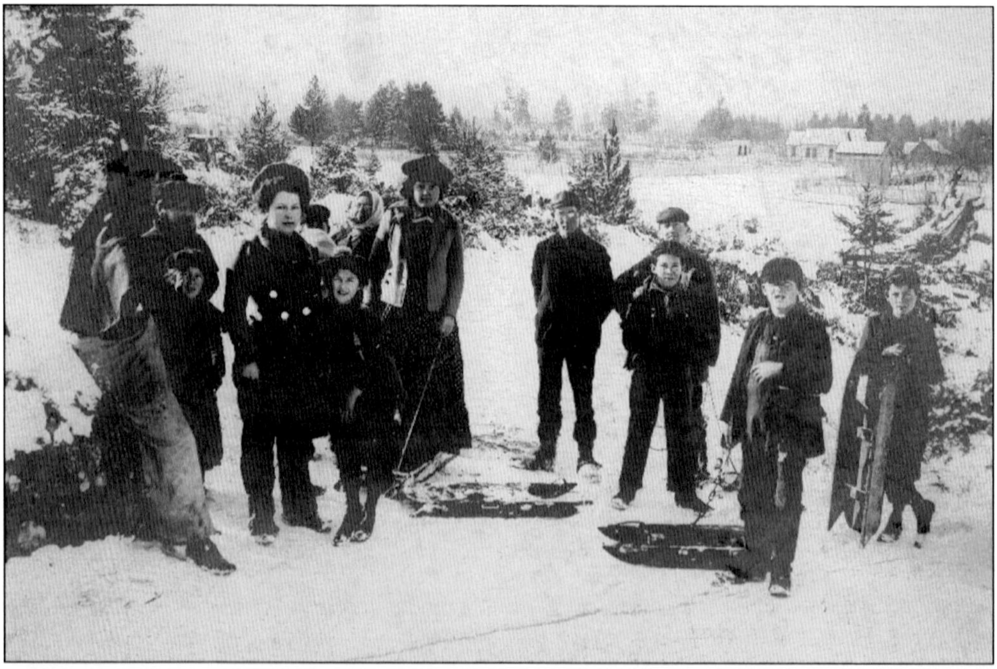

SNOW DAY. Steilacoom children of all ages are ready to enjoy the snow by sledding from Frederick Street to Union Avenue. A bonfire was stoked on Rainier Avenue to keep the sledders warm as they hiked back up the hill to Sequalish Street. If the snow melted on Frederick Street, the children would start at the Catholic church on the corner of Nisqually and Main Streets and sled to Commercial with a "lookout" on Lafayette Street to watch for traffic.

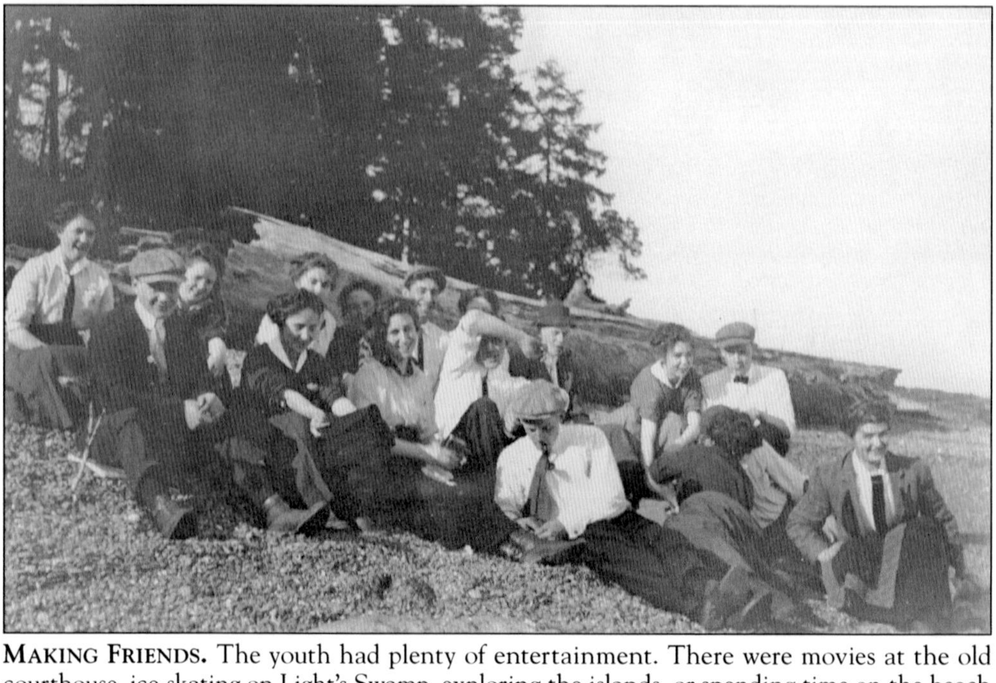

MAKING FRIENDS. The youth had plenty of entertainment. There were movies at the old courthouse, ice-skating on Light's Swamp, exploring the islands, or spending time on the beach with friends.

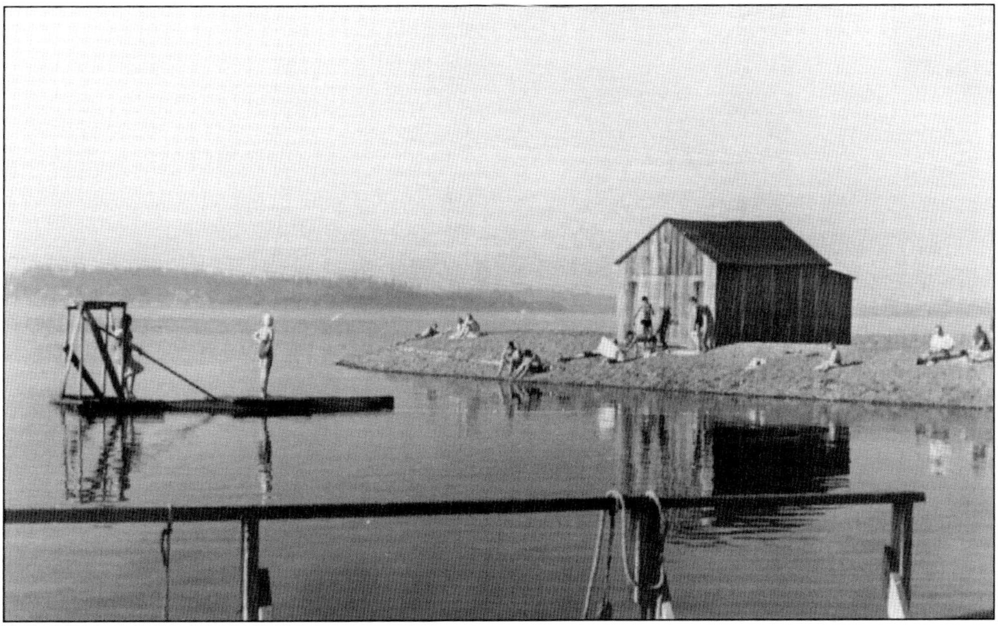

SUNNING AT SALTAR'S POINT. This is one of the preferred sunning spots on the Puget Sound. Swimmers liked to alternate time dipping into the cold water of Puget Sound and warming up on the sun-baked pebbles on the beach.

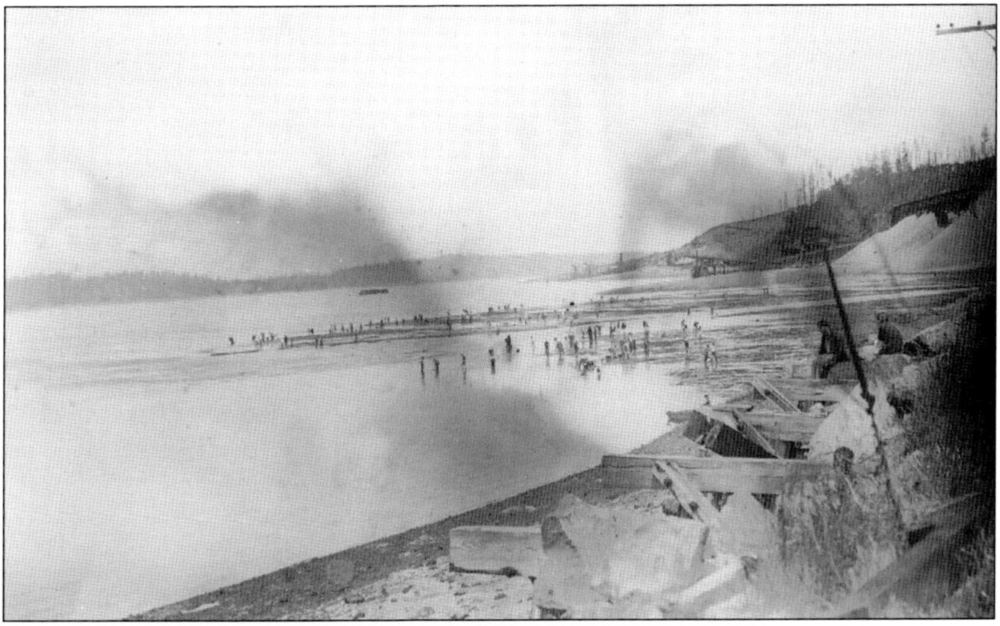

GRAVEL PIT. Steilacoom Sand and Gravel, built by Bill Thompson to compete with Pioneer Sand and Gravel, was in operation just outside of town. As the gravel was separated from the sand, the surplus was washed into the bay, and, over the years, much sand accumulated and filled in to extend the beautiful beaches. After the sale of Steilacoom Sand and Gravel and the property to Pioneer Sand and Gravel, the plant was torn down. The area where the plant once stood is now Madrona Park. The town of Steilacoom benefited with the recreation area now known as Sunnyside Beach.

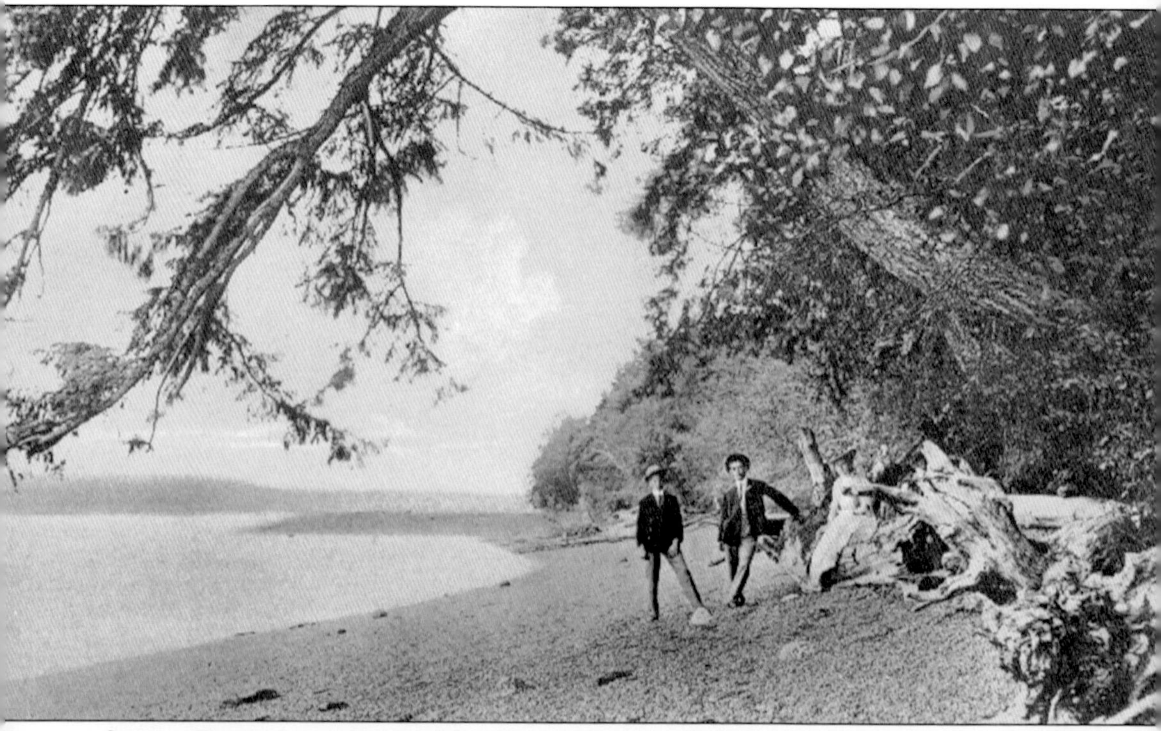

SUNDAY DRESS ON THE BEACH. The pristine beaches of Steilacoom became a place for recreation instead of a major port for trade business. Vacationers and beach cabins replaced maritime traffic and merchandise deliveries via water. The identities of those pictured are unknown.

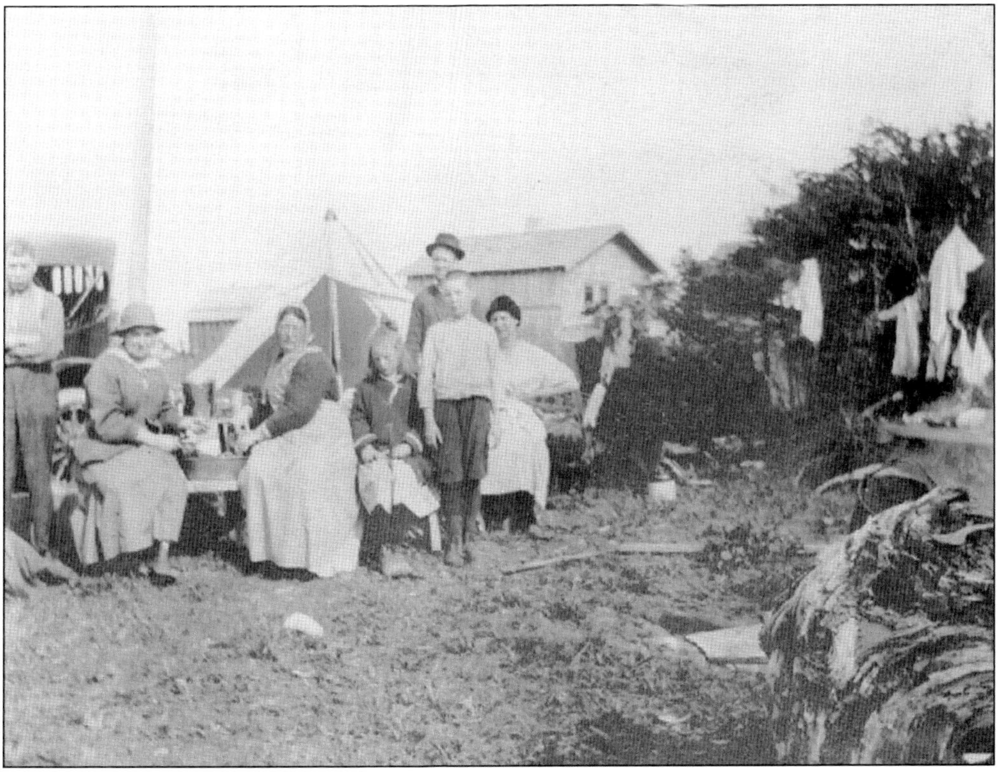

CAMPING. Even before there were modern conveniences at home, families like the Doerings, pictured with the entire family with their laundry hanging in the trees, enjoyed camping in the wilderness. In addition to the regular work done at the Steilacoom Transfer Company, the family worked seasonally by chopping and hauling wood, pulling stumps, and even plowing gardens for Steilacoom's residents.

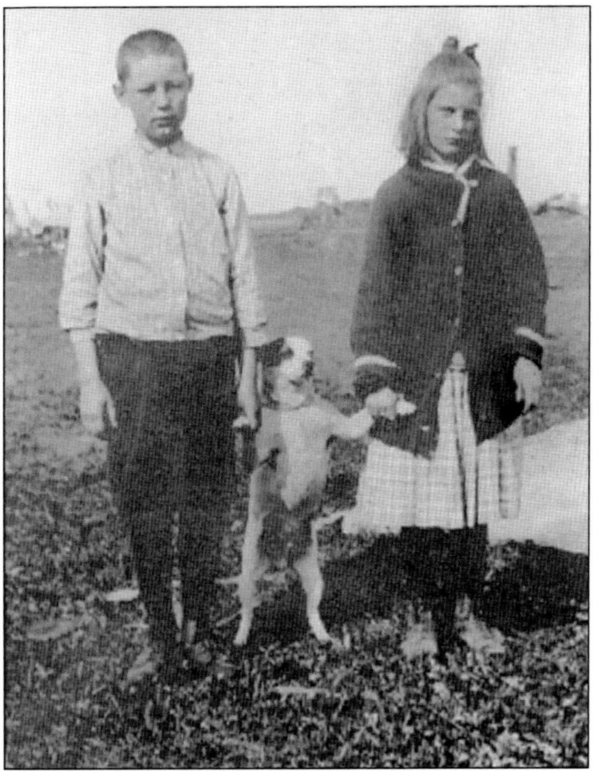

CAMPING KIDS. Here are the Doering children with their terrier. It doesn't appear as though the children enjoy the camping experience very much. The Doering children would go on to help their father work through the Depression. Russell Doering founded and then sold the Lakewood Fuel Company.

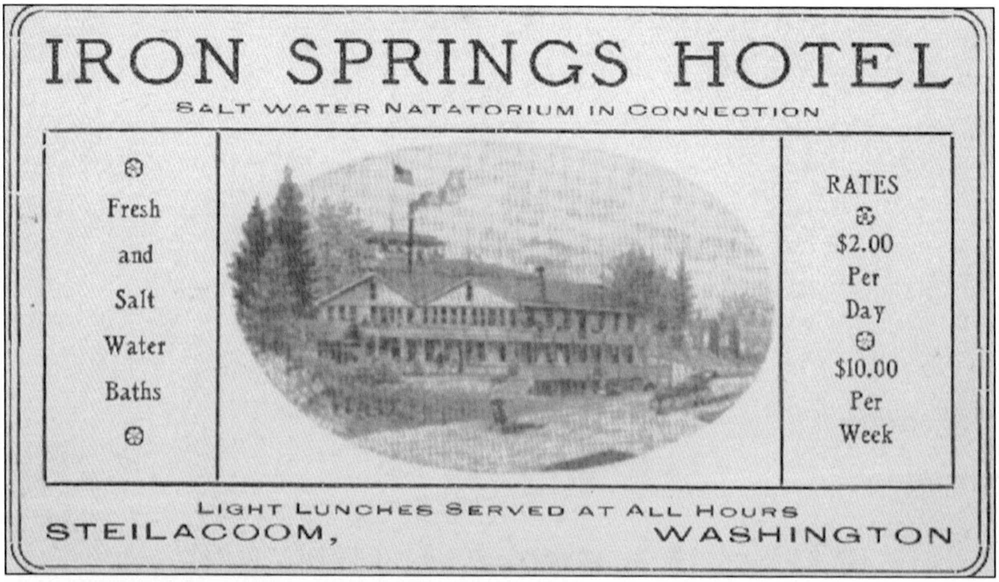

BUSINESS CARD. In an effort to draw new tourist business, the Iron Springs Hotel business cards were printed with all the necessary information to plan a relaxing getaway.

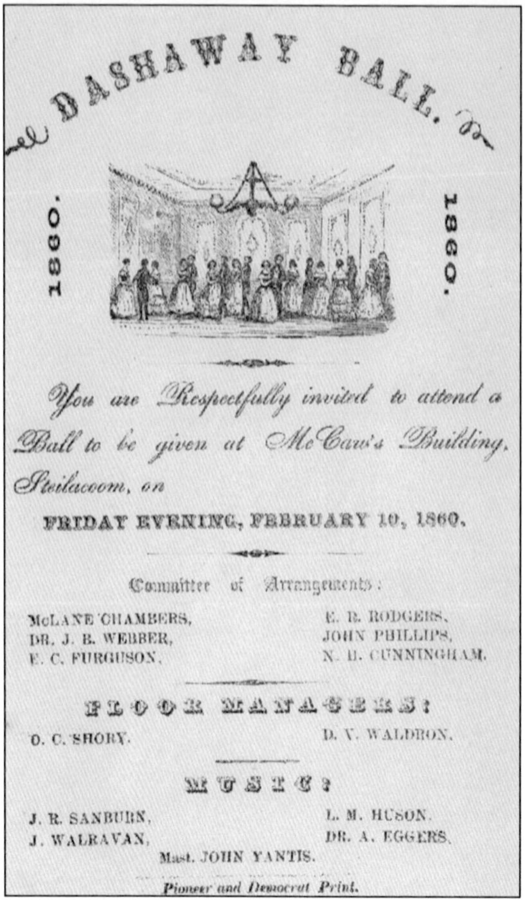

DASHAWAY BALL. This is an invitation from 1860 to join other townspeople for a Dashaway Ball at the Sam McCaw Building. The Dashaway was certain to be a well-attended and festive Friday night event for the entire town.

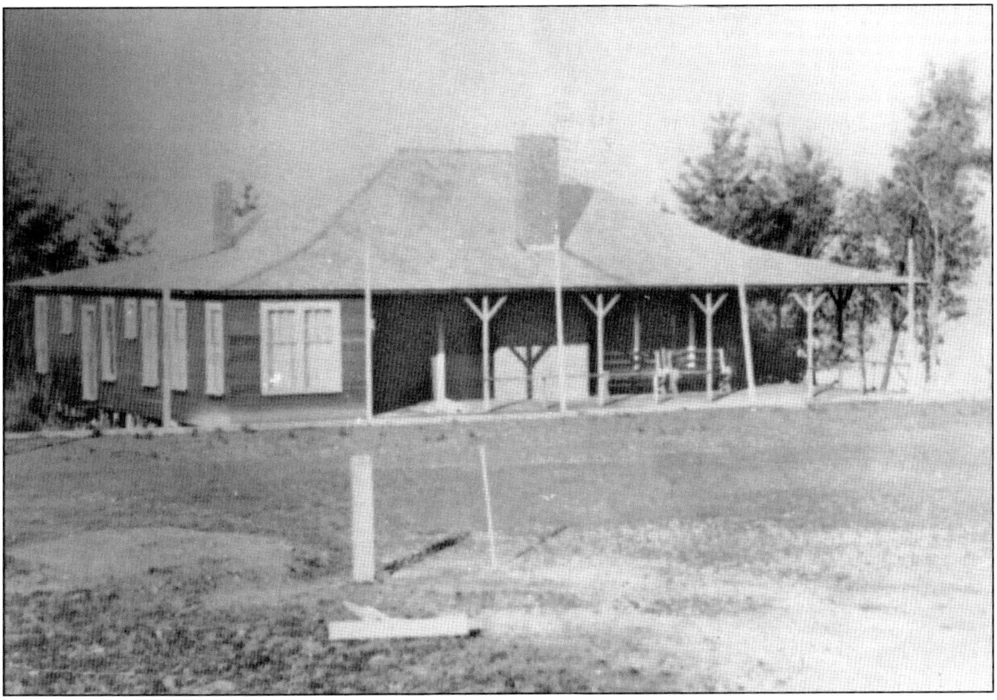

TENNIS ANYONE? Recreation is a part of life in Steilacoom; pictured is the former club, located on Fourth and Martin Streets. There are still two public tennis courts in town built on land that Dr. Taylor had donated for that purpose.

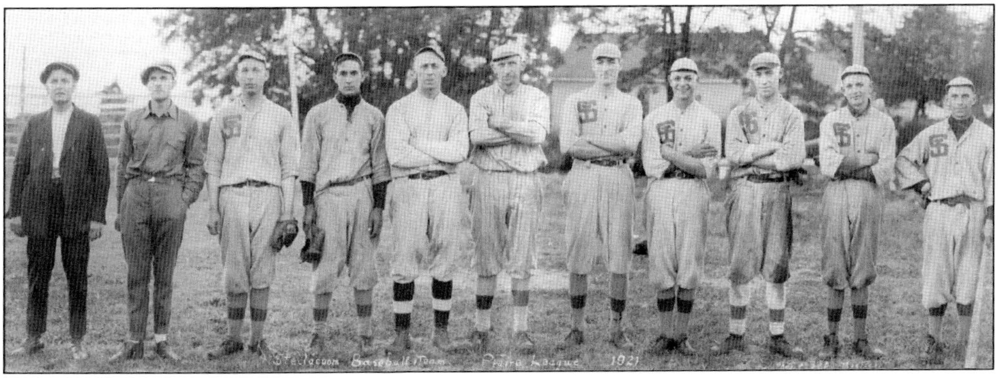

PLAY BALL. The Steilacoom Baseball Team participated in the Prairie League. Opposing teams included Bucota, Tenino, and DuPont. In 1921, Bucota won the league pennant with Steilacoom in second. Jess Baker (sixth from the left) was a former major league pitcher for the Chicago Cubs.

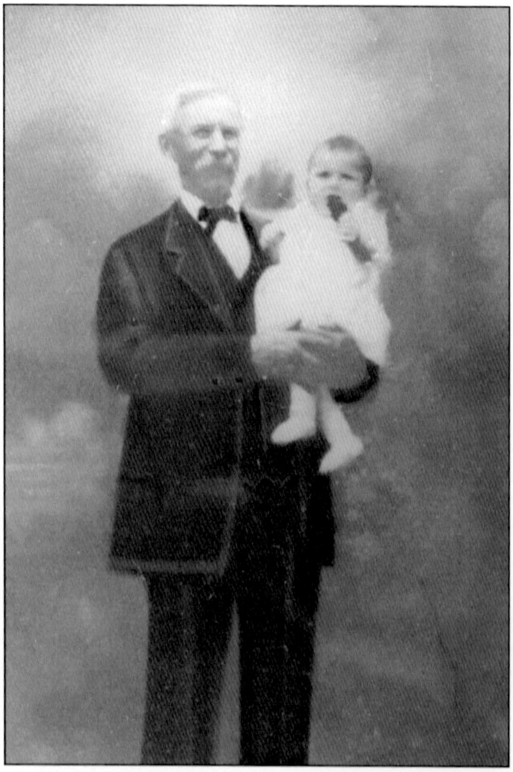

GRANDPA BAIR. Here we see an older W. L. Bair with one of his grandchildren. Like many residents of Steilacoom, Bair spent his relaxation time at the Masonic Lodge. He was an active member of the Steilacoom Masonic Order, serving as master five times.

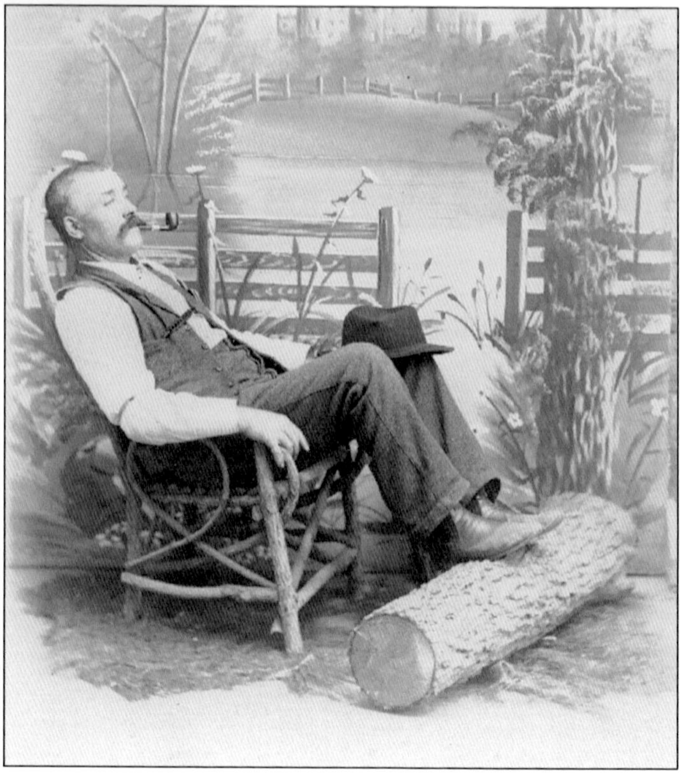

JOHN BAIR. A brother to W. L. and Edward Bair, John was an amateur photographer. Because of John Bair's love for photography, the Steilacoom Historical Museum Association has an extensive glass-negative collection of pictures taken by him.

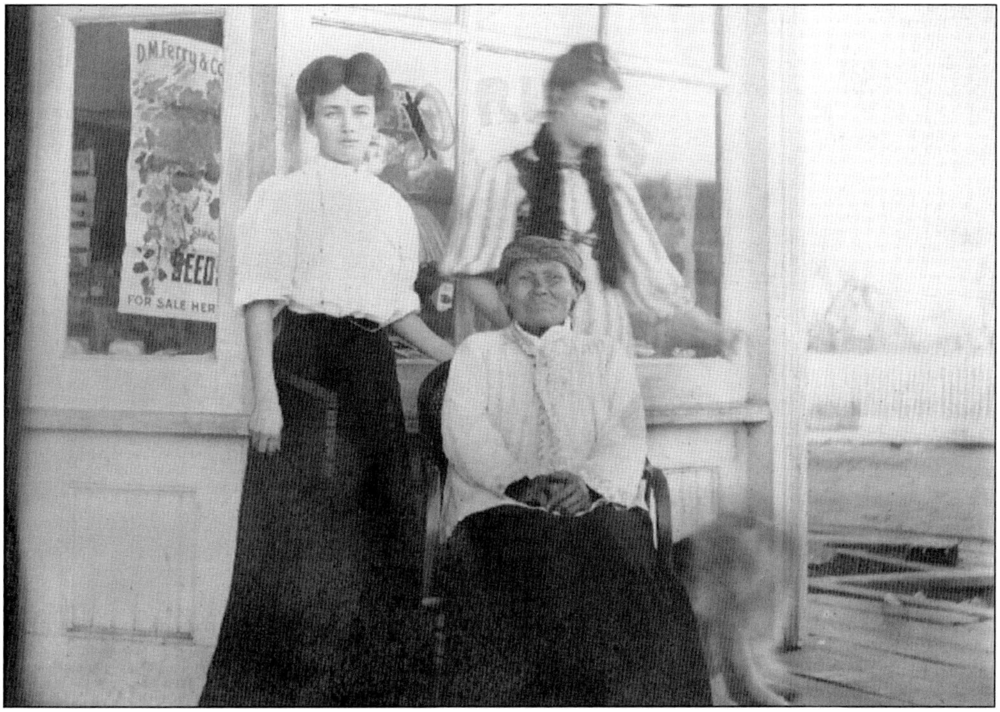

STEILACOOM ANNIE. Helen Rookledge is standing behind Steilacoom Annie on the corner of Lafayette and Wilkes Streets. The woman on the right remains unidentified. It wasn't uncommon to sit and pass the time in front of the Bair Store.

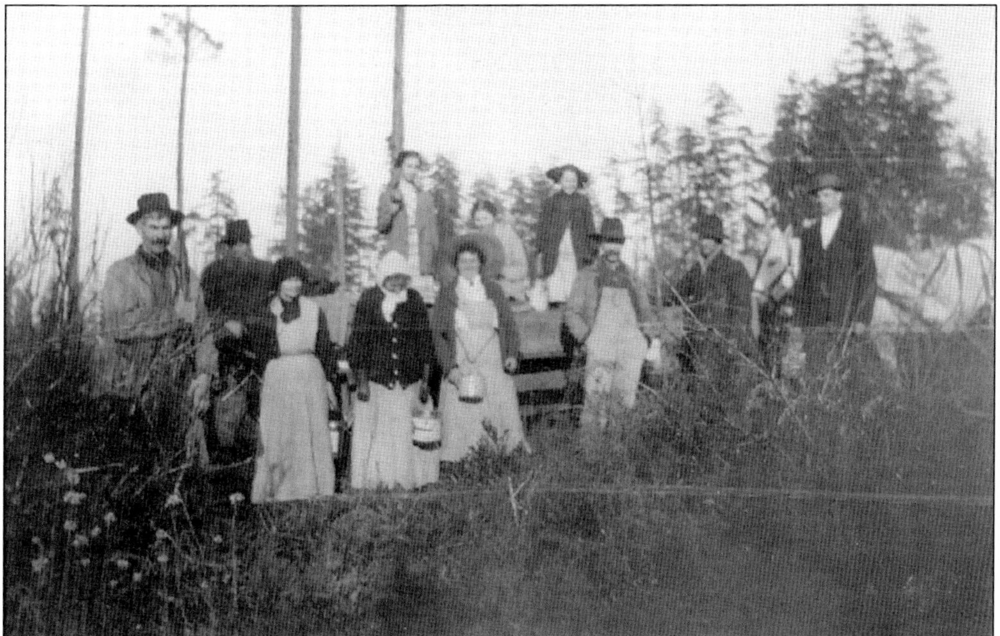

BERRY PICKING. Picking Olympic huckleberries continues to be a favorite pastime wherever the berries grow. Pictured here in 1913 are the Hammond, Fletcher, and Green families with Henry Chaler and a horse.

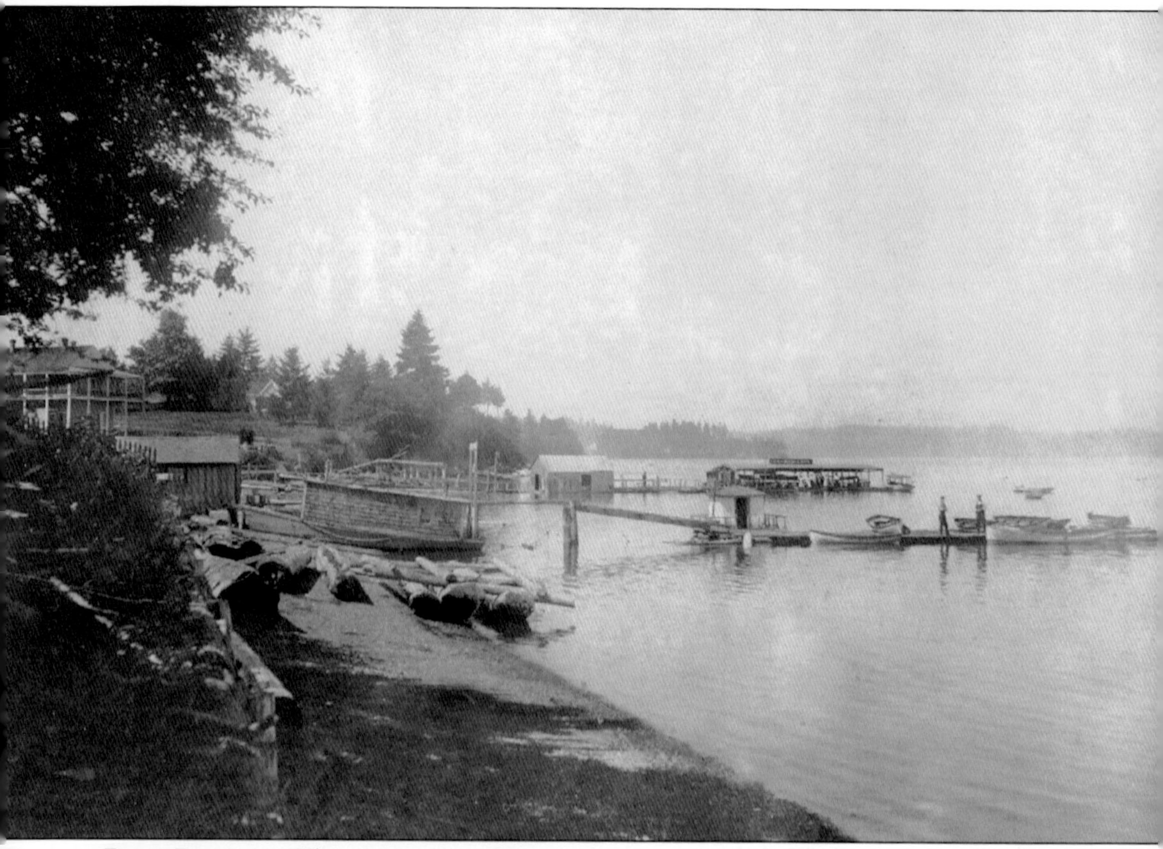

Boat Rentals. What was once a major port evolved into a destination for relaxation. One could rent a rowboat from John and Edwin Hoff or Charlie Murbarger for a paddle around the Puget Sound. According to the late Cub Bair, Hoff and Murbarger, both owners of boathouses, were extremely competitive with each other for business. One day, a customer confused the two and rented a boat from Charlie instead of John. Later that day, Charlie was in front of the Bair Store. John confronted him and began twisting his nose, and Charlie punched John through the window of the store.

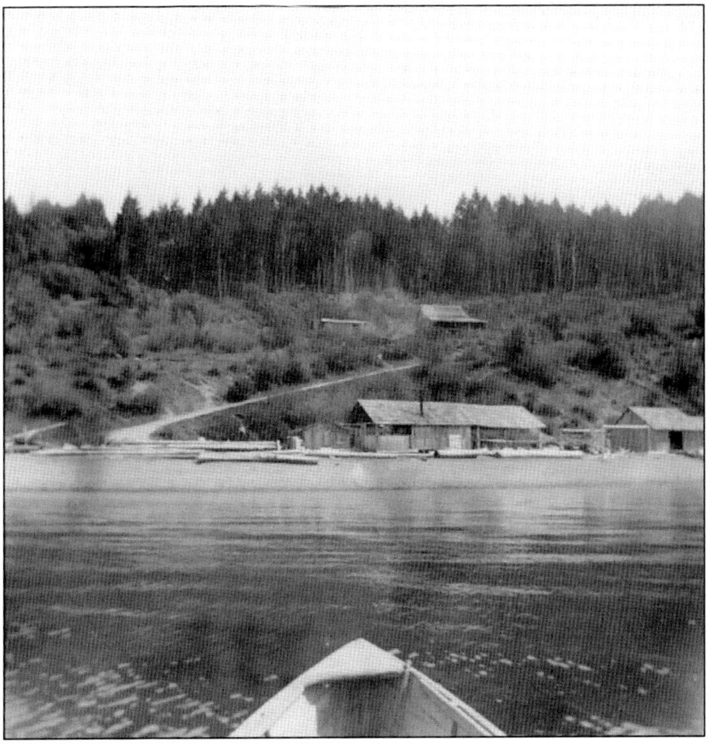

BOATING ON THE SOUND. Boating for those who live near water will always be a source of recreation. This 1895 photographer included the bow of his or her boat in the picture of the Gravel Pit Wharf in the nearby town of DuPont.

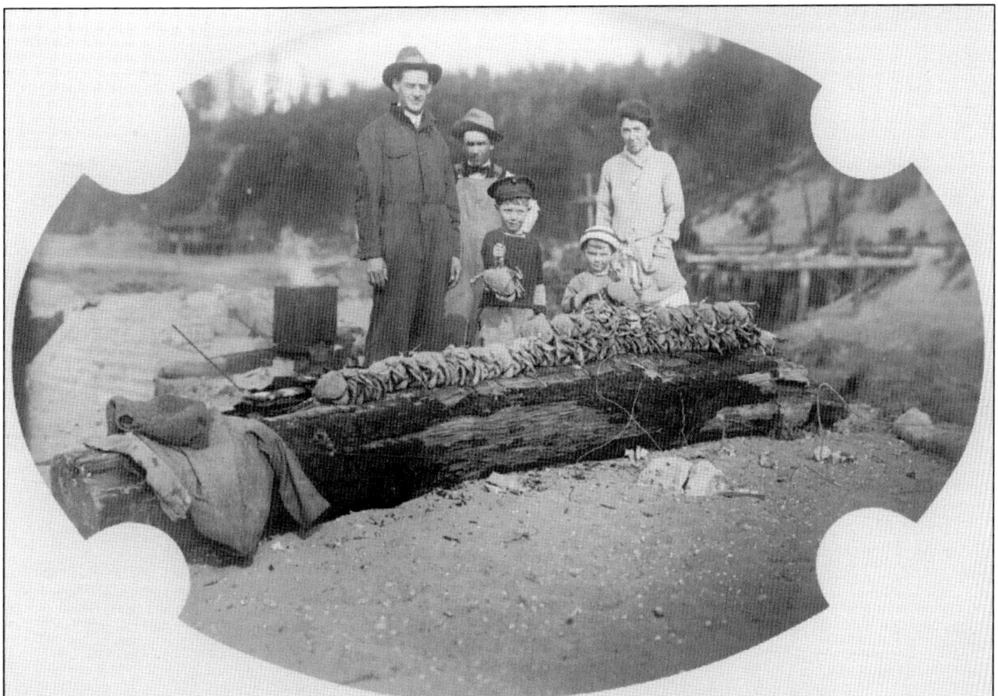

MARSH FAMILY. The Thomas Marsh family is pictured here on the shores of Steilacoom after what appears to have been very successful day of crabbing on the Puget Sound. It is unknown if they planned to eat the crab right then or if they were steaming all of it with the intention of selling it.

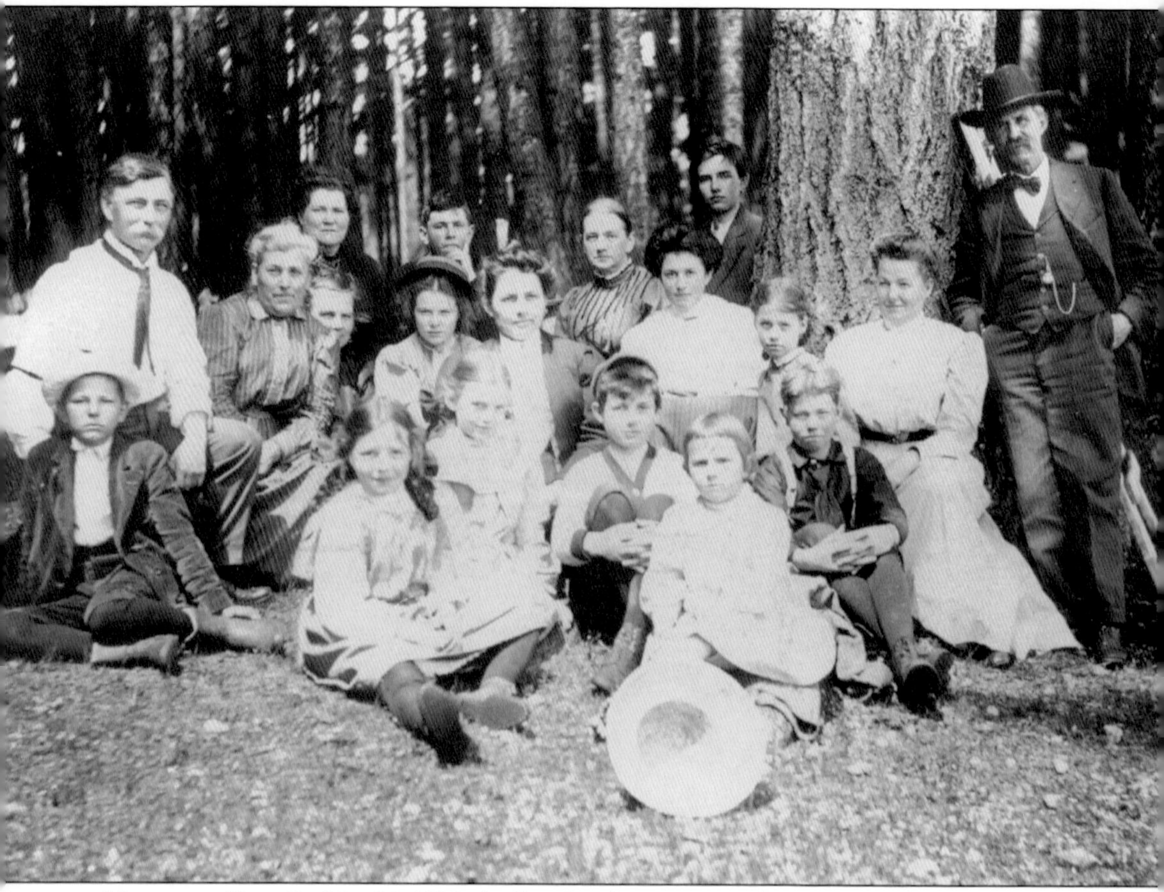

Memorial Day. On May 30, 1909, the Bair family is enjoying their Memorial Day picnic at the Masonic Cemetery. The annual event consisted of paying their respects to their loved ones before traveling to a nearby park to have lunch. W. L. Bair is leaning against the tree.

Six
THE TOWN OF FIRSTS

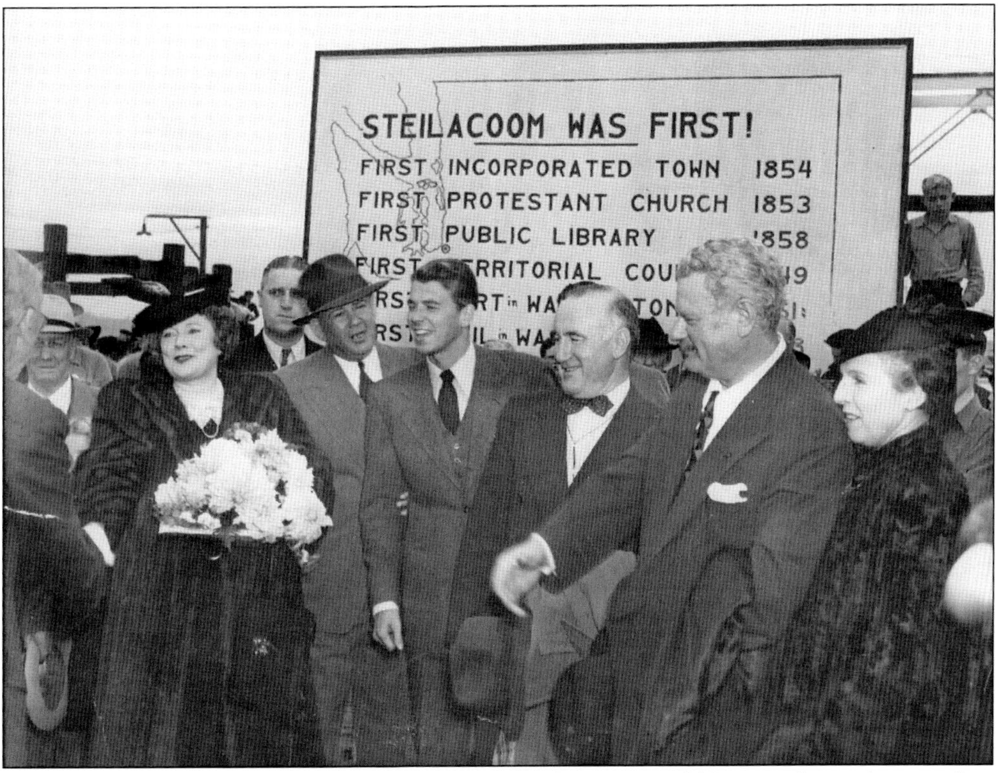

RONALD REAGAN. On a press tour through the Northwest, Ronald Reagan (center) stopped on February 18, 1940, in Steilacoom to promote *Tugboat Annie Sails Again*. The movie premiered at the Roxy Theater in Tacoma. Foss tugs were used in the filming of the movie. Other celebrities pictured are Marjorie Rambeau (with flowers) and Alan Hale Sr. (second from right).

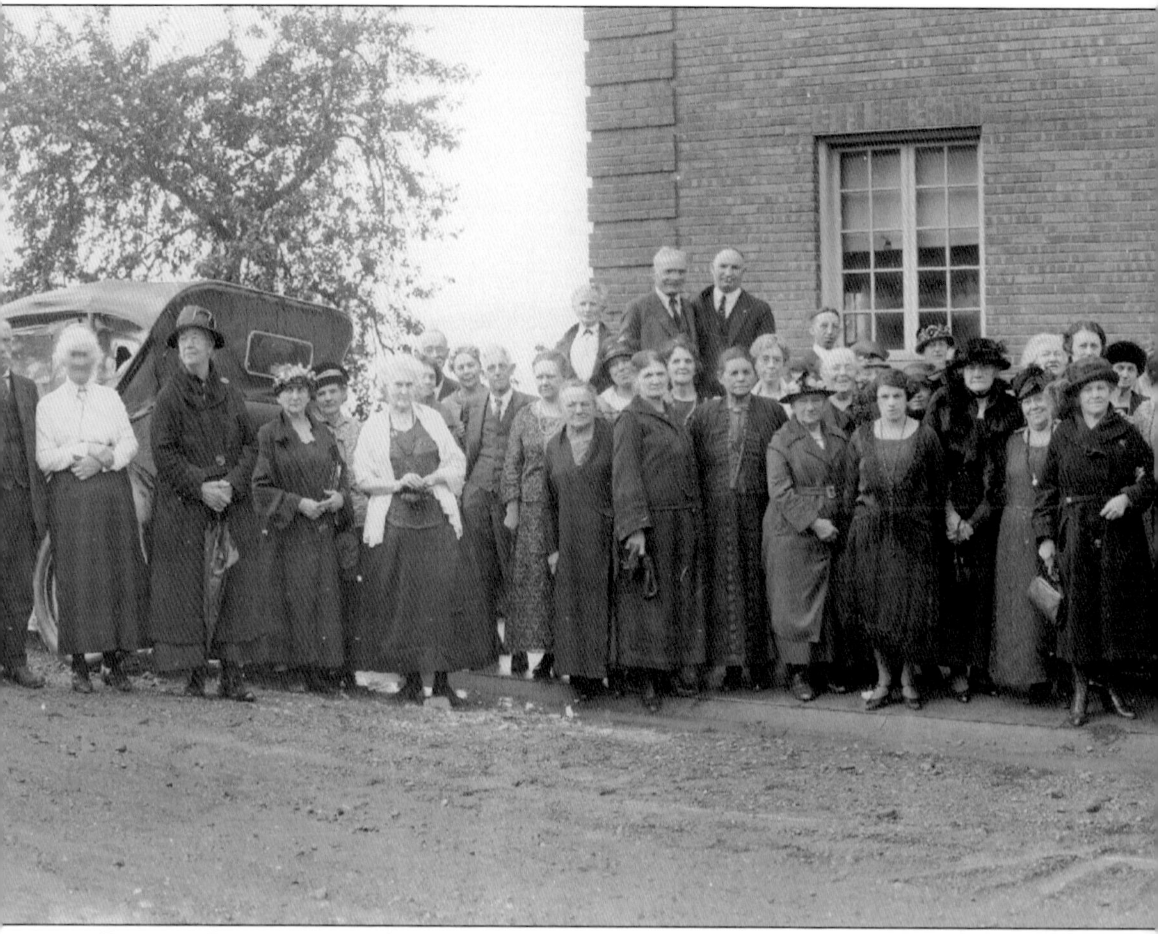

PIONEER GATHERING. Steilacoom is a favorite spot for Pierce County pioneers to gather. This 1920s photograph was taken in front of the brick Masonic Lodge on Lafayette Street. Steilacoom pioneers and their descendants have understood the need to preserve their unique place in

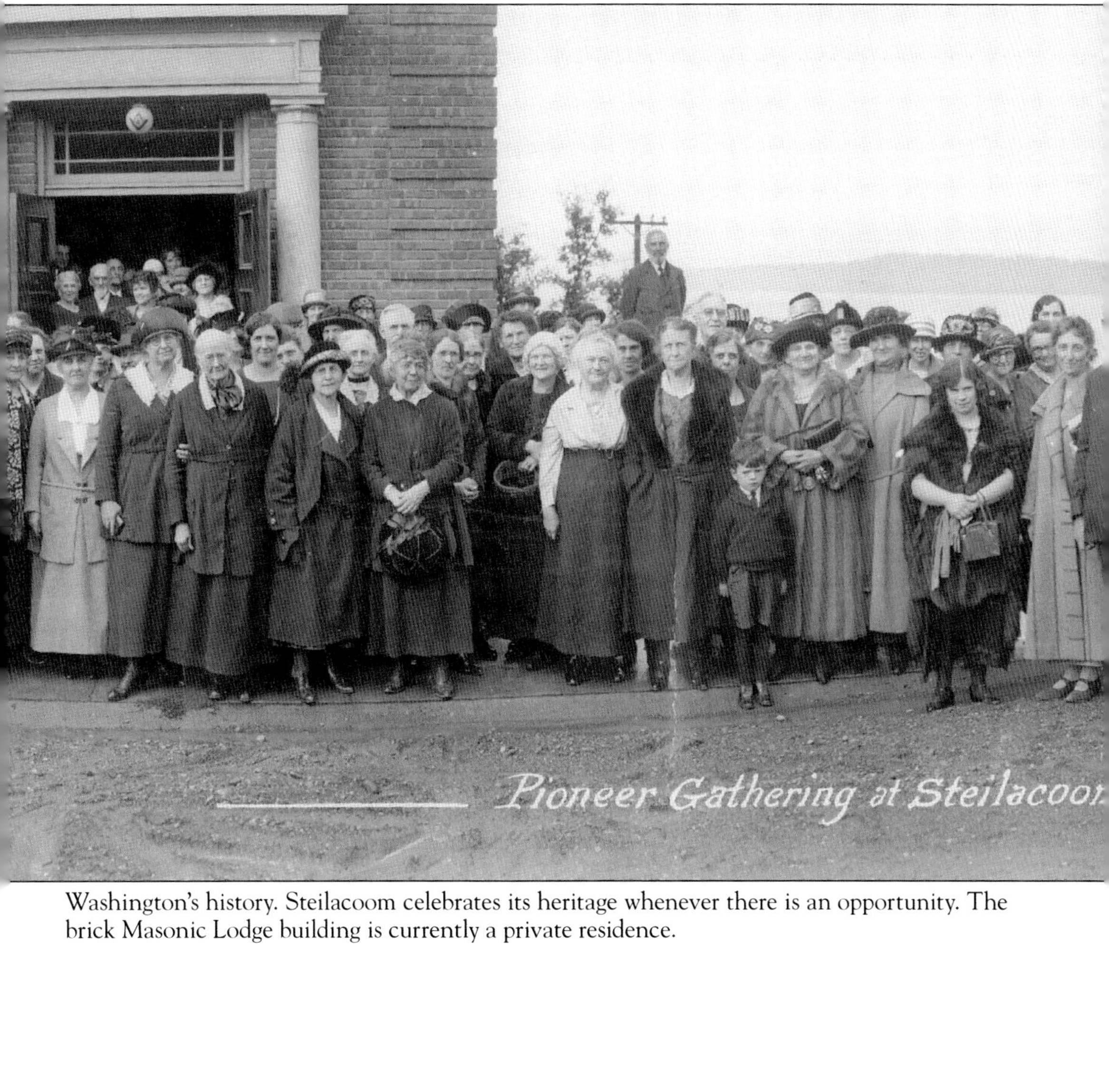

Washington's history. Steilacoom celebrates its heritage whenever there is an opportunity. The brick Masonic Lodge building is currently a private residence.

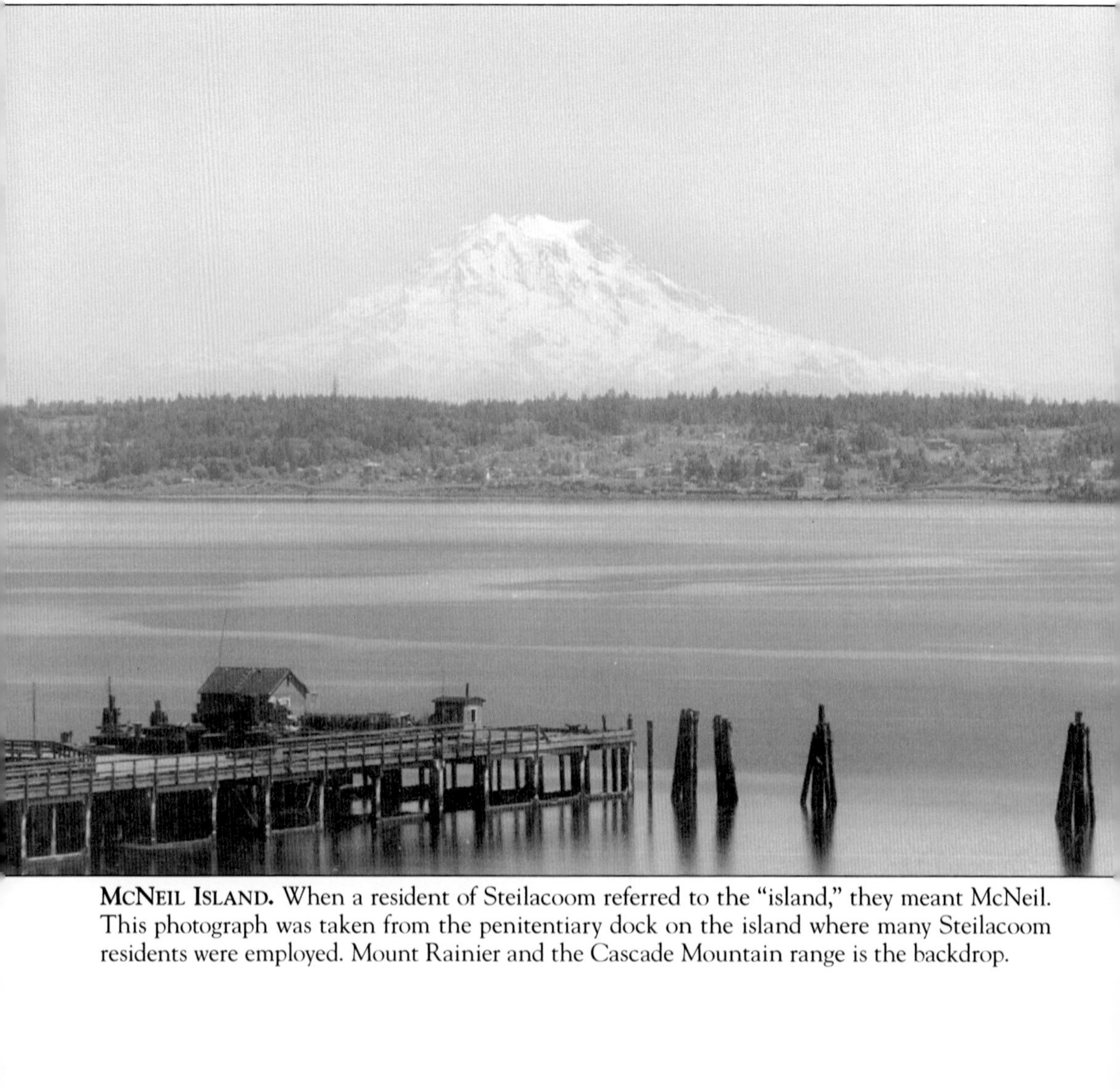

McNeil Island. When a resident of Steilacoom referred to the "island," they meant McNeil. This photograph was taken from the penitentiary dock on the island where many Steilacoom residents were employed. Mount Rainier and the Cascade Mountain range is the backdrop.

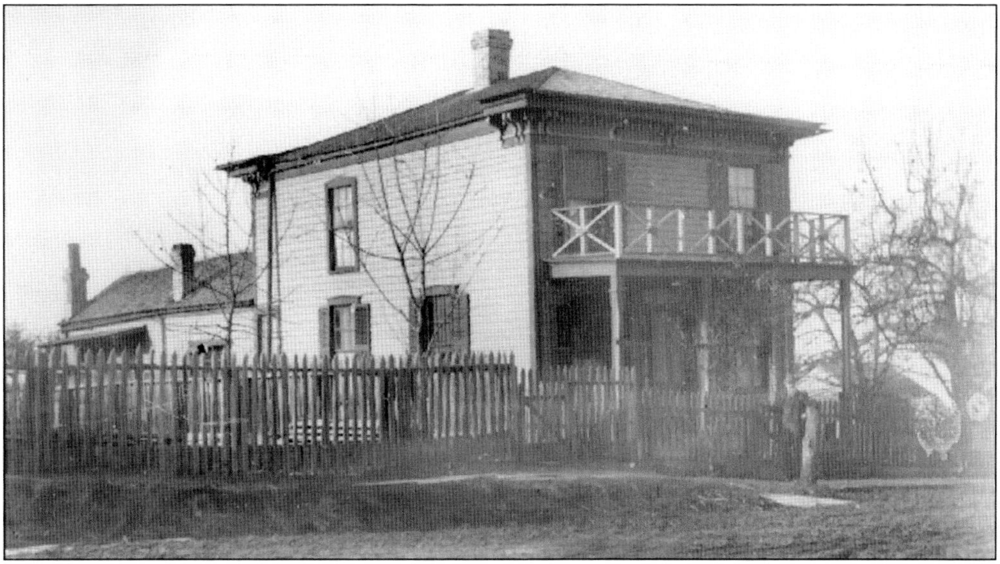

KNOWN FOR THE HOMES. Driving through Steilacoom, one cannot help but to take notice of the charm and character that exudes from the homes, especially within the historic district. The Town of Steilacoom and the Steilacoom Historical Museum Association worked closely to establish the Steilacoom Historic District, one of the first in Washington state. The district was placed on the National Register of Historic Places in 1974. At present, there are 67 structures on the list. Unfortunately, all of the old structures that depict the history of Steilacoom are no longer standing. "Granny Blyth's" house, which stood on the corner of Commercial and Wilkes Streets, is one such example.

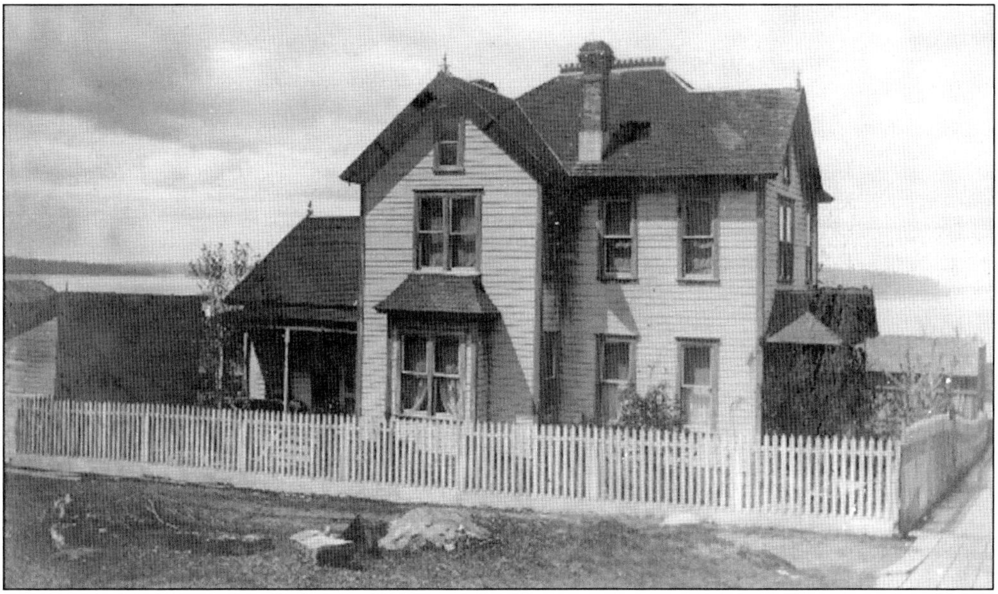

MYERS/SMITH HOME. Joel Meyers built his home on the corner of Rainier and Main Streets directly across the street from the Steilacoom Historical Museum. Jake Smith, a local grocer, also lived in the home. The house was torn down in 1971 and replaced with an apartment building. The idea for a review board was born out of the razing of the Meyers home. Many houses were lost, but many have been saved and preserved.

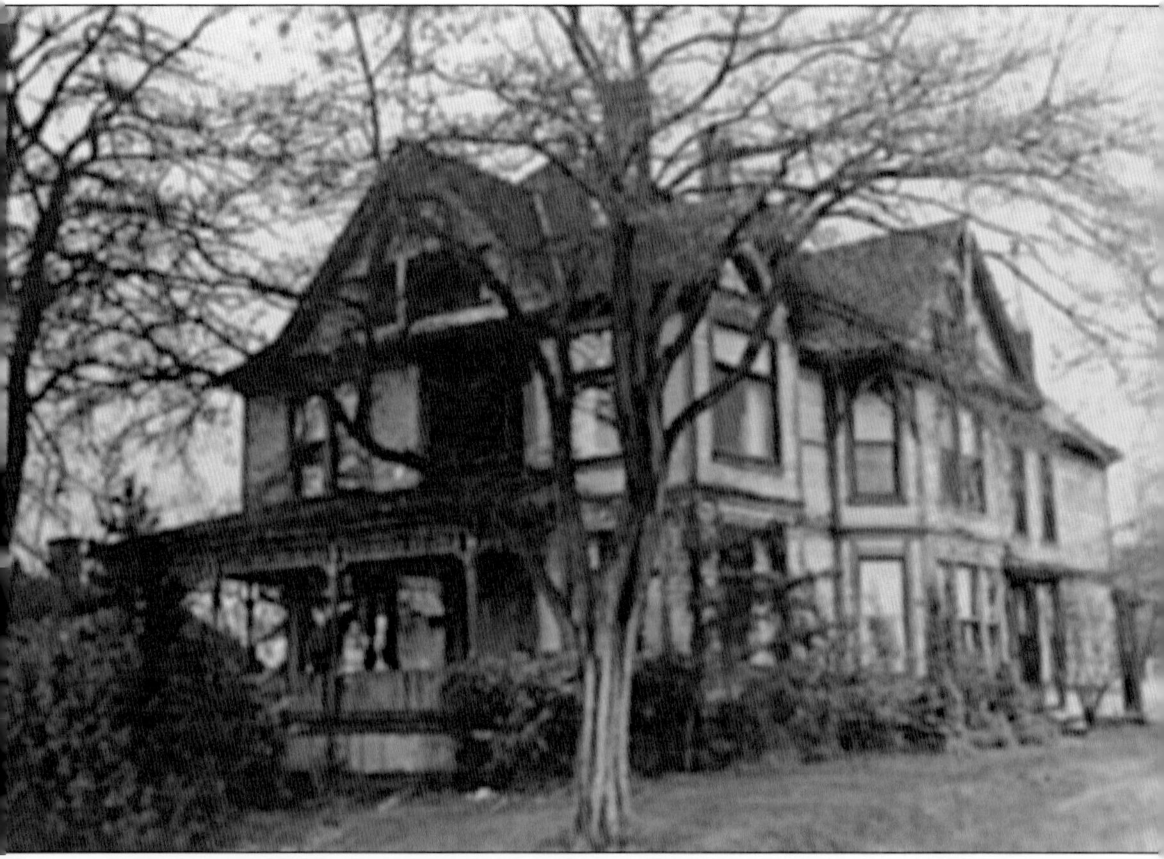

E. R. Rogers Home. This 17-room mansion was built by E. R. Rogers in 1891 for his wife, possibly to rival the Ezra Meeker home in Puyallup. The family did not enjoy the home long, as there were delays in construction and the Panic of 1893 wiped out the title on their mortgage. Shortly after that, Mr. and Mrs. Charles opened a boardinghouse. She named the building Waverly by the Sea after her bicycle. In 1920, Hattie Bair purchased the Waverly by the Sea. The hotel hosted many soldiers and their wives during World War II, when housing was difficult to come by. Hattie Bair lived in the home until she died in 1948. Like many of Steilacoom's beautiful homes, it was somehow forgotten and began to fall apart. Then in the late 1970s, the great home was once again full of people dining on fine cuisine as a destination restaurant named for the home's original owner. The E. R. Rogers restaurant closed its doors in 2005, and the building was sold. The landmark structure has since been renovated.

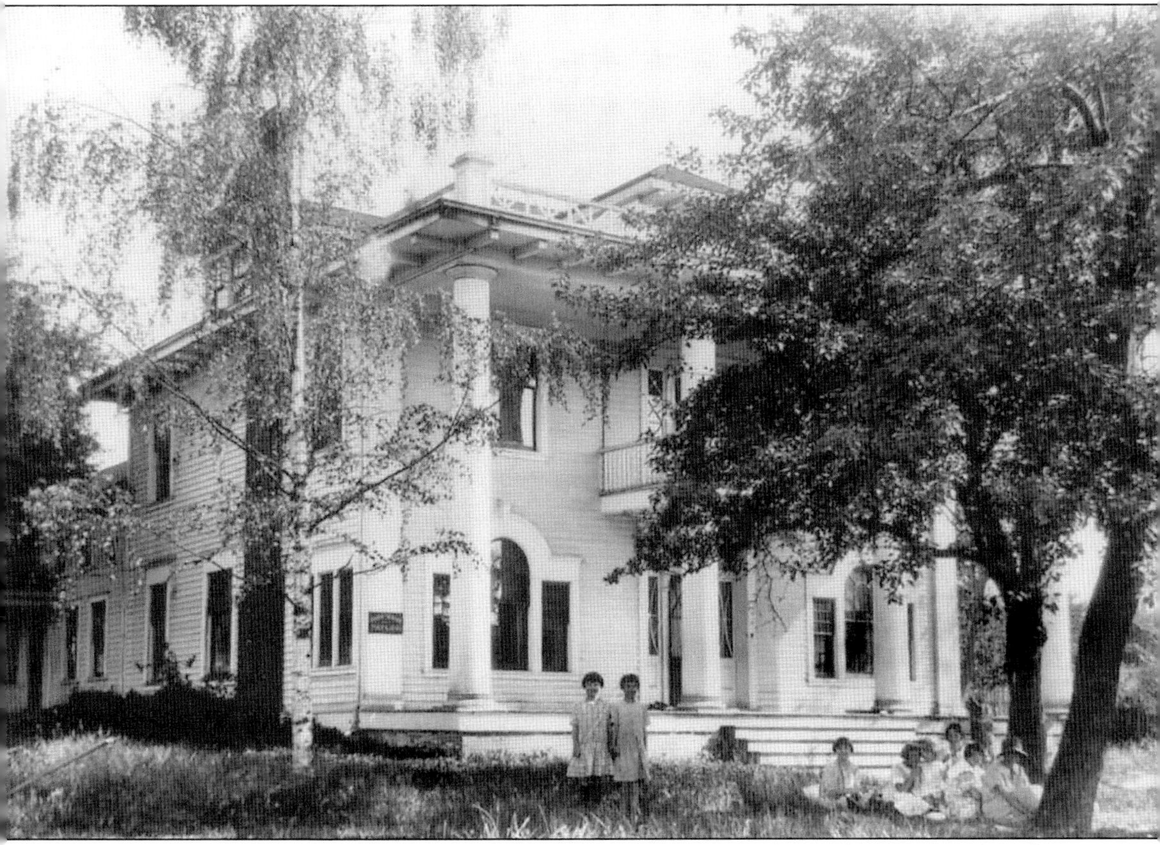

Dr. Taylor Home. The Colonial-style home belonging to Dr. Charles Taylor once stood on the corner of Lafayette and Wilkes Streets. The home covered half the block with a greenhouse on the alley. It had a sleeping porch that could accommodate eight and a billiard room. The Taylor children enjoyed a musical merry-go-round along the side of the house and a Shetland pony with a cart to occupy their time. Dr. Taylor continued to add onto his house for his extended family; grandparents, children, aunts, and uncles all lived there. The Taylor home was purchased by Hattie Bair and was converted into apartments. Upon her death, her son Cub inherited the property and sold it to Art Hudtloff. The impressive home was torn down and replaced by Steilacoom's first shopping center. The post office now operates in the Steilacoom Center.

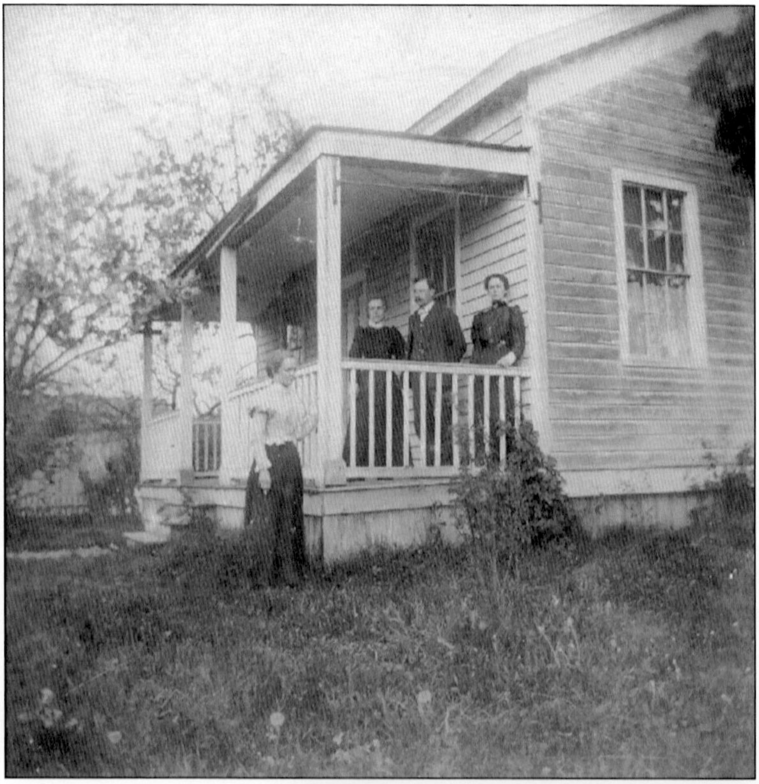

O'Donnell House. The Steilacoom office of Western Union was operated out of this home from the 1880s to 1911 by the Rigney twins. The family owned the home until it was demolished in 1969. Nellie (left) and Fred Chelius and an unidentified woman are standing on the porch, and Dora Steelwell is standing on the ground.

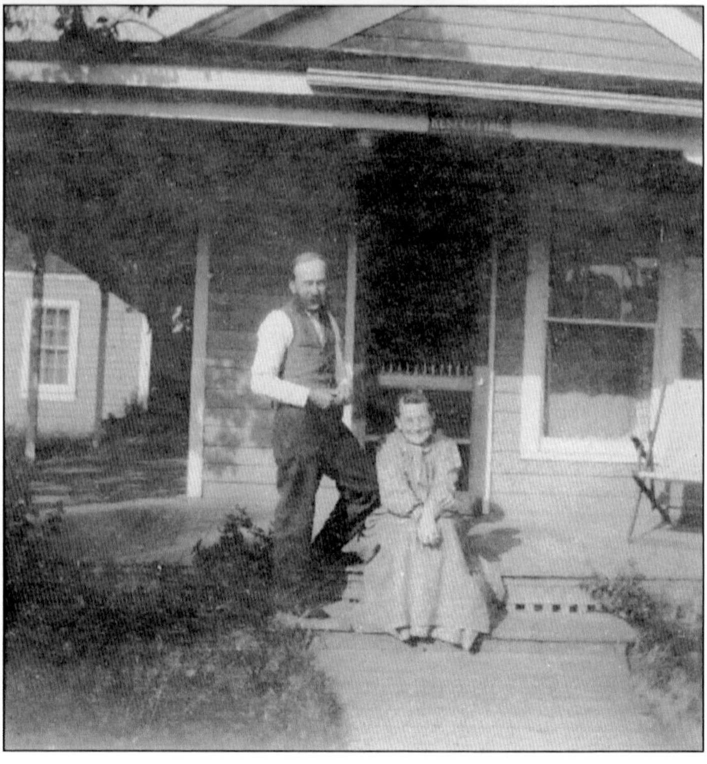

Resting on the Porch. Silas and Flora Harvey are smiling for the camera on the porch of their Steilacoom home. Silas was a clerk at the Oberlin church in the early 1900s.

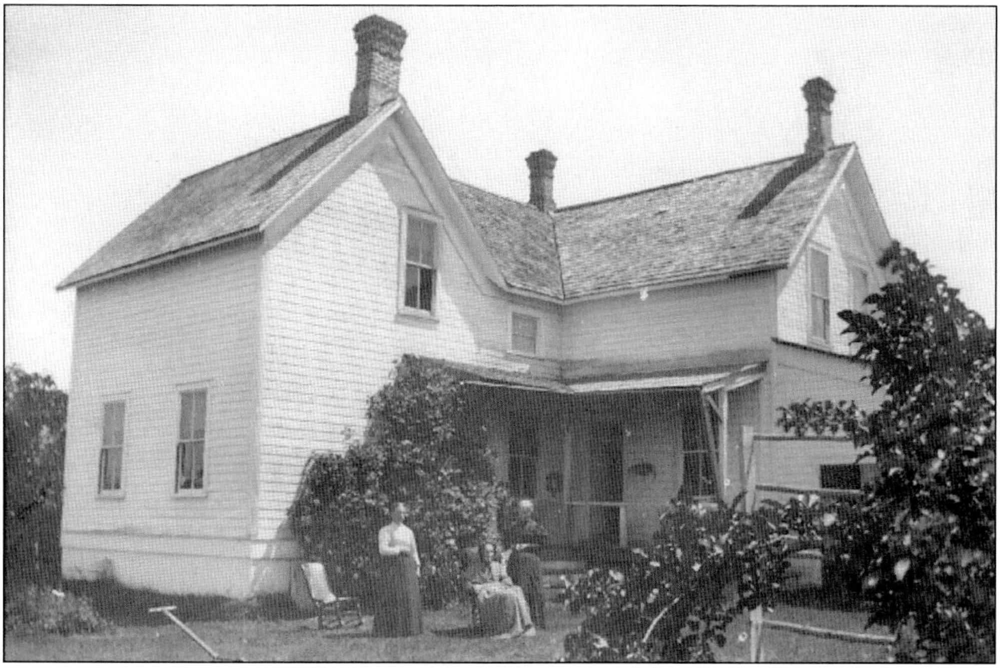

STEILACOOM ARCHITECTURE. Many of Steilacoom's first homes that are still standing have wooden clapboard siding painted in muted colors with tall windows that make the most of the view of the bay. The historic homes mix a Northeastern design adapted to the Northwest terrain. The house pictured no longer stands, and the women in the yard are L. Minerva Shults (left), Nancy Weston (seated), and unidentified.

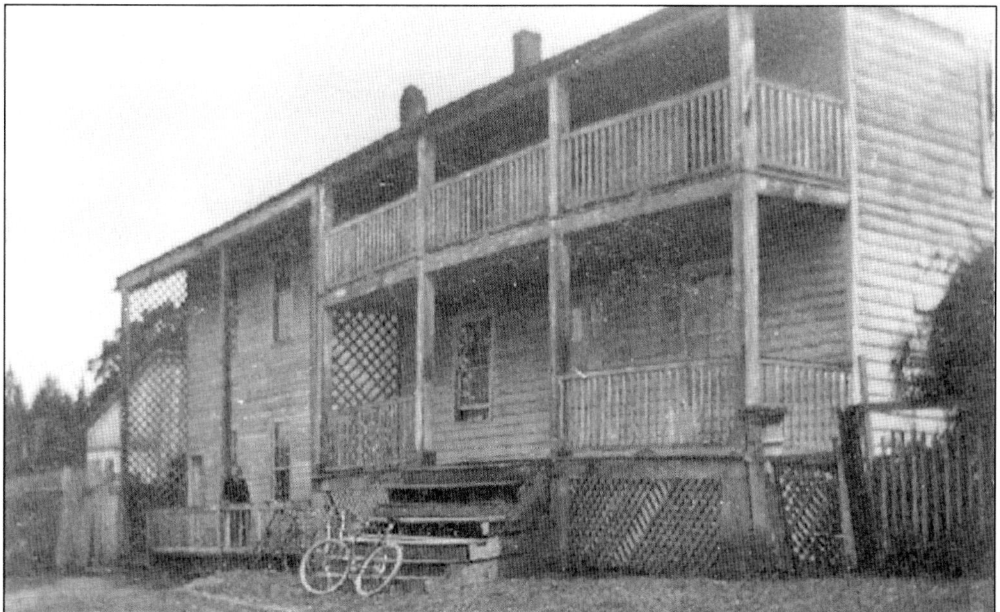

ST. JOSEPH'S ACADEMY AND CONVENT. Before the building was razed in the early 1900s, many Steilacoom families, including the Doerings and the Cheliuses, used it as a rental. Note the bicycle leaning up against the side of the building.

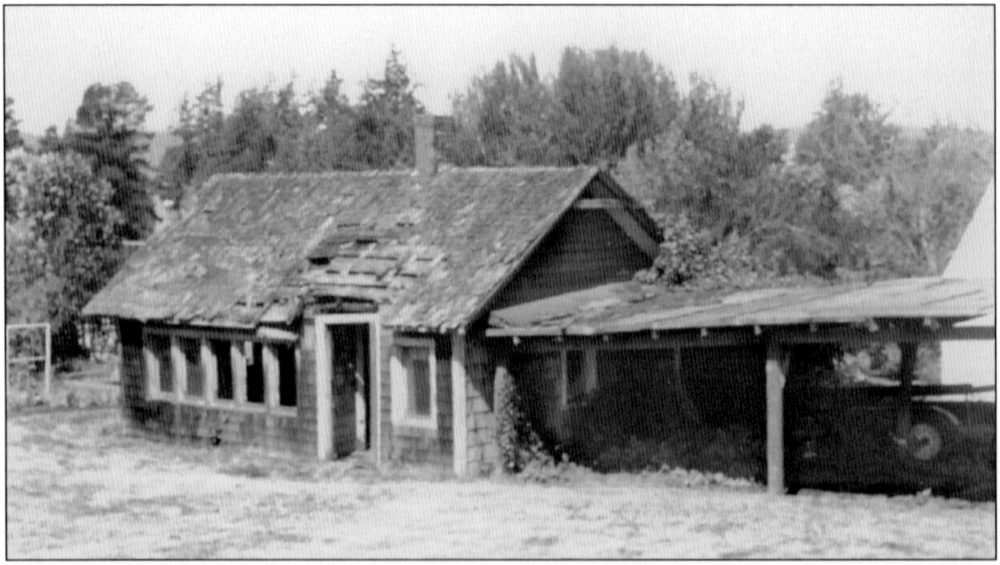

COZY COT. Though it was not exactly living up to its given name at the time the picture was taken, this home and others were named either for their location, such as Cottage-by-the-Sea, for the feeling the home evoked, such as Snug Harbor, or for the family that occupied the home, like Green Lantern. Other names included Blink Bonnie, the Columns, Outside Inn, the Waverly by the Sea, Rolling Hill, Appletree Cottage, and even Neenamoosa (meaning "dearest possession").

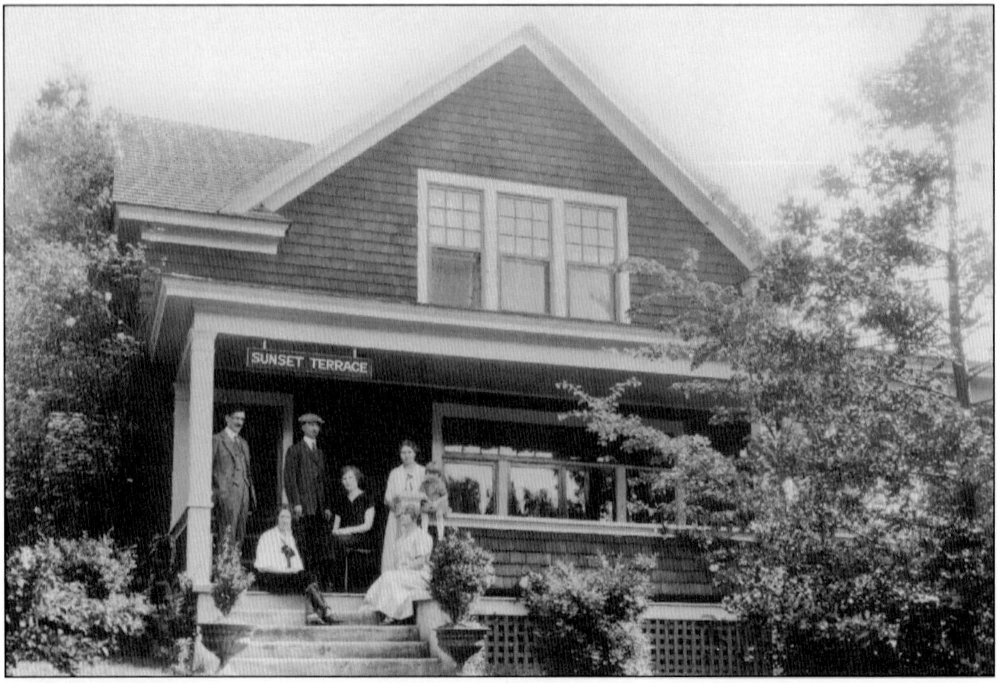

SUNSET TERRACE. Around 1900, as Steilacoom transitioned to a vacation destination, it became fashionable to name homes. Homeowners painted the names on wooden signs and hung them in a prominent location on the house. Mayor Willis Morris and his family lived at Sunset Terrace. Currently the sign is still fastened to the porch, but the home has been modified since this photograph was taken.

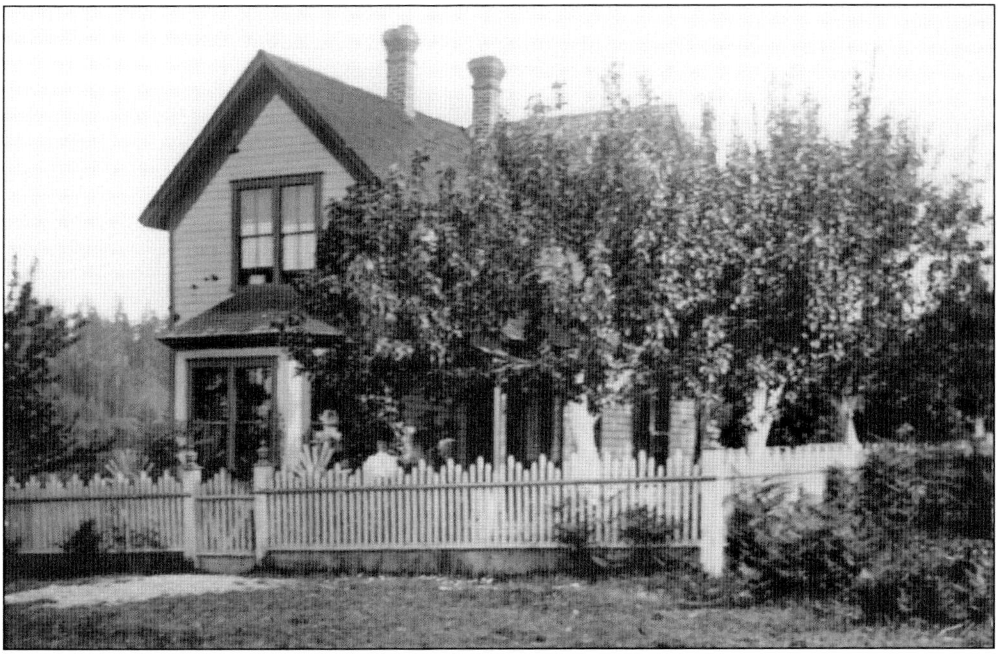

ROBERTS/BARBER HOUSE. This was built for the Roberts brothers, who owned and operated the Roberts Brothers' Grocery in North Tacoma. When it became popular to rent a home for the summer during the 1890s, the families were residents. The father would ride the streetcar into town and come home in the evening, giving his family time to enjoy the beach and the countryside. The picket fence was a common sight around the homes, as they kept the roaming cattle out of the gardens. The Barber family later owned the house.

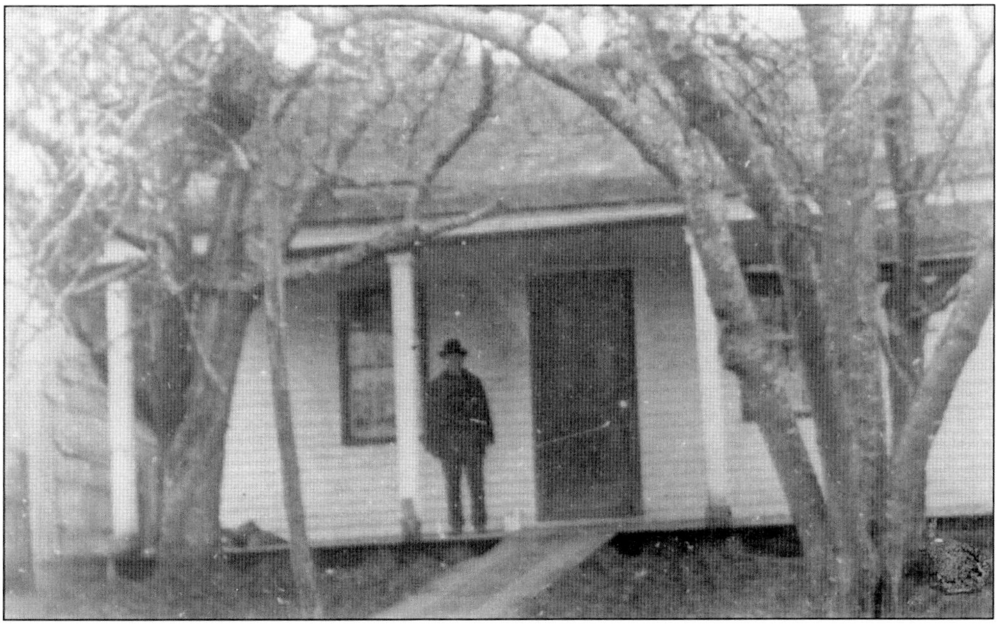

THE BREWER'S HOME. Martin Schmeig established Schmeig's Brewery in 1858. By 1865, Schmeig had sold it to John Locke, pictured at home next to the brewery on Lafayette Street. Locke later leased it in 1878, and the brewery operated under different brewers until 1890.

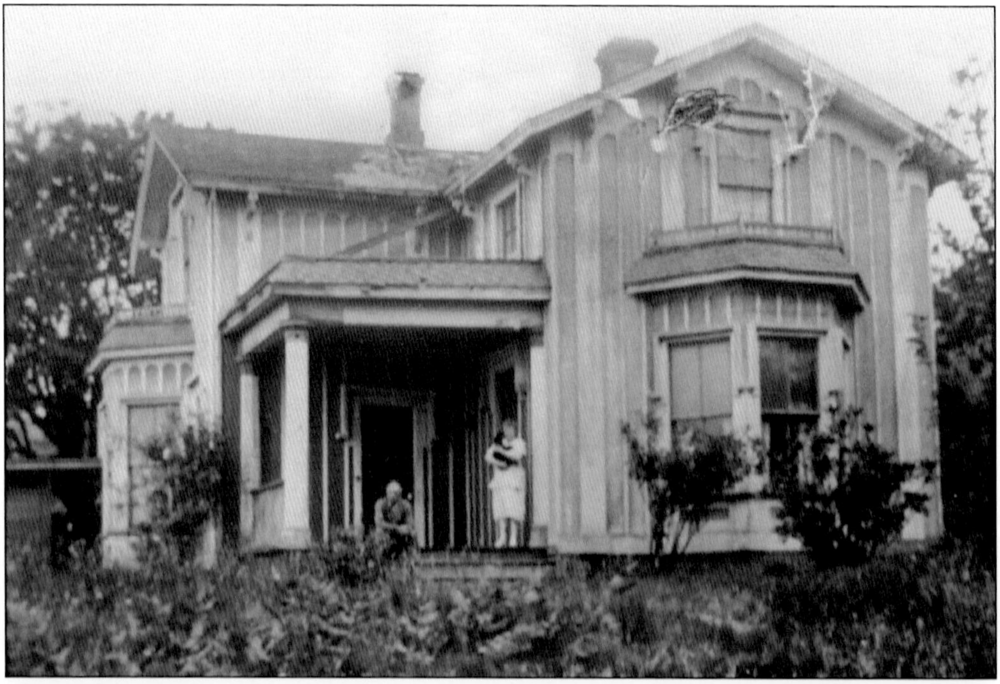

JUDSON HOME. This is one of the first homes belonging to original pioneer Stephen Judson. Judson was sheriff for a time and served on the school board. He lived a long life in the town he helped build. The house no longer stands on the corner of Starling and Main Streets.

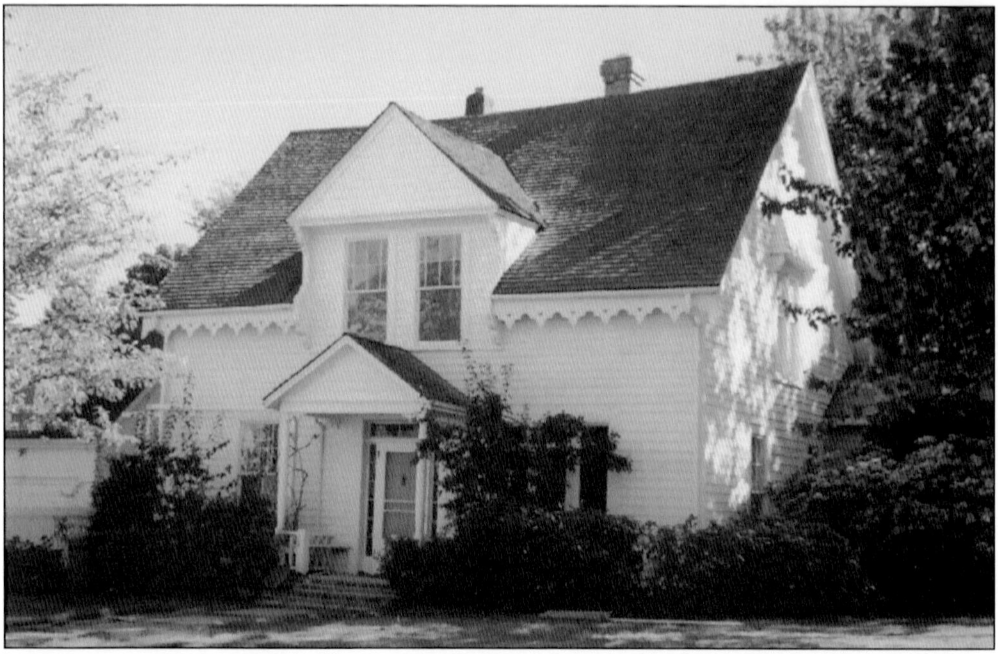

THE CAPTAIN BLACK HOME. The home that was built by Capt. George Black has had the same owners since the 1980s. The home's current owners are committed to historic preservation and as a result have restored the home to its original character inside and out. Today the Captain Black House represents Steilacoom's authentic appreciation of history.

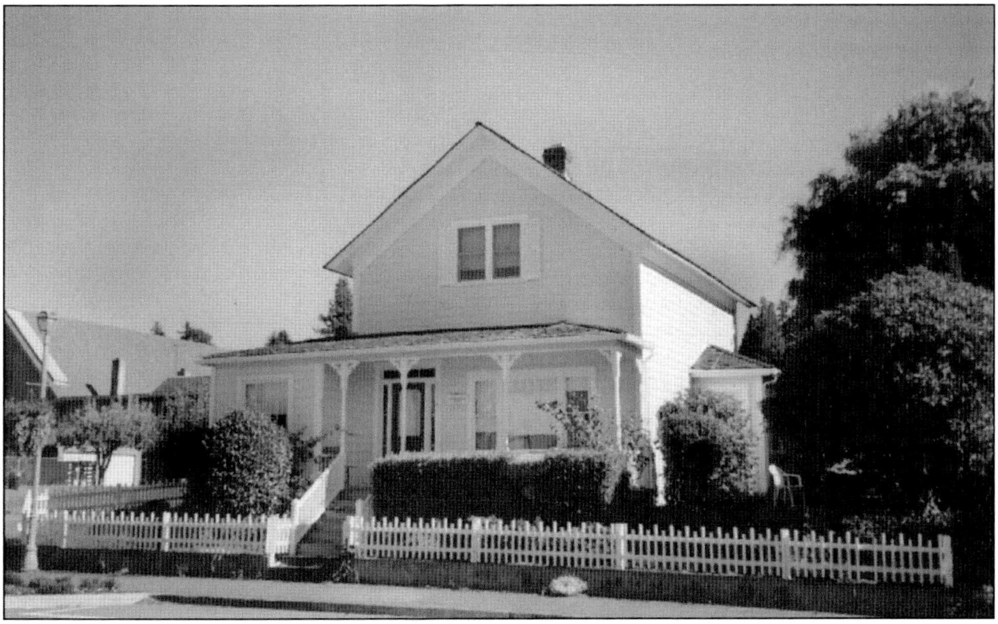

THE GARDINER HOUSE. James Gardiner, a black soldier from Pennsylvania, built the house in the 1870s and opened a barbershop. Gardiner was well known for his vegetable and flower gardens. In the late 1800s, the Hatcher family purchased the home and occupied it for many years. It later was the parsonage for the Oberlin Congregational Church. The home is located on Lafayette Street.

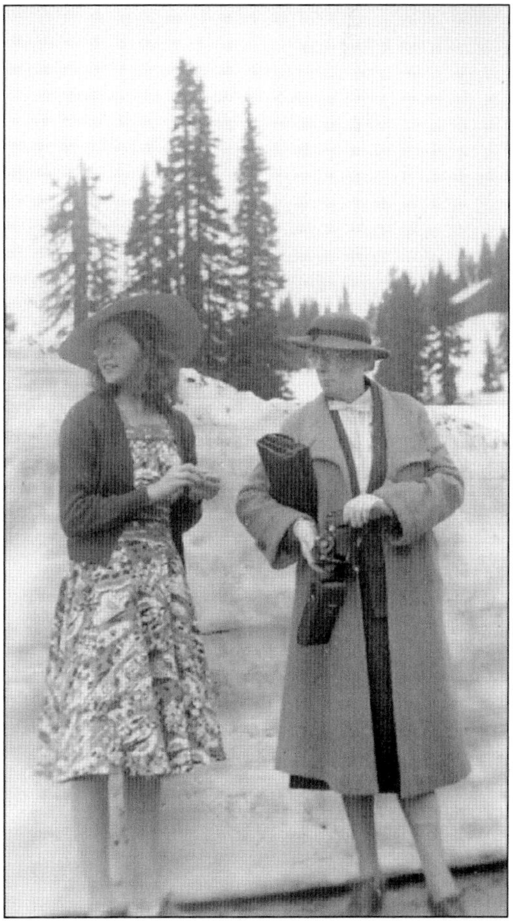

"STEILACOOM HAS CHARM." Gladys Parker, pictured on the right, was a former Lincoln High School business teacher. She moved to Steilacoom in the 1930s, and in retirement she became a real estate agent. Parker's love of Steilacoom was contagious; many families moved to town with her encouragement. Parker was a savvy marketer, coining the slogan "Steilacoom has Charm." Gladys Parker died in an automobile accident in 1956, and over 100 people attended her memorial in front of town hall. "Steilacoom has Charm" became a statewide slogan to describe the town she loved so much.

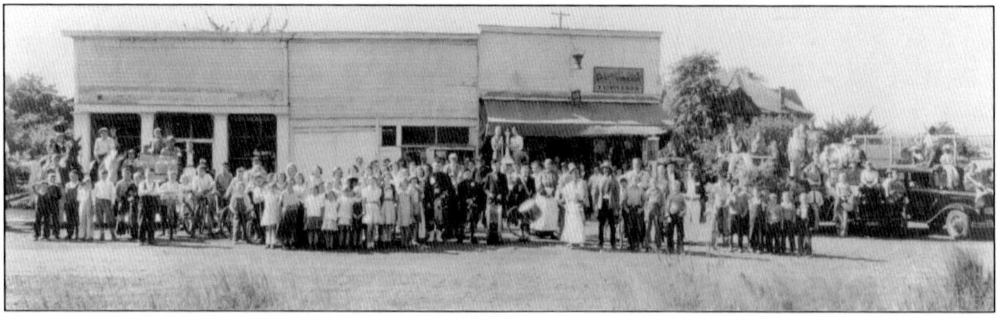

FUND-RAISING. The "boosters" staged this parade in support of the minstrel show that was performed on May 12, 1934. The proceeds of the performance were added to the book purchase fund for the library association. The festive evening began with dinner served by the Steilacoom Library Association. At 8:00, the show started at the Pioneer School auditorium.

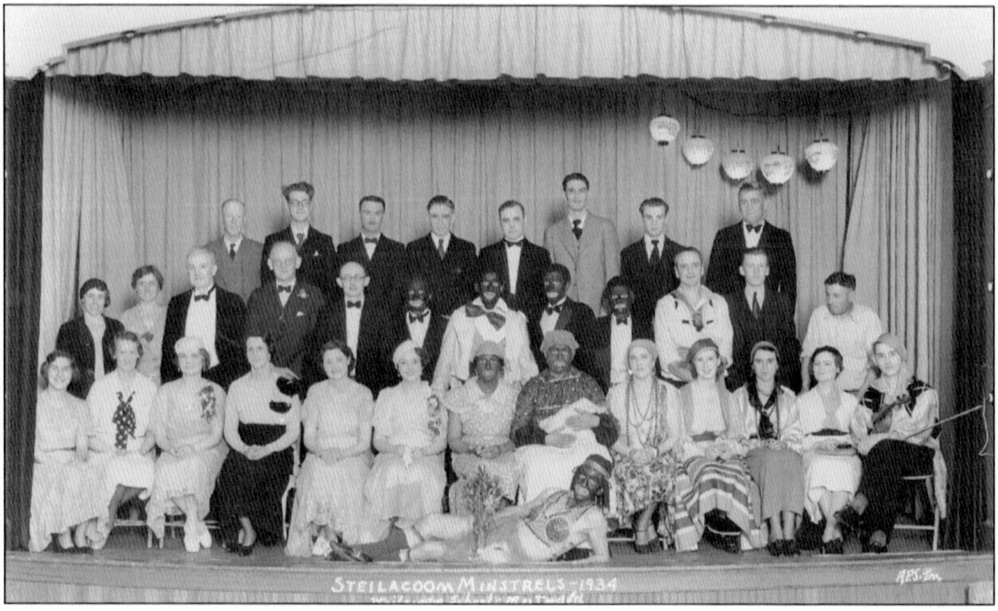

STEILACOOM MINSTRELS. On May 12, 1934, the Steilacoom Minstrels performed at Pioneer School. They are, from left to right, the following: (first row) unidentified, Helen Buzzard, Carol Larson, Mary Bair, Bill Drew, Katherine Hatcher, Hallie Dimmick, Tima McCutheon, Eudocia Leech, Bernice Scholes, Geraldine McClelland, Frieda Whitaker, and George Johnson; (second row) Sigrid Grondahl, Gladys Parker, John McCutheon, Fredrick Rosevear, Harold Scholes, (with blackface) Fred Beckwith, Darrell Smith, Sigurd Grondahl, unidentified, Harold Balabanoff, Franklin Larson, and Cub Bair; (third row) Herbert Bell, Moody Bacon, "Barney" Drew, Kenneth Bryan, James Jack, Bert Strang, Anders Hanson, and unidentified. The belly dancer lying on the floor is Dr. Homer Tollefson. (Courtesy of Tacoma Public Library.)

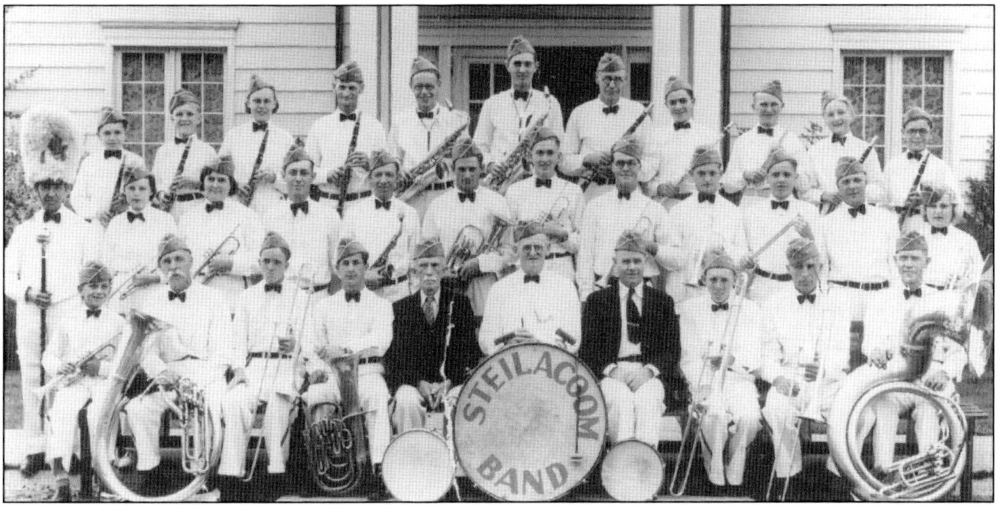

THE STEILACOOM BAND. During the 1930s, Steilacoom had an organized band with 30 boys and girls and 10 adults under the direction of Roger Laybourn. They are, from left to right, the following: (first row) William Frondahl, Robert Saxton, Glenwood Rosevear, Earl Kerr, Capt. Neil Henly, Fred Rosevear (bandleader), William Leech, Elmer Gaul, William Saxton, and James Nelson; (second row) Dr. Homer Tollefson, Betty Swanson, ? Martin, Russell Doering, Darrel Smith, Manley Welfringer, Bill McLean, Moody Bacon, Charles Rosevear, Ernest Hedlund, Leland Smith, and Doris Martin; (third row) Gene Pitts, James Dyer, Mary Swanson, John Evanger, Tom Pignott, James Jack, John Pignott Sr., Jack Leech, Ralph Baker, Shirley Barkley, and Byron Bookhyser.

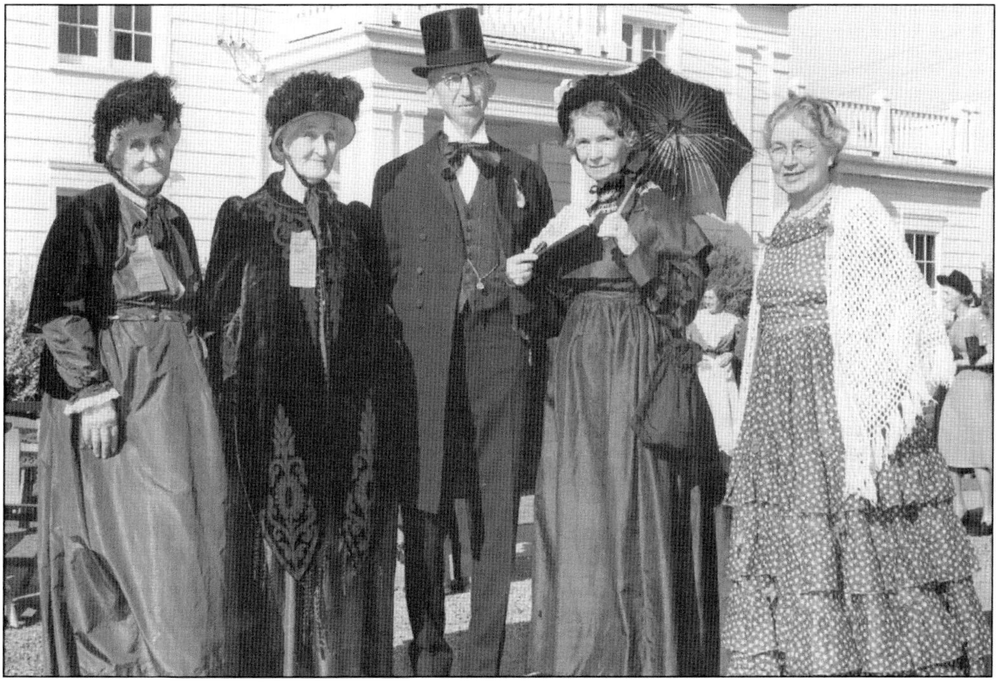

THE 1939 PIONEER CELEBRATION. Marcella Rigney Henly and Rose Rigney O'Donnell pose with Mayor Morris and his wife, Mabel, for the pioneer celebration in downtown Steilacoom. This picture was taken directly in front of the town hall. The Pierce County Pioneer Association frequently used Steilacoom as a meeting place.

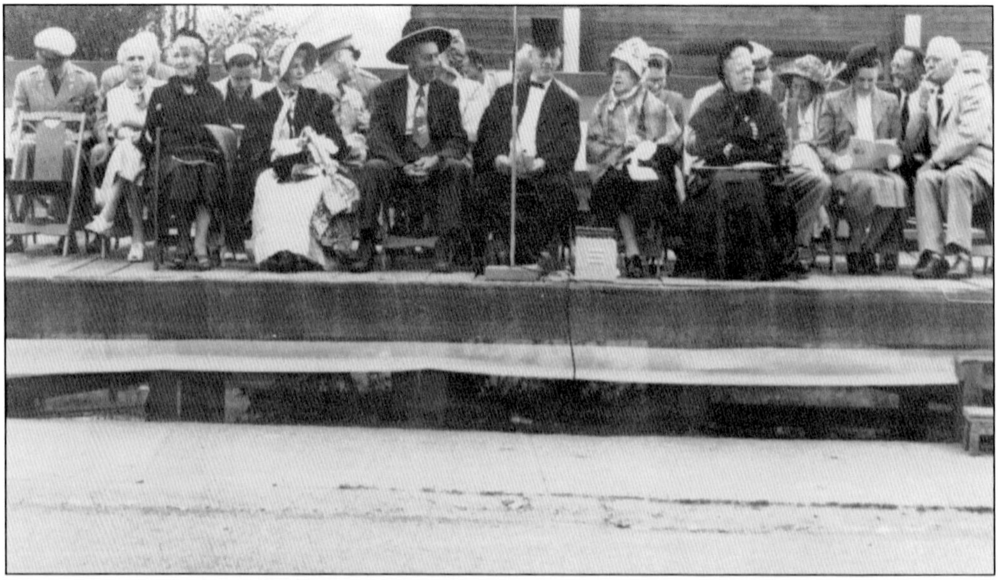

Celebrate Steilacoom! Steilacoom had four centennial celebrations: 1951 (founding of town), 1952 (first post office), 1953 (first Protestant church), and 1954 (first incorporated town). Each celebration was complete with food, activities, and entertainment. A Steilacoom centennial celebration was not complete without a parade. The event organizers provided a resting place for those who wanted to reminisce about bygone days in Steilacoom.

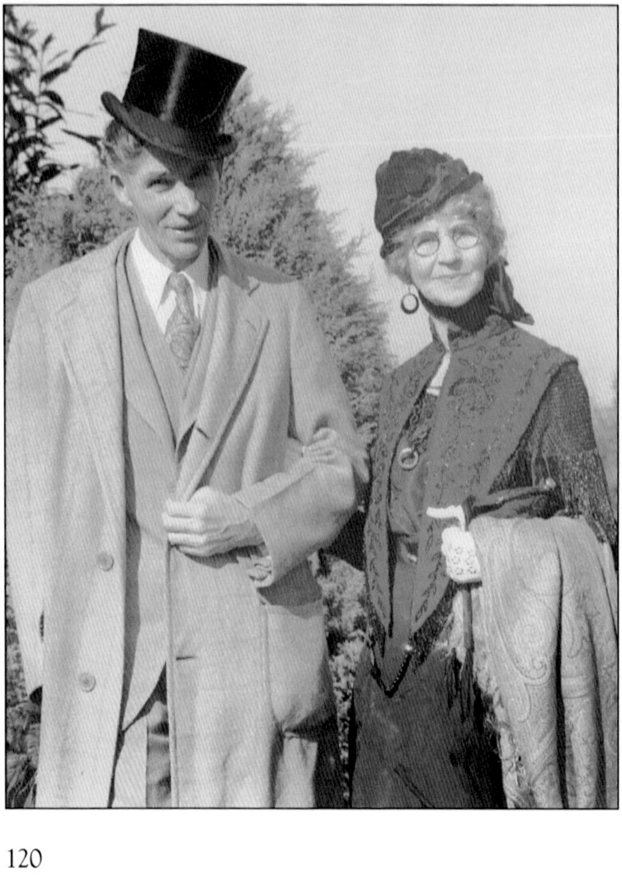

In Costume. In honor of the centennial celebration, Gertrude Johnson Baker and Charles R. Johnson are adorned in their finest. On August 14, 1952, the *News Tribune* reported, "Centennial fever burns brightly as townsfolk prepare for the most ambitious birthday blowout in the history of this normally quiet little community. . . . Steilacoom will once again boast the preeminent title it held in bygone days: No. 1 City in Pierce County."

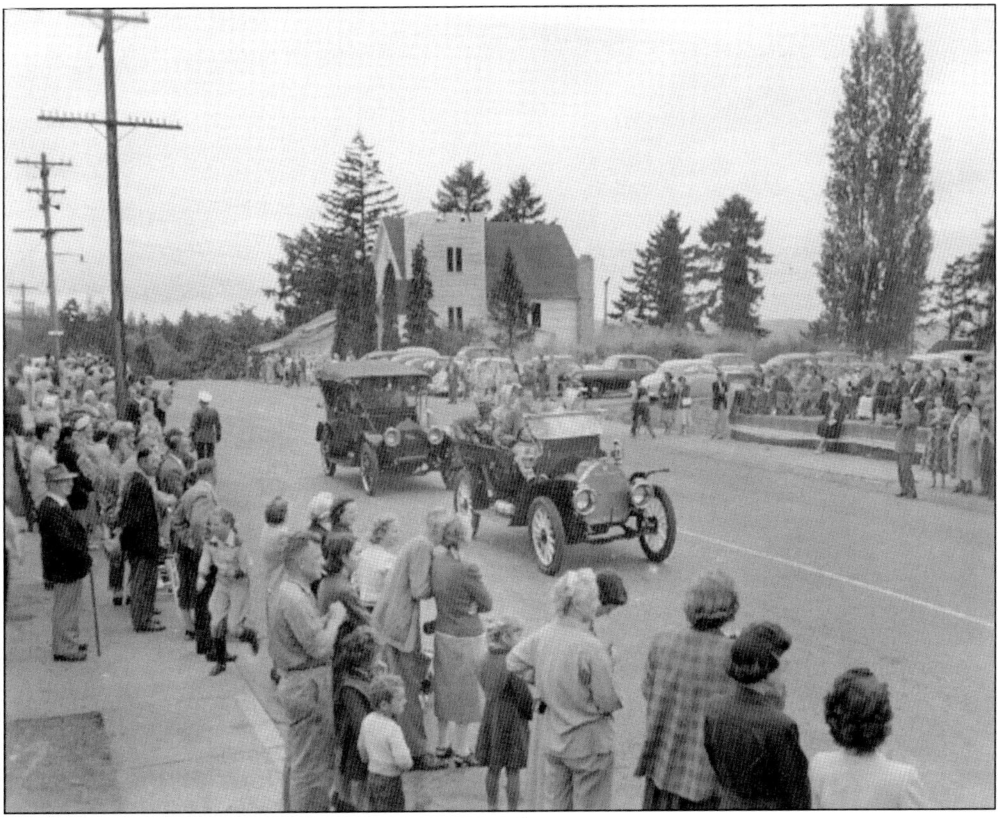

CENTENNIAL PARADE. With so many townspeople participating in this parade, it is a mystery as to where the spectators came from. Beyond the parade, festivities integrated games including tug-of-war and a hog-calling contest. The August 14, 1952, *News Tribune* described the parade: "Saturday morning's parade promises to be the biggest stunt Steilacoom has pulled since it outsmarted Olympia and Whidbey Island and that young upstart, Seattle, back in 1853 and got the first Protestant church north of the Columbia River."

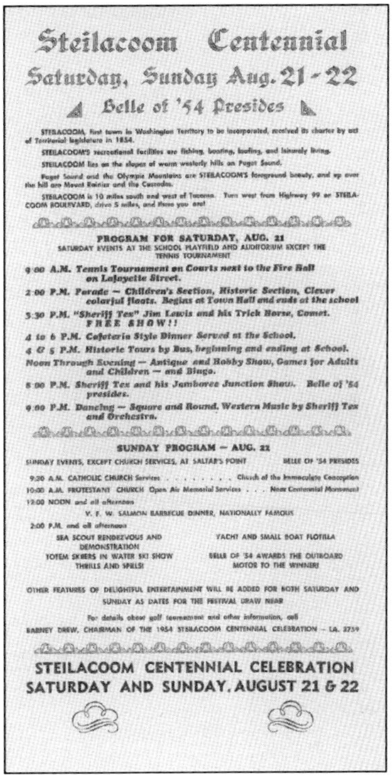

Steilacoom Centennial

Saturday, Sunday Aug. 21 - 22

Belle of '54 Presides

STEILACOOM, first town in Washington Territory to be incorporated, received its charter by act of Territorial legislature in 1854.

STEILACOOM'S recreational facilities are fishing, boating, loafing, and leisurely living.

STEILACOOM lies on the slopes of warm westerly hills on Puget Sound.

Puget Sound and the Olympic Mountains are STEILACOOM'S foreground beauty, and up over the hill are Mount Rainier and the Cascades.

STEILACOOM is 10 miles south and west of Tacoma. Turn west from Highway 99 or STEILACOOM BOULEVARD, drive 5 miles, and there you are!

PROGRAM FOR SATURDAY, AUG. 21

SATURDAY EVENTS AT THE SCHOOL PLAYFIELD AND AUDITORIUM EXCEPT THE TENNIS TOURNAMENT

9:00 A.M. Tennis Tournament on Courts next to the Fire Hall on Lafayette Street.

2:00 P.M. Parade — Children's Section, Historic Section, Clever colorful floats. Begins at Town Hall and ends at the school

3:30 P.M. "Sheriff Tex" Jim Lewis and his Trick Horse, Comet. FREE SHOW!!

4 to 6 P.M. Cafeteria Style Dinner Served at the School.

4 & 5 P.M. Historic Tours by Bus, beginning and ending at School.

Noon Through Evening — Antique and Hobby Show, Games for Adults and Children — and Bingo.

8:00 P.M. Sheriff Tex and his Jamboree Junction Show. Belle of '54 presides.

9:00 P.M. Dancing — Square and Round. Western Music by Sheriff Tex and Orchestra.

SUNDAY PROGRAM — AUG. 22

SUNDAY EVENTS, EXCEPT CHURCH SERVICES, AT SALTAR'S POINT — BELLE OF '54 PRESIDES

9:30 A.M. CATHOLIC CHURCH Services . . . . Church of the Immaculate Conception

10:00 A.M. PROTESTANT CHURCH Open Air Memorial Services . . . Near Centennial Monument

12:00 NOON and all afternoon

V. F. W. SALMON BARBECUE DINNER, NATIONALLY FAMOUS

2:00 P.M. and all afternoon

SEA SCOUT RENDEZVOUS AND DEMONSTRATION

YACHT AND SMALL BOAT FLOTILLA

TOTEM SKIERS IN WATER SKI SHOW THRILLS AND SPILLS!

BELLE OF '54 AWARDS THE OUTBOARD MOTOR TO THE WINNER!

OTHER FEATURES OF DELIGHTFUL ENTERTAINMENT WILL BE ADDED FOR BOTH SATURDAY AND SUNDAY AS DATES FOR THE FESTIVAL DRAW NEAR

For details about golf tournament and other information, call BARNEY DREW, CHAIRMAN OF THE 1954 STEILACOOM CENTENNIAL CELEBRATION — LA. 2759

STEILACOOM CENTENNIAL CELEBRATION
SATURDAY AND SUNDAY, AUGUST 21 & 22

SCHEDULE OF EVENTS. The four centennial celebrations had a printed events schedule. The weekend was complete with chiming from the beloved town bell. In addition to scheduled events, spectators would enjoy a decorated boat parade led by the *James V. Bennett* of McNeil Island.

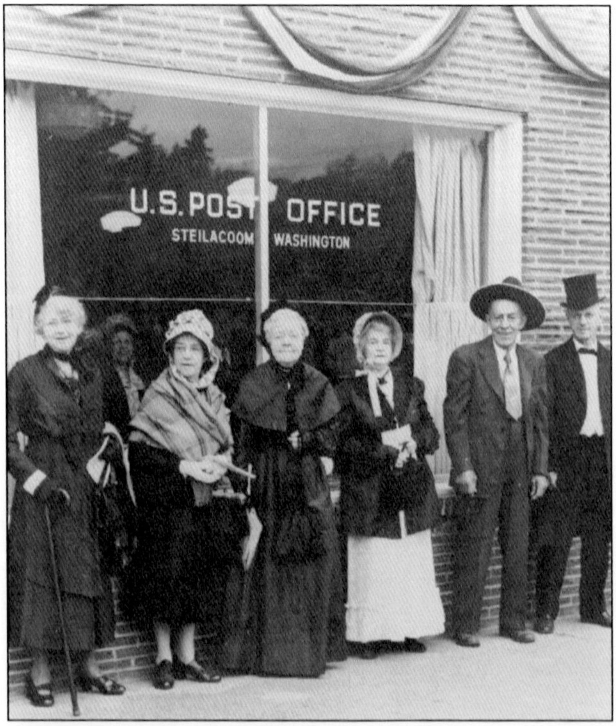

POST OFFICE CENTENNIAL. Like the centennial celebrations before, the post office celebration had an event schedule, including a parade, food, costumes, and speeches honoring pioneers. Festivities included square dancing on the tennis courts and a chowder lunch. The celebration commemorated 100 years of continuous U.S. Postal Service.

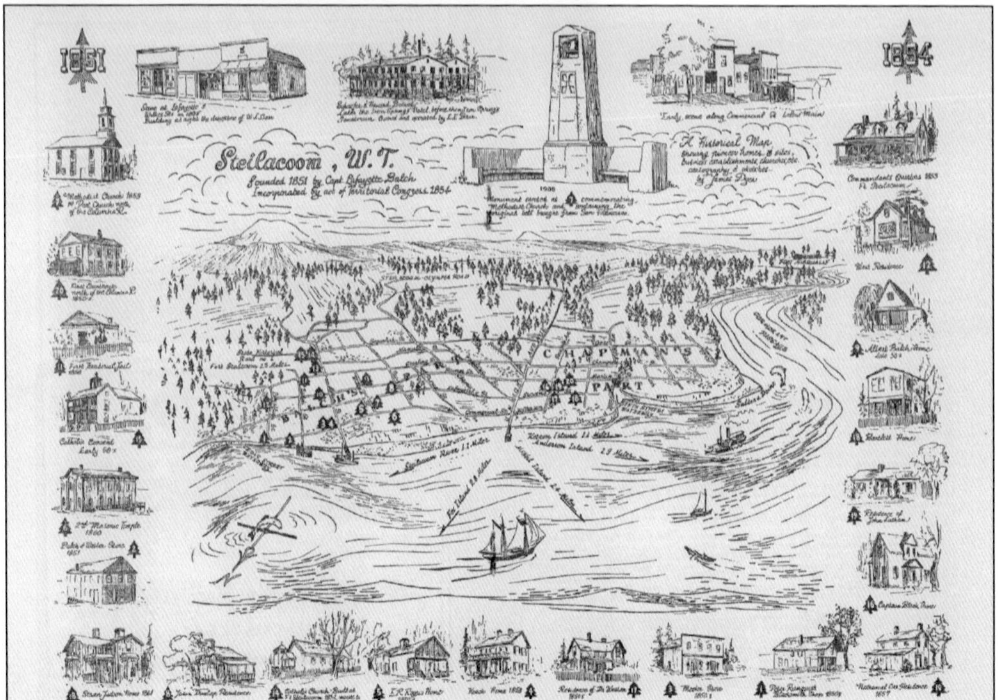

SELF-GUIDED TOUR. Each centennial celebration had a map for a self-guided tour of the historic center of Steilacoom. This historically accurate hand-drawn map provided all points of interest.

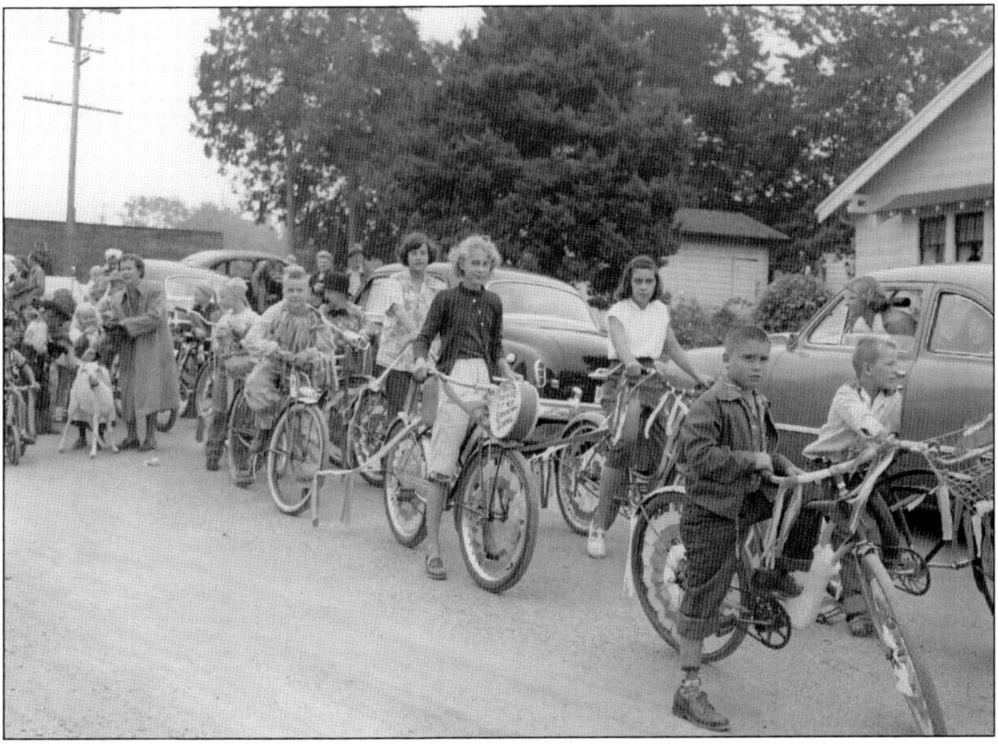

BICYCLE PARADE. The town participated in the parade with every available mode of transportation, goats and bicycles and sneakers included. Neighboring towns participated in the centennial parades with floats, bands, and bugle corps. The streets were decorated and elderly citizens honored. In 1952, Glenn Orr and Frank Runquist marched in the parade at age 72 and 77, respectively.

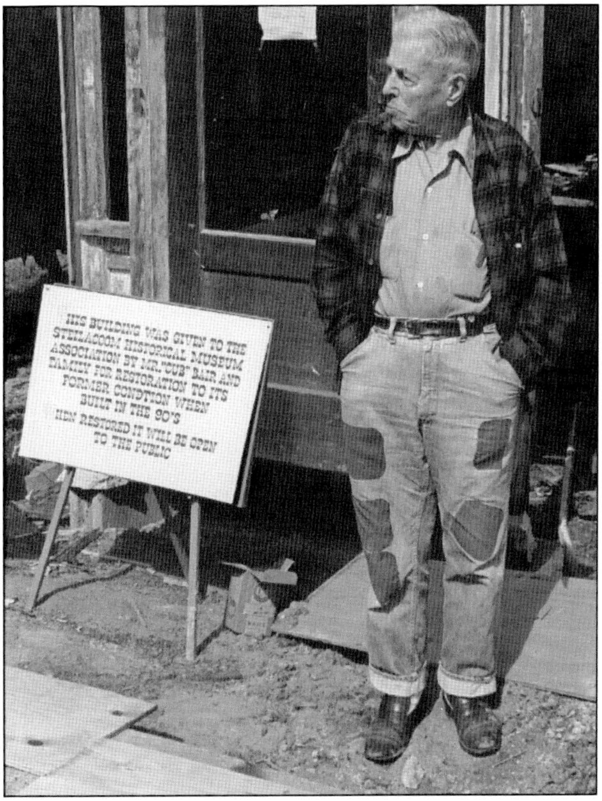

DONATION ACCEPTED. Cub Bair is possibly having second thoughts about his family's generous donation. In 1973, Eudocia Bair Leach and Cub Bair donated the Bair Drug and Hardware Store building and the adjoining lot to the Steilacoom Historical Museum Association in memory of Hattie and W. L. Bair.

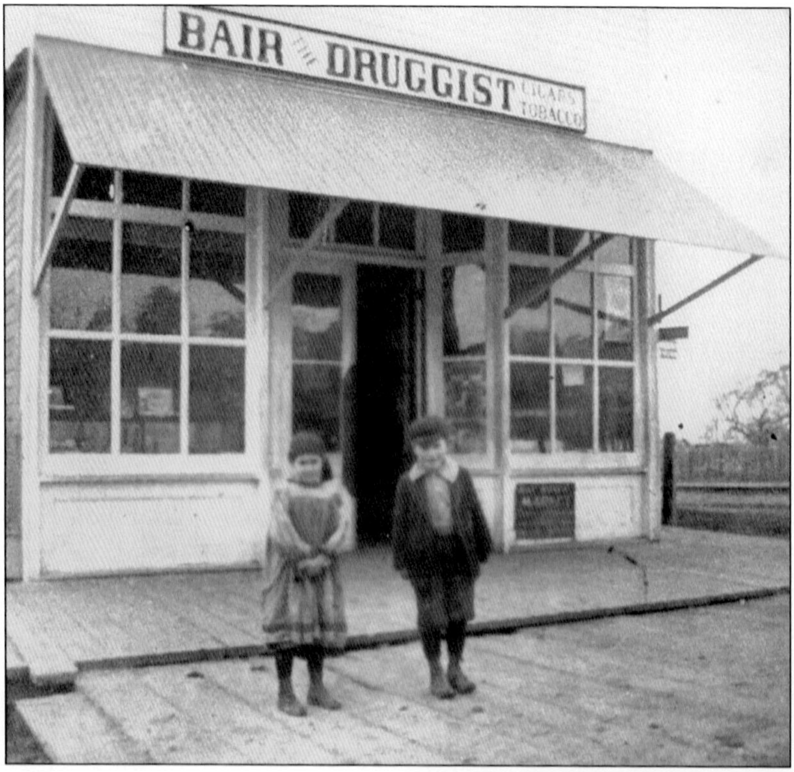

EUDOCIA AND CUB BAIR. The children of W. L. and Hattie Bair are pictured in 1896 in front of the Bair Store. Both children spent their childhood working in the family store, beginning at the candy counter.

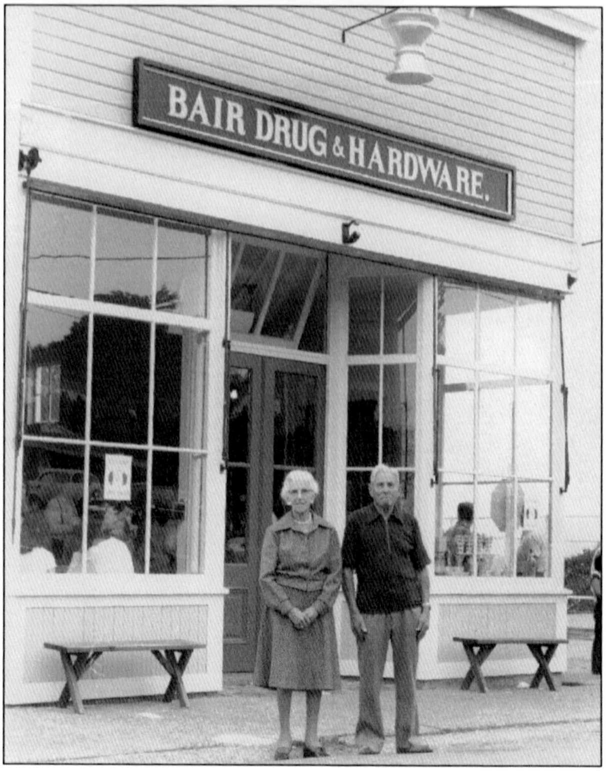

HISTORY REPEATING ITSELF. Many years after the above picture was taken, here we see the siblings reliving their past in front of the newly remodeled Bair Drug and Hardware Store. The Bair children lived their lives in Steilacoom. The impression that they left on the town will be remembered always.

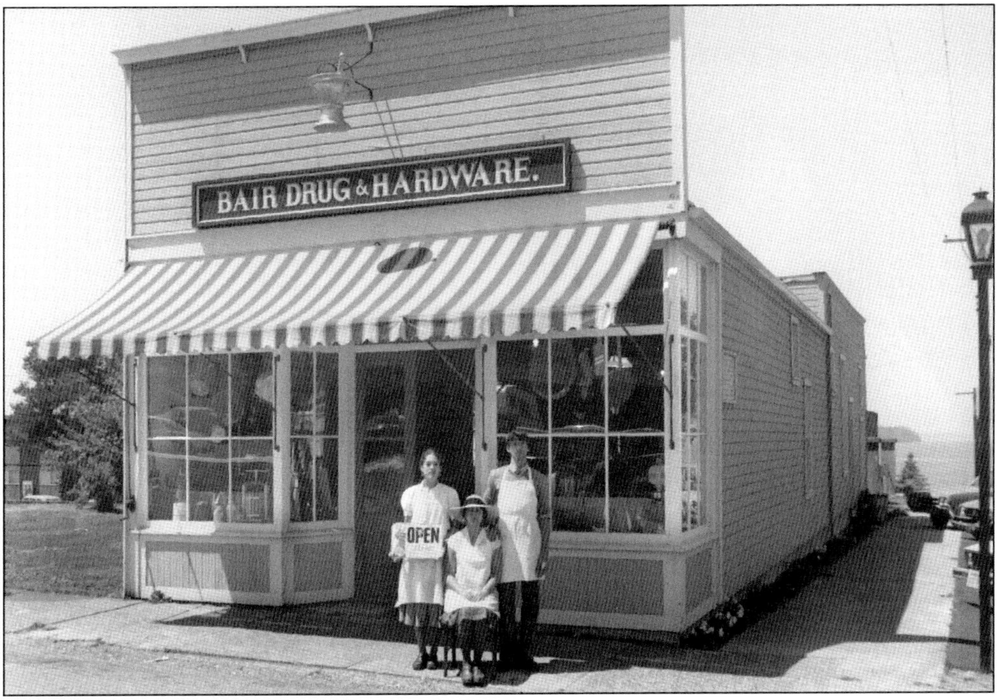

THE WAITSTAFF. The building was renovated by the Steilacoom Historical Museum Association to like-new condition with help from countless volunteers. The Bair Drug and Hardware Store once again opened as a soda fountain and expanded as a restaurant inside a working museum. The three servers in the picture were among the staff to work at the restaurant.

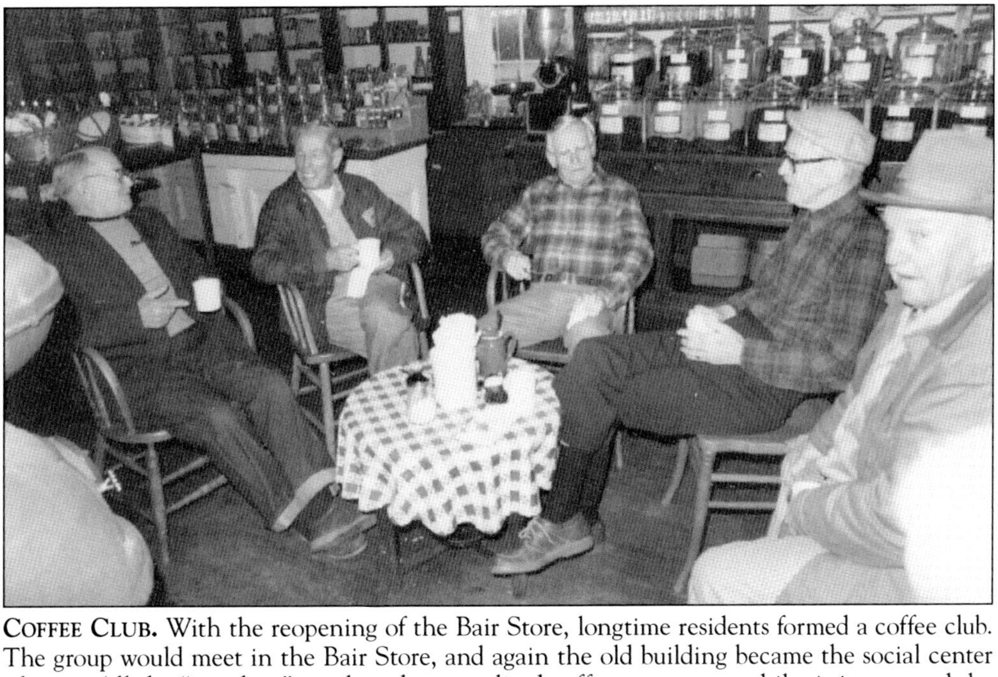

COFFEE CLUB. With the reopening of the Bair Store, longtime residents formed a coffee club. The group would meet in the Bair Store, and again the old building became the social center of town. All the "members" purchased personalized coffee cups to use while sitting around the potbellied stove; the cups were stored on a shelf nearby.

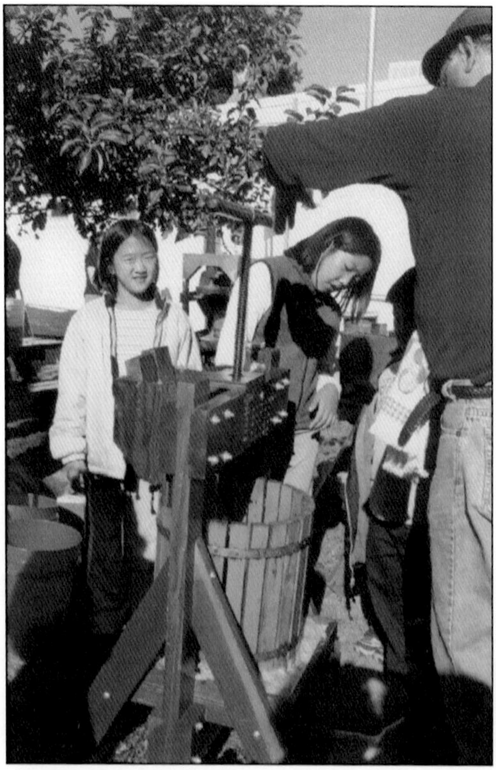

APPLE SQUEEZE. The Apple Squeeze is an annual event in the town of Steilacoom that takes place the first Sunday in October. The first fall event was held on October 21, 1973. People can enjoy a walk through history and a lesson on how apple cider is made. The first few events used apples from Steilacoom's oldest orchards.

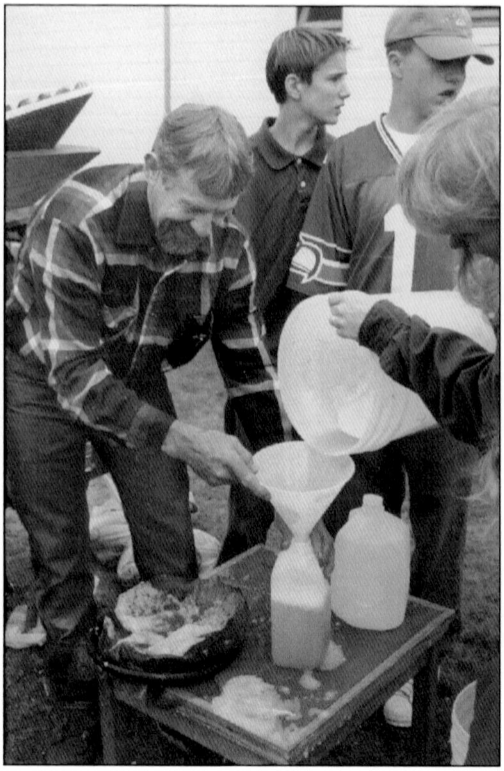

DOWN THE HATCH. What began as a town of Steilacoom event has grown into a Puget Sound event. The "Squeeze" at Perkins Park has since evolved into a festival on Lafayette Street with crafts, entertainment, and apple products for sale. Together visitors and residents squeeze the apples and funnel the sweet juice into cartons they bring from home. Hands get sticky, but the fresh juice is worth the mess.

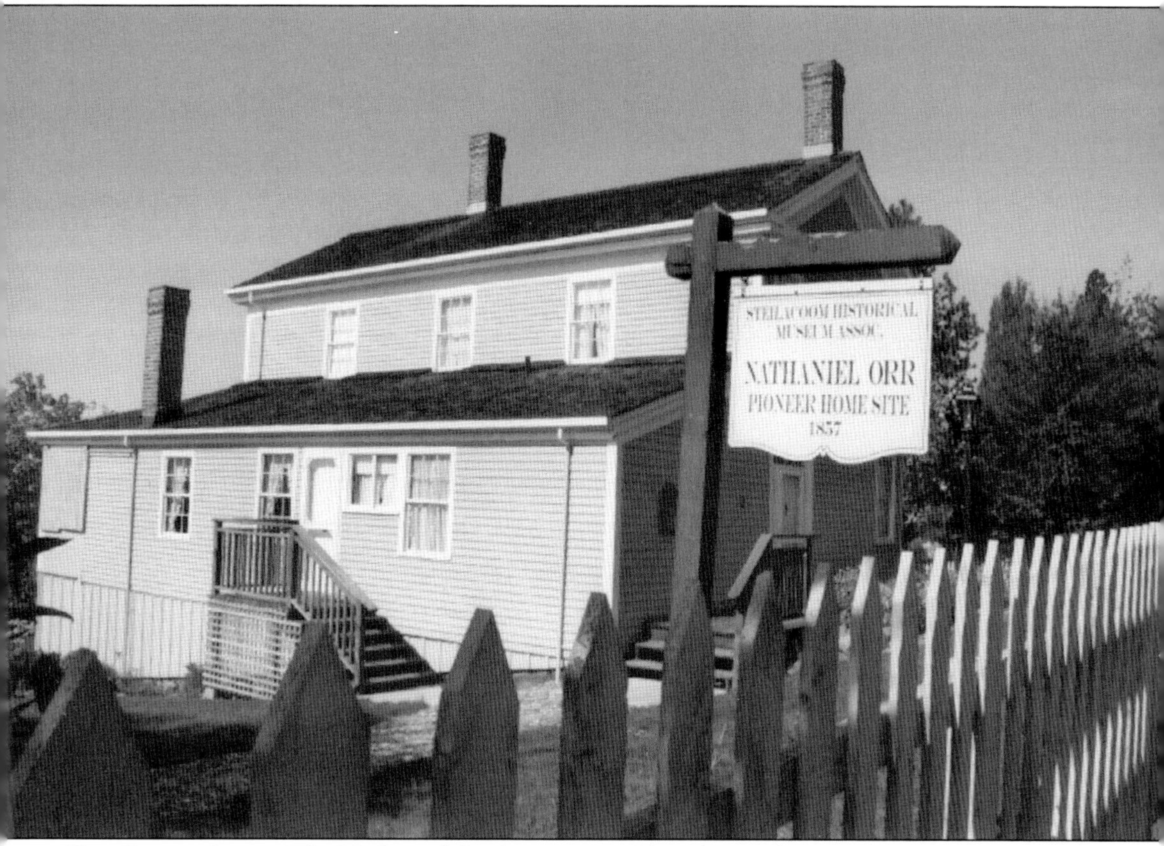

THE CROWN JEWEL. The Nathaniel Orr home was sold to the Steilacoom Historical Museum Association by Nathaniel and Emma's son Glenn and his wife, Bertha, in 1974. With its original furniture and artifacts, it provides a vivid illustration of life in late-19th-century Washington. The property encompasses a one-half block with the old orchard, a reconstructed wagon shop, and a museum constructed in 2000. Since 1970, the association has had a firm commitment to preserve the history of Steilacoom and to preserve and protect its historic properties, including the 1857 house and the Bair Store, the only commercial building predating 1900 in town. The buildings are open on a regular basis and are available for specialized tours.

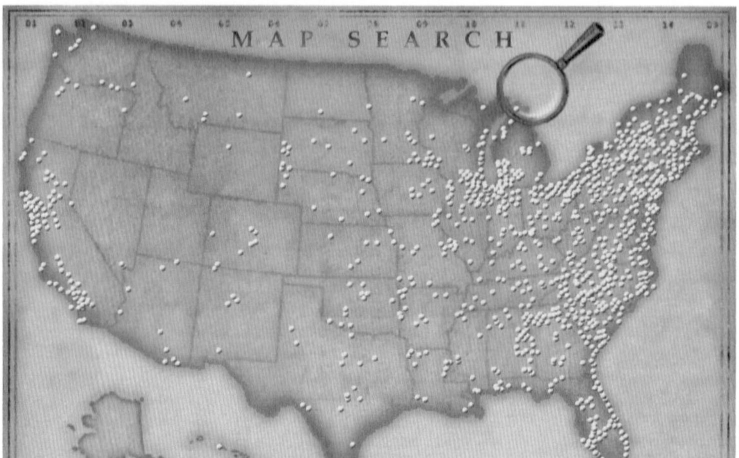
MAP SEARCH